Playing Games
Is Serious Business

STEPHEN W. ZUCKER

AMP&RSAND, INC.

Chicago • New Orleans

ISBN: 978-0999477519
ISBN: 978-0999477526 (E-Book)

Author: Stephen W. Zucker

Book Cover Design: Dorey Kronick

Text Design: David Robson

Managing Editor: Ira Berkow

Managing Line Editor:
Howard Schlossberg
and Suzanne T. Isaacs

Front Cover Photo Credit:
Mitchell Canoff

Published by:
Ampersand, Inc.
515 Madison Street
New Orleans, Louisiana 70116

First Printing: 2019

Printed and bound in Canada

To my wife, Shelly, who has given me more than I ever could have dreamed.

Steve and Shelly Zucker, Palm Springs, 2017
(Photo: Lance Gerber)

Steve and Jim McMahon

FOREWORD
BY JIM MCMAHON

It's safe to say I would not have had the football and business life that I have had, or a lasting friendship, if I had not asked Steve Zucker to be my attorney at the start of 1984.

Not just an agent. If you're associated with me, you should have a relationship that goes beyond contracts. And from the day I got to know Steve, we have been friends. We had a hand-shake agreement. And that's why I am honored to contribute to his book of memoirs, which covers his youth — certainly wilder than mine — and his long career that stretches from the riot-torn streets of Chicago to its courtrooms to NFL general managers' offices and well beyond. I'm happy I helped launch his career as an agent.

When I met Steve he was a criminal defense attorney. He pretty much knew everyone in Chicago. But he wasn't in the sports agent business yet. Going into my third year with the Chicago Bears in 1984, I had to have an attorney/agent. I told Steve at the time I wanted him to negotiate my upcoming new contract. Steve told me he had never done a sports contract before. I simply told him, "I trust you." Our relationship was born. Except for the first 18 months of my career, I looked to Steve for assistance on many aspects of my life, on and off the field.

Even before Steve did my second Bears contract, he and his wife, Shelly, were extremely helpful to my family in adjusting to Chicago, a far different environment from my youth in the Bay Area and college days in Provo, Utah. We hung out as family together and traveled abroad together. I attended Zucker family weddings, bar/bat mitzvahs and holiday suppers.

You must understand that Chicago fans live and die with their teams. Almost everyone is a Bears fan, and everything the quarterback does or doesn't do attracts attention. That was proven when I did an autograph appearance on Chicago's Northwest Side, and our limo was rocked back and forth by very enthusiastic fans waiting for us. My life got really hectic starting in the Super Bowl XX season, and Steve helped me handle its controversies and the commercial demands that followed. Thanks to Steve I made millions of dollars in endorsements following the Super Bowl.

With some exceptions, Steve kept the endorsement load off me during the 1985 season so I could concentrate on football. And he helped me during the wild buildup to the actual game in New Orleans, the Bears' only Super Bowl title to date.

I did not particularly want to do all those commercials. But I needed an income supplement with a growing family. My first contract in 1982 as a high first-round pick was $100,000. We had a strike, so it was really adjusted to $50,000. Steve finally re-negotiated my deal after the third year.

As endorsement offers poured in, I gave Steve full authority to say no. Once in a while, neither he nor I could reject an offer. William Perry, the "Fridge," backed out on somebody, so they asked me if I could stop by for a "meet and greet." They offered $10,000 for an hour. I said no. Soon they're up to $15,000, and I still can't do it. They finally called back and offered $20,000. You can't say no if they're going to keep showering money on you.

Most of us '85 Bears are still well known for doing the "Super Bowl Shuffle" video. I did not want to do it. The promoters came to us with an idea to raise money to feed the homeless. The players who decided to do it taped it the day after our only loss of the season to the Miami Dolphins. Walter Payton and I did not show up the day of filming. Eventually, Steve advised me to do it. It was a pain in the ass to tape Walter and me, and our image was superimposed on our teammates dancing in the background. But it worked far beyond anyone's expectations. People still talk about the video.

When I first met Steve, I told him that I did not want to work after football. He probably thought that I was kidding. I wasn't. Steve made sure that I had a great financial advisor who ensured that I made the proper financial decisions so I wouldn't have to worry when my career ended.

I wish I could have had a longer run with the Bears. But between injuries and what I believe was the thrifty management philosophy, I left after the 1988 season. Steve helped me through a long journey in the NFL, between starting jobs and backup gigs behind the likes of Brett Favre. My best payday came in 1990, when I signed a seven-figure deal with the Minnesota Vikings. I was fortunate to play in the league for 17 years. Steve was with me the entire way.

We're both amazed that the shelf life for the 1985 Bears — from which we both benefited so much — continues into its fourth decade. What a bunch of characters.

And it's unbelievable how that team and its personalities still generate controversy. Going into the 2017 season, Hall-of-Famer Dan Hampton, who still has regular TV/radio gigs in Chicago, claimed the Bears could have won several Super Bowls with quarterback Jay Cutler, whereas I won just one, in '85. To be frank, Dan has had a hard-on for me for years. Maybe that's because he thinks I got too many endorsements. He apparently is still jealous. I thought my relationship with Dan was good until we won in '85. I'll say this for Cutler: he would have been in the doghouse in my opinion if he'd played for Mike Ditka.

I'm giving you just the tip of the iceberg here. I greatly enjoyed getting together with Steve and Shelly at their home to reminisce for this book in the summer of 2017. *Playing Games Is Serious Business* will be entertaining and informative as you keep turning the pages. I will be back in upcoming chapters with a few more opinions and remembrances. Thanks for reading!

Jim McMahon
Chicago, Illinois

CHAPTER 1
RIDING THE RE-CREATED MONSTERS
OF THE MIDWAY

E ven after more than three decades, the unforgettable 1985
Super Bowl XX season still feels like a dream.

Indeed, it was a dream come true, to have watched the Bears
finally assemble a complete team on both sides of the ball. As
a fan-turned-agent in '85, I represented a quarterback in Jim
McMahon who clearly had more than enough savvy to win
it all, so long as he remained healthy. And with McMahon
at the helm, the Bears led the NFL in scoring while allowing
the fewest points. The two units clearly fed off each other all
season, reminiscent of the 1940's "Monsters of the Midway"
Bears' championship squads. So many people benefited from
the '85 Bears, especially the ever-loyal fans.

But the NFL and its TV partners were grateful beyond belief.
"They were a gift from God," WBBM-TV (now CBS Chicago)
news anchor Bill Kurtis said of the team's unparalleled effect on
his Chicago CBS-owned station's ratings and revenue. Attracting half the households with TV sets on — levels of sports viewership rarely matched in the country — will evoke such feelings.
Even the most casual fans blocked out their Sundays, starting
usually at noon central time for a Bears game. More avid fans
were regularly entertained an hour earlier on WBBM TV via
the appetizer of former Bear great Johnny Morris hosting old
teammate Mike Ditka, the Bears coach, who was delightfully
unpredictable in his pregame, taped interviews.

With just one Super Bowl appearance ever since "XX," via a
defensive-heavy 2006 team and having started 30 quarterbacks

during the 25-year period when the Green Bay Packers virtually only fielded prospective future Hall-of-Famers Brett Favre and Aaron Rodgers, the '85 Bears still stand out as one of the greatest football entries in Chicago sports history. The team that backed up its audacious prediction via its popular, mid-season "Super Bowl Shuffle" video, could also compete with the 1996 Bulls and 2016 Cubs as the best-ever Chicago franchise. Should the Bears have had won it again in the intervening three decades, the '85 champions still would have distinguished themselves in fans' ratings based on their personalities and their primacy as Chicago's first Super Bowl winners.

No wonder some fans, in polling, have named McMahon the greatest quarterback in team history, second only to legendary Sid Luckman. That rating is very generous and appreciated, but who knows what McMahon could have locked down had he remained injury free. The Bears might have repeated given the talent level, and if ownership, in my opinion, had the foresight and generosity of the front-office policies that originally assembled the championship roster.

I won't soon forget my Wednesday trips to the original Halas Hall at Lake Forest College to confer with McMahon after practice and get to know his teammates, many of whom I'd also soon represent as their agent. The winning aura emanating from those cozy quarters had been a long time coming and had been put together with a lot of hard work and competence by executives put in place by the late owner, George S. "Mugs" Halas, Jr.

I had wondered through the long decades whether the Bears could ever field a quarterback who had the base of being a very good game manager and at his peak could pull off spectacular comebacks. My earliest Bears memories at their then-home Wrigley Field centered on Luckman (famous No. 42) and then Johnny Lujack as centerpieces of quality quarterback play. Much lesser lights followed these talented signal-callers, as the Bears let go of youthful quarterbacks Bobby Layne and George Blanda and watched them go on to fame and championships elsewhere.

The odd good season was recorded by the likes of Ed Brown, as well as game manager types Billy Wade and Rudy Bukich, even though Wade guided the '63 championship team. But for the most part, the Bears simply would not ante up a quality contract for a talented veteran quarterback or identify one in the draft's first round for a long time.

A low point might have been the years-long expectation placed on quarterback Bobby Douglass, a lefty, that he could become an All-Pro. A Tim Tebow type of his day, Douglass gained 968 yards rushing — then a quarterback record — in 1972, having been an option quarterback in college, but he never really possessed the throwing touch of a McMahon. He concluded his pro sports career as a gimmicky pitcher on the Triple-A Iowa Oaks of the White Sox organization in 1979.

No one in Bears management, in my opinion, ever put a premium on the kind of passing system that powered other championship NFL teams. McMahon picked this up from Day One as a rare No. 1 Bears quarterback pick in 1982. Attempts to change this came in 2017 with the drafting of North Carolina product Mitchell Trubisky as the No. 2 selection overall.

"It's the mentality," McMahon said in his explanation of the longtime Bears philosophy. "Everyone thinks Chicago is a defensive team. That's what they worry about. It doesn't matter what quarterback was used. The emphasis was a defensive, running team. It's all in the system. If you have a system that wants a guy to succeed, you can have a quality quarterback."

While Papa Bear George Halas revolutionized football with Luckman and the T-formation to start the 1940s, sclerosis set into his franchise by the late 1960s. After Gale Sayers, the Kansas Comet running back, sparked a 9-5 season in 1965, senior-citizen Halas declined to retire from the sidelines and smoothly transition his job as was expected by many to the deserving George Allen, who had crafted an NFL championship Bears defense in 1963, then drafted Sayers and Hall-of-Fame linebacker Dick Butkus in '65. Halas sued Allen, just to make an old-school point, after he broke his assistant's contract to take the Los Angeles Rams' head-coaching job in 1966. Halas actually won the case, then let Allen go anyway to build multiple contenders in various stops around the NFL.

Without Allen to run the franchise, less-than-productive drafts, insufficient quarterback play, and what was considered skinflint pay levels, made the Bears something of a league laughingstock through the early 1970s. The team wandered to any available open field without a permanent Chicago-area practice facility. The overall record was 21-48-1 between 1969 and 1974. Finally, Papa Bear gave son George Halas, Jr. the authority to make a key change in 1974, hiring longtime Minnesota Vikings General Manager Jim Finks.

A former Pittsburgh Steelers quarterback who I followed in my grade-school days, Finks had built up a Super Bowl-caliber program with coach Bud Grant in Minneapolis. He hit the ground running, literally, with the Bears, drafting Walter Payton out of Jackson State with his first pick in 1975. Then Finks set out to build a team the right way, beefing up both lines. But the quarterback position remained in the hands of journeymen veterans like Mike Phipps, a great college quarterback who did not measure up to McMahon.

After taking Dan Hampton in the first round to anchor the defensive line and Otis Wilson—a future client—to play outside linebacker in 1979, Finks selected running back Willie McClendon in round three while passing up Notre Dame quarterback Joe Montana.

Soon afterward, Bears history would be altered for many decades, outlasting a championship and affecting the present team. On December 16, 1979, on the cusp of the Bears' second playoff appearance under Finks, George Halas, Jr. died of a sudden, massive heart attack at 54. His father, then 84, survived him. The line of succession to run the Bears long-term was clear for "Mugs," who had a son and daughter. Now the Bears' future would funnel through Virginia McCaskey, Halas' only other child. Virginia and Ed McCaskey had 11 children.

The elder Halas went back on duty as an octogenarian, re-assuming the Bears presidency and making the ground under Finks a little shakier without his family sponsor. Finks' hand-picked coach, Neill Armstrong, was fired after a poor 1981 season. But Finks did not hire Armstrong's successor. Papa Bear shockingly stepped in to choose Dallas Cowboys assistant Mike Ditka, a groundbreaking Bears tight end of the 1960s who Halas once traded away to Philadelphia after a contract dispute. Ditka once said Halas threw "nickels around like manhole covers," but all was forgiven with Halas seeing many reflections of himself in the intense Ditka. Amid the head-coaching change, Bears players wrote a letter to Halas pleading for him to retain defensive coordinator Buddy Ryan. Halas agreed. Such devotion between Ryan and his defensive players would soon pay off handsomely.

With Ditka on board, Finks finally pulled the trigger on a first-round quarterback with McMahon in the 1982 draft. He had spent the previous two seasons as one of college football's most gifted quarterbacks, holding some 70 NCAA records with LaVell Edwards' pass-happy offense at Brigham Young University. McMahon did not get the broadcast exposure he enjoyed 15 years later. Far fewer games were televised each weekend compared to today's sport network-flooded availability. ESPN had just begun, but did not possess the major college-football deals it has now. The major TV networks focused on the top established conferences.

But McMahon came through spectacularly in college when given national exposure, especially via the 1980 Holiday Bowl in San Diego against Eric Dickerson-led Southern Methodist University. In the final two minutes, 33 seconds, McMahon engineered one of the greatest comebacks in college football history, erasing a 20-point SMU lead. The coup de grace was a Hail Mary into the end zone as time expired. BYU tight end Clay Brown somehow out-jumped four SMU defenders to snare the McMahon pass. The miracle pass never got the promotional play through the years that Doug Flutie's sleight-of-hand for Boston College against Miami got in a 1984 regular-season game, but it was just as effective. The extra point kick by Kirk Gunther completed the 46-45 final, as McMahon completed 32 of 49 passes for 446 yards.

The "game manager" under duress, needing to keep his team together under impossible odds, obviously impressed the Bears' scouting staff, then the smallest in the NFL—consisting of Bill Tobin and Jim Parmer, with Finks chipping in when he could get away from the office. The number five choice in the 1982 draft, McMahon endured the usual tussle over money, with the historically tight-fisted Bears.

"If it was up to me, you should go up to Canada to play pro football," McMahon recalled as Halas' lecture. "If we give you 200 bucks per game, you're overpaid. You've got a bad arm, a bad eye, bad knees and you're too small."

But the contract eventually was signed. Bears treasurer Jerry Vainisi, who had been assigned to pick up McMahon at the airport, appealed to the vanity of McMahon's then-agent that he'd miss getting the signing on that day's 10:00 p.m. news if he dallied any longer. The deal then was reluctantly cut and McMahon was announced as a Bear. McMahon was turned over to rookie coach Ditka to begin his NFL apprenticeship.

Through a mutual friend, I met McMahon, again with no inkling I'd be involved in sports professionally. In one trip through town before he played a down, McMahon stayed at my house because his then-agent was an old friend of mine, and McMahon and I hit it off. He lost crucial development time, though. The first-ever NFL strike wiped out seven mid-season games and gave birth to new rosters with strike line-crossing around the league, whose results counted in the standings.

McMahon started seven of the nine games the "real" Bears actually played, finishing with a 57.1 percent completion rating and nine touchdown passes. Then, in 1983, the Bears started poorly at 3-7, but finished strong, winning five of their final six games. McMahon started all but three games, amassing a 7-6 record with a 59.3 completion percentage.

Steve meets Jim for the first time at our house, 1982

But the Bears' biggest news was off the field in '83. Finks' final draft as general manager was probably his best overall, helping round out the starting lineup of an NFL powerhouse. He landed Pitt tackle Jimbo Covert and Tennessee wide receiver/Olympic sprinter Willie Gault in the first round, Arizona State defensive back Mike Richardson in the second, Notre Dame safety Dave Duerson and guard Tom Thayer in the third and fourth rounds, respectively, and Tennessee State defensive end Richard Dent and Iowa tackle Mark Bortz in the eighth. Duerson and Bortz eventually became clients, and I would go on to represent eventual Hall-of-Famer Dent in a policy-impacting NFL drug case.

After he fulfilled his '83 draft duties, Finks resigned from the Bears, resurfacing later in the year as Chicago Cubs president. On August 24, 1983, Halas appointed Vainisi, by then an 11-year front-office veteran, as Finks' replacement. Like me, Vainisi played youth sports at Chicago's Green Briar Park. Vainisi grew up in the St. Hilary's parish — Halas' former longtime neighborhood — four blocks south of my childhood home. Vainisi had additional football blood in his family, as his late older brother Jack Vainisi had been drafted in the 1950s. Concurrent with Vainisi's appointment, Halas granted Ditka the final word on future drafts.

But the co-founder of the NFL did not live to supervise either Vainisi or Ditka in their roles long-term. Halas died at 88 on Oct. 31, 1983, a 63-year Bears era concluding with both spectacular success and failure, but also with the longest family tradition in pro sports.

That Halas-McCaskey ownership would approach a century in length as this was written. Halas' son-in-law, Ed McCaskey, had worked in the Bears business department since 1967, but oldest son Michael, just 39, would take over as president from his grandfather. A business-school professor at Harvard and UCLA, and Peace Corps alum with no sports management experience, Michael McCaskey had previously told George Halas he wanted to work for the Bears. Virginia McCaskey, a 1935 St. Hilary's grammar school alum, also had made her father aware of her intention to elevate her son to team leadership eventually.

Michael McCaskey's appointment as president was announced November 11, 1983 at Halas Hall. He publicly discouraged any bids to buy the Bears, fulfilling his grandfather's vow stated to McMahon during his rancorous contract talks the previous year. "No matter how difficult it is to run this team, we want to keep it in the family. The Chicago Bears are not for sale," Halas told McMahon during his 1982 contract talks.

Finally, with far more experienced football men in charge of player personnel, McCaskey first set out to boost interest in the Bears, who had taken a beating in public appeal the previous four seasons. He staged a series of community meetings to chat with fans.

Meanwhile, as I transitioned out of criminal-defense work, my and McCaskey's personal timelines would intersect over the coming decade, affecting my life, that of my clients and my passion for my childhood team.

I had walked away from criminal law after 13 years due to my representation of porn publisher Larry Flynt. Actor-evangelist Marjoe Gortner contacted me through a mutual friend who had asked me to handle Flynt's case, who was being detained in Chicago by federal agents. At a federal court hearing, December 6–7, 1983, I was sickened by Flynt's behavior. He aimed profane outbursts at the judge and exposed himself; it was enough to make me walk away from my practice.

I took a holiday break, then entered Rush Presbyterian-St. Luke's Hospital for back surgery. On January 2, 1984, McMahon — with whom I had developed a rapport after being introduced two years earlier — staged a surprise by visiting me in the hospital with a football signed by his Bears teammates. But the welcome visit wasn't just social. McMahon needed to change agents. McMahon did not use the word "agent," though. He said he needed an attorney.

Although I cautioned Jim I had never done sports representation before, he responded, "Don't worry, I trust you." I guess we were kindred souls. We shared an August 21 birthday. We were both optimists and romantics. We bent rules and defied conventions to varying degrees, and we were rebels against authority.

I had to catch up on sports contracts fairly quickly. Going into his third season after a nice 1983 performance, McMahon was logically due for an extension. I quickly did a lot of research about comparable contracts for other quarterbacks and carried it into negotiations with Vainisi.

"I had met Steve at practices and such with Jim," said Vainisi. "We had casually gotten to know each other by the time the contract negotiations had started. We had somewhat of a rapport. We knew McMahon was our guy. As Finks would have said, he had pelts on the wall by that time. We had a belief in the program. I'm the GM and there was complete unity within the organization at that point. We were all in this together. We had players who were coming on. Halas had given us his baby. We did things in his memory, and I was the guy who put the 'GSH' on the uniform sleeves."

Later, Vainisi said McMahon was "the first real quarterback this team has had since Sid Luckman. Jim McMahon, we could build around. He's the future."

So the first major sports deal I negotiated was with Vainisi. Growing up in the same neighborhood helped us get along immediately, coupled with Vainisi's friendly personality and football background. The talks stretched out for a while, the five-year contract completed in June 1984, simply because Vainisi and I had reasonable differences about McMahon's value.

"It was not acrimonious," Vainisi said. "We know what we're dealing with. Even though this was Steve's first contract, he was a seasoned attorney. He knew how to negotiate. He had done his homework, and knew what the (quarterback) values were. It was a very professional, arms-length negotiation. We got the deal done. My attitude was get the player signed before camp."

All through the negotiating sessions, Vainisi had full authority to do the deal and did not repeatedly have to check with the back office. I enjoyed the process. Similar to defense law, I had to sell myself and my client. Another benefit of dealing with Vainisi was access to good Bears season tickets, for which I gladly paid. Meanwhile, I took care of the contract for Bears receiver Ken Margerum, whom I met through McMahon. I would go on to amicably negotiate a number of contracts with Vainisi.

While my negotiating skills were sharpened, I also had to keep an eye on the relationship between McMahon and Ditka, especially because, early on, the pair butted heads over play design and selection. McMahon prided himself on his field awareness and leadership skills. Ditka was strictly old-school. But Ditka and McMahon should have had a meeting of the minds. Ditka had been an All-Pro pass-catching tight end under Halas in the 1960s. "Iron Mike" coming out of his blocking stance to serve as a go-to target was exactly the type of play-calling McMahon savored.

"I wish he'd been in my huddle," McMahon said of Ditka. "I knew what the hell I was doing. I used to tell him to his face, I wish I would have played with you, you would have understood me more.

"He thought I was doing things to piss him off. But your offense has got to believe in you. They knew I knew what I was doing. I never had a problem changing plays. Knowledge is confidence. You know what you're doing. If other people around you know what you're doing, they'll follow you. I never had a problem with people following me. The quarterback position is a leader by title. I knew where everyone was going."

Proving his leadership qualities did not stop when the game clock did. In his Bears tenure, McMahon would get together with his offensive linemen every Thursday night at a local bar. The group became as tight-knit as any line-quarterback combo in the NFL.

One Bears staple McMahon wanted to tweak as he established himself in Chicago was the overuse of Payton, who finished as the Bears' all-time leader with 492 receptions, let alone his spectacular then-league record rushing yards. As Payton amassed that total, McMahon still wanted to employ him more in the passing game. Sweetness, as he was known, had the ability to gain yardage that could have been enhanced by isolating him on a linebacker or safety coming out of the backfield. And McMahon wanted to save Payton from unneeded wear-and-tear as he entered his 30s, going up against run defenses massed against him. He respected Sweetness for his status and sublime skills and desired to protect him as much as possible. Payton seemingly had to take on an entire opposing defense by himself once he got to his blockers.

"Walter got tired of running into a brick wall," McMahon said. "Third and long, he runs a sweep. You go up to the line of scrimmage, there were nine on one side waiting for the sweep."

Even with the somewhat-stodgy offensive game plan, the talent assembled by Finks finally jelled in 1984. The "46 defense" guided by coordinator Ryan rose to elite status, ranking third in the NFL, so-named for the unusual positioning of safety Doug Plank, who wore that number. The Bears won the NFC Central before pulling a stunning 23-19 road upset of the

Washington Redskins in a divisional playoff game. Even with a loss to the San Francisco 49ers in the NFC title game, the defense firmly believed it was Super Bowl-ready.

But the offense lagged in such levels of success, and McMahon's injuries played a factor. On November 4, 1984, at Soldier Field, McMahon suffered a lacerated kidney midway through a victory over the Los Angeles Raiders. I rushed into the locker room, where McMahon was peeing blood. I would arrange to get him treated by a urologist at Northwestern Memorial Hospital. He recovered, but was lost for the season because he could not absorb contact in the afflicted area.

I firmly believe the Bears would have reached Super Bowl XIX if McMahon had not been disabled. In his absence, and with backup Steve Fuller also hurt, the Bears literally had to improvise at quarterback. On December 9, 1984, third-stringer Rusty Lisch played so poorly Ditka inserted Payton from the shotgun position at quarterback late in the first half against the Green Bay Packers at Soldier Field. Payton threw a short touchdown pass to backfield mate Matt Suhey in the third quarter of the 20-14 loss to the Packers, the Bears' fiercest rivals.

McMahon's value to the offense, elevating it to championship level, definitely was proven when he was upright and available to play, starting out the magical 1985 season. His offensive sparks got the team off to a great start and they've never been diminished in the fans' minds ever since. In game one on September 8, amid tropical weather conditions at Soldier Field, McMahon simply had to outscore the Tampa Bay Bucs, who held a 28-17 halftime lead before crumbling. McMahon completed 23 of 34 passes, including two TD strikes. He also scored on a pair of one-yard runs.

Then, after a more pedestrian 20-7 home victory over the New England Patriots a week later, McMahon heroics — a bit reminiscent of the 1980 Holiday Bowl miracle — really put him and the Bears on the map in a nationally televised Thursday night game in Minneapolis.

He literally came off a sickbed to break Ditka's rule of "no practice, no play" after playing on only a few days rest on September 19, 1985. McMahon had been confined to Lake Forest Hospital, in and out of traction for upper back spasms earlier in the week. The day before the Vikings game, he suffered an infection in his right leg. Fuller filled in as starter, but the Bears trailed 17-9 with 7:22 to go in the third quarter.

Ditka figured despite McMahon's sketchy physical condition, he was tired of acquiring a tin ear from the quarterback's continual sideline pitches to return to action. He'd put him in the game in a "put up or shut up" fashion. But McMahon was in the habit of practicing what he preached. On his first play, he called an audible, sensing a Viking blitz coming. With Payton making a key block, McMahon hit the speedy Gault perfectly in full stride for a 70-yard TD bomb. Minutes later, after a turnover, McMahon's second pass of the evening was a 25-yard bullet to Dennis McKinnon to give the Bears the lead. Soon he connected on a third score, a lightning bolt striking the entire viewing audience in a 6½-minute span. The Bears had a 33-24 victory and a 3-0 record. A bit of McMahon selling himself to Ditka had worked and relations began to warm between them. And my sports agent's phone began ringing with endorsement inquiries for McMahon.

He was far from finished with spectacular on-field artistry. His back and leg much better, he showed he had sticky hands amid a 31-point second quarter against the Redskins at Soldier Field on September 29, 1985. Breaking left after handing off on an option play, McMahon streaked toward the end zone, reached out and snared a Payton pass for a 13-yard TD. He returned the favor in the third quarter with a 33-yard scoring strike to Payton, a cherry on the sundae of the 45-10 victory.

By now, I had made a habit of waiting in the tunnel to greet McMahon and his teammates as they ran off the field to the locker room. My smiles were returned, and then some, as the narrative of '85 blossomed. Meanwhile, McMahon earned the specific affection of one McCaskey male.

"Ed McCaskey was always great to me," he said of the

then-Bears chairman. "Every time he came into the locker room, he left a cigar for me."

As the season proceeded, McMahon ensured Payton had plenty of help. The greatest player in Bears history did not have to be the sole mule pulling the wagon. The defense battened down its hatches, militantly carrying out the dictums of the hyper-admired Ryan, almost an alternate head coach in his own right.

And now Ditka would unveil the best-remembered gimmick of '85.

Opposing head coaches immediately learned the angered Bear in Ditka never forgets and his personal statute of limitations does not exist. After a road victory at Tampa Bay, the Bears had a rematch with the San Francisco 49ers on October 13 at Candlestick Park. Taking a measure of revenge for a long-remembered playoff loss against 49ers Head Coach Bill Walsh, Ditka inserted rookie defensive tackle William "Refrigerator" Perry into the offensive backfield. Clemson product Perry was Ditka's pet No. 1 pick—for whom Ryan had little use, but was overruled on playing time simply because Ditka outranked him. Football's only 300-pound running back became an immediate sensation, but the country hadn't seen anything yet.

On October 21 at Soldier Field, a Monday Night duel pitted the Bears against the Packers. The embarrassment would only be on the visitors' behalf this time. On two first-and-goal plays, Ditka again inserted Perry into the backfield. Obliging, "the Fridge," as he was known for his size and appetite, he flattened Packers linebacker George Cumby for a pair of touchdowns. Any indignities Packers coach Forrest Gregg, a former offensive lineman, and his then-Green Bay teammates had inflicted on the Bears and Ditka in the Packers' championship 1960s years had been searingly stored away in Iron Mike's soul. Now they'd be paid back, with compound interest, no matter how many decades it took. Perry scored a third TD in '85—via a four-yard pass from McMahon in Green Bay 12 days later.

Bears radio analyst Dick Butkus screamed, "He's OPENNN!" as the Fridge lumbered into the end zone. Although only a six-point loser, the frustrated Packers tried to fight the 9-0 Bears, committing what many considered dirty plays against Payton and fullback Matt Suhey.

Now though, The Fridge was emerging in a popularity all his own, besieged with outside offers to compete with McMahon's. But my lifelong friend Rick Fizdale, now a creative executive with the Leo Burnett ad agency, advised me to defer accepting major deals for McMahon, popularized as the "Punky QB" thanks to a fluke haircut, until after the season. In other words, until after a potential Super Bowl. Financial and marketing value would wind up being maximized by such patience.

Already the Bears had grabbed the imagination of much of the country. They were known by their nicknames. Sweetness and Iron Mike had been established for years. McMahon had his unwanted "Punky QB." The Fridge stormed to the fore-front. Danimal (Dan Hampton), Mongo (Steve McMichael), Mama's Boy (outside linebacker Otis Wilson), Samurai (middle linebacker Mike Singletary), LA Mike (defensive back Mike Richardson), Silky D (wide receiver McKinnon) and Butthead (place kicker Kevin Butler) soon became household words.

Projections of a potential undefeated season began to sur-face. Pushing back against what was a sore shoulder McMa-hon suffered in the 49er victory, he then aggravated it in Green Bay and did not start the following weekend against Detroit. McMahon frustratingly missed the much-hyped game in Dal-las on November 17, 1985, when the Bears further established themselves as the NFL's premier team with an unexpected 44-0 demolishing of the Cowboys. A second straight shutout, this time 36-0 against the Atlanta Falcons, hard to accomplish in any era, came a week later at Soldier Field and turned atten-tion squarely on Ryan's stifling defense.

Their performance still seems amazing after all these decades, and you could make the argument that they were the greatest in NFL history, better than the four-time champion

Pittsburgh Steelers' "Steel Curtain."

But the '85 Bears played the entire season without holdout defensive end Al Harris and safety Todd Bell. Ryan wanted the two players back, at the very least for depth. But backup quarterback Fuller and Hall-of-Famer Payton kept the offense in fine tune. However, a leader like McMahon would be missed at an opportune moment. That took place in the most promoted game of the regular season, a Monday Night Football encounter, December 2,1985 in the Orange Bowl against the Miami Dolphins.

Don Shula's perennial contenders took pride in defending the franchise's 14-0 mark (plus three postseason victories) in 1972, the only perfect record in NFL history. At 12-0 with all cylinders clicking in spite of McMahon's sidelining, the Bears were the greatest danger in the ensuing 13 seasons to equal that spotless mark. On national TV in front of a rapt audience and armed with plenty of Dan Marino-led offensive weapons, the Dolphins, with members of the '72 team along the sidelines, had almost a spiritual motivation to stop the Bears.

"We're going to beat their butts," Miami receiver Mark Duper said in the run-up to the contest.

"This game had taken on the trappings of a Super Bowl here," wrote the *Chicago Tribune*'s Phil Hersh. "People were saying this was the biggest thing to ever happen in this jungle outpost of pro sports."

But Marino was dead-on with his passing as Nat Moore snared a pair of TD passes. The "46" defense could hardly stop the Dolphins in the heat and humidity of a late South Florida night as the hosts rushed to a 31-10 halftime lead. The temporary collapse seemingly put Ditka and Ryan at each other's throats during intermission. The early thrashing got Ditka out of his mental game midway in the third quarter after the Bears cut the lead to 14 points. The coach tried an onside kick and failed to recover the ball, even though plenty of time was left for a comeback.

All the while, I believed the Bears had been overly careful

with McMahon. Team physician Clarence Fossier even tried to schedule shoulder surgery after the Dallas game, but McMahon and I agreed to continue with a regimen of medication. Sure enough, in practices leading up to the Dolphins game, McMahon finally could cut loose with his arm. In pre-game warmups, he was observed tossing the football 50 yards.

"People are always telling me to be smart, take care of myself, so for once I did," McMahon said after the game. "I don't want to miss the playoffs. I could have started here tonight. All this thing needed all along was rest. I've had enough of that already."

But Ditka opted to stick with Fuller. Finally, McMahon entered the game early in the fourth quarter after Fuller limped off with a severely sprained left ankle. He was just 3-of-6 passing in a too-little, too-late scenario.

In hindsight, perhaps the Bears were right in holding McMahon out of the game. A playoff berth was hardly on the line at that point. Still, my longtime feeling was the Bears' perfect record might have stayed intact had McMahon started. He could have helped eat up enough clock to keep the ball away from Marino's quick-release style more than what took place in the real timeline of the eventual 38-24 loss.

An all-night flight back to Chicago and short rest did not stop the Bears from re-assembling at a Chicago studio to shoot "The Super Bowl Shuffle," their signature off-field performance of the '85 season. At the time, many figured the players were at best presumptuous, at worst foolhardy, to sing and dance about a Super Bowl so overconfidently before season's end and with three postseason games to win to achieve it.

McMahon and Payton declined to participate in the original taping, but later went before the cameras via close-ups, with their video images superimposed on their shufflin' teammates. The video became a bestseller and was nominated for a Grammy Award. The confidence and some might say arrogance of these colorful characters was a once-in-a-generation phenomenon. McMahon summed it up best in the heat of the post Dolphins-game locker room.

Referencing that the media were perhaps waiting for the Bears to choke, McMahon said, "We kept getting compared to the Cubs. Well, we're not the Cubs of 1984 (who blew a playoff lead to San Diego). We're not even the Bears of 1984. This is a different Bears team than ever before. Do you think guys like Walter Payton, Dan Hampton and Steve McMichael are going to choke? We're really together, this team."

McMahon returned to the lineup unhindered for the final three games of the season, all wins. He even dashed for a 14-yard touchdown in Detroit. With McMahon starting only 11 games, the Bears finished with an NFL-leading 456 points, 11 more than any other team in franchise history. Their average time of possession was 34 minutes, which helped the defense to allow only 198 points. Payton's typical 1,000 yard-plus rushing season was complemented by almost unheard-of franchise balance in the passing game. The defense, however, was the well-remembered trademark of the franchise.

But the Bears' main business of their season would lie beyond New Year's Day, in hard-earned home playoff games against the New York Giants and Washington Redskins. Little could I predict McMahon, playing off my improvised and sometimes crisis management, would virtually share top billing with the defense in the run-up to kickoff of Super Bowl XX.

CHAPTER 2
AN AGENT-TURNED-AUTHOR

My background as a Chicago city corporation counsel and later a sports and media agent have put me in a unique position to have an up-close perspective on the powerful developments that are still rippling through the public discourse that is the world of athletics today.

Two decades later, I negotiated contracts at the start of the revenue and salary explosion fueled by television rights and free agency that made pro sports such a passion to tens of millions. From the colorful, championship posture of Jim McMahon to the stoic, executive realism of my hometown Bears' GM Jim Finks, I was fortunate to see all sides of the top athletes and front-office directors whose actions and words shaped the loyalties of countless fans.

I am doing this book because every time I'm out to dinner telling stories, someone suggests I write a book. So, I am finally doing it. I want to educate young people on how you become an effective, trend-setting agent.

I have spoken at universities all over the country, including Harvard. I had an internship program from Northwestern. I've put a number of young people into the business. It's amazing how many young attorneys want to become sports agents. I tell them I love it. I was lucky. I was a criminal defense lawyer. My last client was Larry Flynt of *Hustler* magazine fame. Three weeks later I met McMahon, then going into his third year as the Bears quarterback.

I negotiated McMahon's second contract. I told him I don't know how to do that. He said, "I trust you." I knew him through his previous agent and he apparently liked me from those meetings. A couple of weeks after doing McMahon's second Bears contract, he asked about my fee. I calculated it at about 4 percent of the contract. I subsequently represented McMahon his entire career and we are still in touch.

I don't emphasize the money aspect of this work. I loved the concept of representing a star athlete so much, I would have done this for free. I still had this as my base philosophy five years later when I landed Deion Sanders as a client and ESPN set up a live telecast featuring Deion from my living room on Draft Day.

As an agent, I had literally turned an avocation into a vocation. I grew up in a sports-crazy family in Chicago's West Rogers Park neighborhood, five miles northwest of Wrigley Field. Some of my earliest memories were going to games with Herb, my father. I recall sitting on his knee at a Bears game at age four in 1944. Three years later, we had front-row seats for Jackie Robinson's debut at Wrigley Field, drawing that ballpark's largest-ever paid crowd, a record that still stands. I watched live sports broadcasts on one of the first televisions in the neighborhood, in our apartment.

Later, as an assistant Chicago corporation counsel, working out of City Hall, for $6,300 a year in my mid-20s, my job was to advise Chicago police on enforcing city laws, and what they could and could not do in handling citizens. I was right in the middle of the tumultuous demonstrations during the 1968 Democratic Convention. You'll read a lot more about that in detail, including some incidents not chronicled in history, later in this book.

Working as a criminal defense attorney, traversing the intricacies of the justice system in Cook and surrounding counties, was the bulk of my city service. I certainly gained much insight into the human character while defending clients and negotiating with prosecutors and judges. By the time I cut the cord of defense work, I had gathered the skills and negotiating acumen necessary to craft multimillion-dollar contracts and book-endorsement work.

Steve's press photo

An agent's work is time consuming and tough, but it can be glamorous. To be able to make your avocation into a vocation is a blessing. I consider myself extremely lucky after working as a criminal defense lawyer. Glamorous, no. Stimulating, yes. You had lives at stake. At first glance, that was the absolute contrast with the seeming toy factory of sports. Later, as I came to understand injury and health issues that really have come into the forefront now in pro football, the long-term wellbeing of my clients also became an issue. Literally, their lives were at stake. Again, much more detail about that down the road in these pages.

One glamorous part of an agent's work is the exposure in the media. I didn't find any tedium. For business, I read *Sports Illustrated,* which I had devoured weekly anyway since my early teens in my avocation. I have the first issue of *SI* from 1954. Going to camp I got *SI.* I read the local newspaper sports section first thing in the morning. Everything I did as a kid in sports I later did in the business of sports.

Negotiating was enjoyable. If I could have limited my agent's work to negotiation, I'd have been in heaven. The worst part was getting clients and keeping them. In that process, you ended up competing with what I considered to be sometimes unscrupulous agents. They often tried to steal your clients, often offering them what I can only call illicit enticements.

I first honed my personal style in negotiating via crisis situations — dealing with demonstrators and their agitators during the 1968 Democratic Convention and the 1969 Days of Rage, a planned riot in downtown Chicago by radical Weathermen. Later, I refined my art of negotiation in trial bargaining in criminal law. The state had to have something, the judge had to have something, and I had to have something. The judge is like the general manager. You learn which judges allow you to have "wiggle" room, same as sports executives.

You study the market. This gave me the insider knowledge to help drive and set the market for athletes. You know what's out there. You know the comparable contracts. So much of the rest of it is by feel.

The most distasteful aspect of the business was agents who attempted to handle players' money. Some were what I considered charlatans in this respect and cumulatively millions of hard-earned dollars were lost. I told the players I would not handle their money. You can use me for one thing, negotiating, and I will refer you to a qualified financial manager. I'd tell clients that all the people who come to you for money or to get into your orbit, just say no. If you need me to say no for you, I'll do it.

You stay as close to clients as you can. I was friendly with Bruce Willis, as was McMahon. A number of people wanted to get close to us. We were careful about who passed our wary defenses.

I had a guy in my Zucker Sports Management office who set up foundations for clients and encouraged them to get involved in charities. Get involved in the community, too. McMahon did so much for charity but did not want it publicized. I tried to go after players who had higher characters, who were the most coachable. I feel almost all my clients followed my advice. I almost always met their families. When a player is going into the draft, families are very important. I really liked my clients. I am friendly with many to this day.

At the start of my representation career, I was generally the only agent allowed in the locker room. I would bring McMahon his mail every Wednesday. We decided what should be responded to. I'd see 11 pairs of eyes on me. My relationship with McMahon and presence in that locker room during the 1985 Bears Super Bowl season resulted in landing 11 more players for representation from that team, including the late Dave Duerson, Otis Wilson, Dennis McKinnon, Steve McMichael, Jay Hilgenberg, Keith Van Horne, Kevin Butler and Shawn Gayle.

Based in Chicago, and being an NFL junkie anyway, I was the first one in my longtime suburban residence to have a big satellite dish. I would watch part of every football game possible. I'd call my clients after a game and say nice catch on 3rd-and-7.

An agent's job and loyalties are to his clients. A lot of people think players get paid too much. That's not the case. They have a unique talent. They get paid whatever the team wants to pay them, what the market says they are worth. Agents often evoke stereotypes of yanking a player from his longtime moorings, angering his fans, and moving him to another team for a few dollars more. That was not my style. With only a few exceptions, I advised every player to stay put. Do not leave your team. Take less money to stay where you're at. You know the system on your original team and could be in a difficult fit elsewhere. The more perceptive sports executives have a similar attitude. The smartest guy I knew was John Hart, general manager of the powerful Cleveland Indians teams of the 1990s. Hart locked up his home-grown players early, keeping them out of both arbitration and free agency, when he did not have to. He nearly won two World Series in that decade as proof thereof.

Bottom line — many fans do not understand it. The sports journalists, who should understand it, can fall victim to leading the fans in misperception, sometimes proclaiming an agent as greedy and the player too. I always go to the players and ask the type of financial package and working conditions they are looking for. It is easy for agents today to misread the market.

Scott Boras, baseball's most prominent agent, is great in his field. He does things differently, but many styles have proven to work. He goes for the maximum contract. I've got all the respect for him. We developed a relationship. When Boras got a football client, he called me. When I got a baseball client, I called him.

Unlike Boras, I never held out for the maximum deal. I never looked for it. You didn't necessarily get the last dollar. I always went into a negotiation with a smile with every general manager. Only a very small percentage of agents have this philosophy. Agents often feel they must get the maximum amount, so when they're recruiting clients, they show they can get that top dollar. But you can also get to lucrative contracts with patience and prudence. I had at one time eight players who were the highest-paid at their positions. Teams liked to draft Zucker players because with only two exceptions — Deion Sanders and Jay Hilgenberg — we didn't hold out.

Fans did not know the reason behind these seeming money-grabs and high-stakes negotiations. An NFL career averages

3.4 years, while baseball and NBA careers are somewhat longer. The player has to make the money when he can, as much of it upfront as possible with signing bonuses.

With only a few exceptions, NFL contracts are not guaranteed for multiple years compared to five-year and longer ironclad deals in baseball and basketball. You have "dead" money in the back end of contracts, as the Cubs and their fans discovered to their consternation with Alfonso Soriano. Football players get nothing at the end except horrible, sometimes crippling physical and emotional injuries. If you hear of a multi-year NFL contract, it's really a series of one-year contracts. I can tell you many players got cut at age 28 with a lot of money owed to them, because of the language in their non-guaranteed deals. Injury was the big factor.

Our work is portrayed in sports media frequently. Agents are among the biggest traffickers of information, much of it off-the-record, in all pro sports. But only one significant movie has ever been filmed about the profession—the popular 1996 production *Jerry Maguire* with Tom Cruise. I was frequently asked my opinion of its realism. *Jerry Maguire* was very accurate, portraying Cruise's relationship with his one client, a fictional Arizona Cardinal played by Cuba Gooding Jr. "Show me the money," was the Gooding character's best-remembered quote, and it was certainly on target. The relationship Cruise had with the one client was the one I believe I had with all of mine. You have to treat your client as if he's the only athlete you are representing.

I'd like to believe that my successes far outweighed any failures. My number one regret was not pursuing more seriously a partnership in the New England Patriots with the Sullivan family owners in the late 1980s. That would have been a $200 million deal. My top investor was Chicago architect Helmut Jahn. I saw sports was going to be the business of the '90s. But I had no idea it would become this big, with franchises valued into the billions.

Other regrets are clients who fell into my lap—and I did

not lock up. Early in her career, the hyper-talented Halle Berry wanted me as her agent. I turned her down, recommending she get a Hollywood-based rep. I was certainly off-target, especially after seeing her accept an Oscar for *Monster's Ball*. Another time, a young Joe Girardi sat across from me in my office while I was on the phone, half-ignoring him. Eventually, Girardi understandably left and got another agent. He had a nice career as a big-league catcher and a far better one as a manager, including a World Series title with the New York Yankees in 2009. And there were others I let slip through. Nobody bats 1.000, but you still look back at "what if?"

Overall, I was proud to be an agent. My phone rang off the hook with lawyers wanting to be agents, to even be interns. They kept inquiring how do you become an agent. Some of my friends experienced some of the same inquires with attorneys wanting to become sportswriters. Well, they would not want to take the pay cut and stand around locker rooms waiting for one interview subject. The majority of would-be sports-industry participants should stay where they are, as it takes a special dedication and motivation to stick it out through inevitably frustrating times.

But if they are as persistent in getting into sports as they'll need to be in the client-recruiting and contract-negotiating processes, I have a few pointers:

> • If they have a love of sport, they must handle the job as if they don't have a lust for money. When I did McMahon's contract, I did not talk about my fee. I never billed hourly. I billed a flat fee. If you had the clock running, you did not have the client's best interests at heart.
> • Know the market. Know what the player is worth. The worst thing an agent can do is overestimate the client's value. If the value is $150 million and the agent wants $200 million, you won't get that amount and won't get the $150 million either.
> • Always try to keep your player on his existing team.

He may get more money elsewhere, but his career could be negatively impacted.

- Be accessible to the media. I made it a point when negotiating a contract to talk to the media. Get the player's story told.

I grew up kind of a bad boy. If I saw something I wanted, I just grabbed it. By my late 20s, I grew up by necessity and made a good life for myself, my family and my clients. I wouldn't exchange my life with anybody, no matter how wealthy or accomplished.

CHAPTER 3
A REBEL WITH A FEW CAUSES
WHO EVENTUALLY GREW UP

I was a wild child. And a wild young adult, to boot.
If you looked at Stephen Wade Zucker circa 1956 or even 1964, you would not have projected a future negotiator and "people person" who tried to strike deals with one of the country's top anti-war radicals [Jerry Rubin in the wake of the Chicago riots] or with sports moguls attempting to keep as many of their mega-millions as possible.

I was carefree and footloose, sometimes to the point of reckless. How I behaved moving about my native West Rogers Park neighborhood with the utmost confidence, if not arrogance, would have seemed incomprehensible to my wife Shelly, my four children and six grandchildren. Not to mention platoons of judges, prosecutors, criminal-law clients, athletes, general managers and media members with whom I dealt, starting in my early 30s.

But maybe I was the proverbial caterpillar. Although there was a solid base and a good foundation waiting to be born inside, my cocky, protective shell got me into some trouble with family and at school. That metamorphosis, though, was not a lonely journey. So many of us started out barely in control, behaving badly, yet growing out of it at various times. Some of it is the crowd with whom we hang out. Some of it is a combination of parenting and physical environment.

The heartening factor is life often provides second and third chances and room to grow out of a wobbly start. And I am dead certain that in that embryonic base, waiting to burst out, was a good heart and a caring attitude about others which manifested itself even as I pulled off hijinks that were pretty brash for a middle-class Chicago neighborhood in the years after World War II.

Some amateur philosophers also suggest we need to "sow our wild oats" before we settle down. If so, then I was stitching like mad, all the way through an era when I even dated Playboy Bunnies and served as wingman with the same for the crown prince of Chicago's royal political family. More on him shortly.

Starting out though, you might have classified me as a late-Depression baby. There weren't a ton of us, like the Baby Boomers of 1946-and-beyond vintage, given that one of the few growth industries of the 1930s was condoms. Countless couples who scraped for a few dollars on relief or in 10-cents-on-the-dollar jobs during our country's worst economic crisis simply could not bring more mouths to feed into the world.

Maybe my parents, Millie and Herb Zucker, were tougher or more carefree than most when I was born in the late summer of 1940. My mom, known as "the sunshine girl," came from a gilded Jewish background. My grandfather, Alex Passen, was one of the wealthiest men in Chicago. Each of his children had a million-dollar trust fund. When the stock market crashed in 1929, Alex locked himself in a room in the family mansion in the Albany Park neighborhood. He heard of associates who killed themselves, having lost everything. When he came out of the room, he told the family they all had to go to work. Eventually they all rebuilt their lives.

My father came from more modest roots. He was literally a "tin man," selling aluminum siding. And Herb Zucker also worked for Hiram Walker liquor distributing. He worked all his jobs around a lucrative pastime as a gin rummy master. Even the likes of gin giant Bob Elson, the White Sox broadcaster, could hardly match my father's acumen in processing cards.

"His dad had a photographic memory," said my friend and Chicago-based creative success Rick Fizdale. "He was a card-counter and made money doing that. Like my father, they were trying to see how little work they could do to make as much money as possible."

Mind you, this late-Depression product did not have in any way a financially deprived childhood. Herbie Zucker hustled up a living, but did not put his shekels into a spatial mansion like Alex Passen did. He had good clothes and good cars, yet we lived in a tenement-style apartment at the corner of Rosemont and Western avenues. That's where we hung out with fellow tenants like Fizdale's family. Fizdale was my lifelong friend who went on 45 years later to become CEO and chairman of the giant Leo Burnett ad agency. Fizdale and I would be on opposite sides during the 1968 Democratic Convention, despite our strong relationship. To this day, he and I still attend Chicago Cubs games together in the 2016 post-World Series championship era we both feared would never come after a lifetime of waiting.

Sports was a big part of our childhoods, providing some of my first conscious memories, and fittingly providing a long-held goal of turning an avocation into a vocation. My father was a huge football fan who had played center and linebacker for famed coach Bob Zuppke at the University of Illinois and later at Wisconsin. Of course, Herbie Zucker bought season tickets at Wrigley Field during the Bears' Monsters of the Midway/Sid Luckman-led championship era of the 1940s. I still vividly remember sitting on his lap at Wrigley for a 1944 game in Box U76, behind the south end zone, next to all-time Bear Jack Manders, who then was working as a scout.

More than 2½ years later, on Sunday, May 18, 1947, my father and I attended one of the most historic games in the famed debut season of Jackie Robinson, when the first African-American to play Major League Baseball was likely the second-most famous American after President Harry S. Truman. On the morning of the Brooklyn Dodgers' first 1947 season visit to Chicago, I drove with my dad and we parked for $2 at a Standard station on Addison Street.

In an astounding sight never forgotten by any in attendance, tens of thousands of African-American fans made perhaps their first-ever trips to the North Side to watch Robinson's first game at Wrigley Field. The new fans packed the right-field grandstand. I had only seen one black man in my life—Jim, the deliveryman at the Schoffman's drug store in our apartment building.

"Dad, what are all those Negroes doing here?" I asked Herb Zucker. It was only much later that I would truly understand the significance of this game. But Herb Zucker understood at that moment. He loved Robinson and believed the big leagues should be integrated.

My father employed a lot of angles in his life and ringing up first-row Cubs box seats was one. We usually sat in Box 24, between first and home. The ticket-seller at the box office would hold it for my father. We never sat in the second row. The seats were $2.50 with a $1 tip to the ticket seller. We were in front of an absolutely massive crowd. The 47,101 standing room only was the largest paid crowd in Wrigley Field history. People were standing in the aisles. My buddy Fizdale had come to the game with us, but had to sit further back in the grandstand. The black fans were all dressed up in their Sunday best, as media accounts of the crowd noted. I also remember all the hats, the wide-brimmed fedoras of the time, that they wore. At the time, when you went out in public, even for ballgames, you dressed up.

Robinson's presence stuck in my memories. Playing first base, he was by far the fastest man on the field. I remember tremendous cheers for Robinson from the assembled throng. Herb said he loved him. And Fizdale and I weren't the only future sports and media types in the mob. Many reports had future baseball commissioner Bud Selig and buddy Herb Kohl, an eventual Wisconsin U.S. Senator and department store magnate, traveling from Milwaukee for the game. And tucked into the standing-room section behind the grandstands was the eventual Babe Ruth of Chicago columnists, a teenage Mike Royko.

When Robinson died shortly after the 1972 season, Royko wrote of that memorable 1947 afternoon. He said in a future column that he snared a Robinson foul ball which had deflected off of other fans. Almost immediately, an enthralled African-American fan offered Royko $10 for the ball. The sawbuck was a small fortune for a young person in 1947, but in my view, it was a bad move by Royko. Six-year-old Steve Zucker would not have sold that ball.

Fittingly, setting the tone for the rooting interest of Fizdale and me until we were senior citizens, the 1947 Cubs were 29-21 and in first place on June 14. But they endured the first of many mid-season collapses spanning the rest of the 20th century and beyond. The '47 Cubs fell under .500 by mid-July and continued dropping to a final 69-85 record. Meanwhile, Robinson — the first-ever National League rookie of the year — played in the first of six World Series in his 10-year career against the New York Yankees. That was an early lesson for which I applied my deal-making as a middle-aged man; get the best talent and you will likely win. But skimp on scouting/player development and player payroll and your results will be far less positive. I had to wait until I was 11 years past Social Security age to witness a World Series winner for the Cubs in 2016, who previously always appeared to be understaffed, underfinanced and undermanaged.

The 1947 Cubs also put their home games on WBKB-Channel 4, Chicago's first TV station. Jack Brickhouse, at $35 per game, teamed with Whispering Joe Wilson on the telecasts. I was fortunate to be able to watch these very early telecasts. Although our living quarters were modest, Herb Zucker spent his money on furnishings, in this case $1,000 on an RCA console TV set/radio/phonograph. The picture tube was just 10 inches wide — but still much bigger than the video screen on iPhones that now mesmerize Millennials. We had one of the first TVs not in a bar in West Rogers Park.

I thus was able to watch the Cubs, then the White Sox when WGN-TV signed on in 1948, and early football telecasts that would stir my passion for the rest of my life. In 1949, Cubs owner Phil Wrigley put into place, in my opinion, one of his few adept philosophies — extensive video exposure of the Cubs. He allowed three stations — WBKB, WGN and ABC-owned WENR-TV — to televise his team simultaneously. I gloried in being able to flip the channels and see the different camera angles in the primitive coverage compared to today's high-definition, graphics-and-replay-filled efforts. WENR-TV aired the games just in one season — 1949.

Their chief announcer was Hall-of-Famer Rogers Hornsby. I remember Hornsby had a ruddy kind of face on TV. As a play-by-play man, let's just say he was sufferable — but he was still Rogers Hornsby. Brickhouse was my favorite for his 34 years broadcasting the Cubs on WGN. I later understood why he did not criticize the Cubs even though they richly deserved his scrutiny. WGN got the Cubs' TV rights for under market rate. Brickhouse could not kill his station's golden revenue goose. Again, market rate was a byword I'd live by in my agent's career.

But I performed a weird "DXing" routine with this early TV. I'd hold the dial between channels 3 and 4, and pick up the audio of a Champaign radio station airing University of Illinois basketball games. The airwaves weren't that crowded before hundreds of TV stations signed on in the 1950s.

On Oct. 3, 1951, I just missed watching the "Shot Heard 'Round the World" — Bobby Thomson's pennant-clinching homer for the New York Giants. The Giants-Dodgers three-game playoff was the first coast-to-coast live telecast of a baseball game. I was waiting in line with my fifth-grade class-mates to leave Clinton School for the day and someone said Thomson already hit his historic homer. Brickhouse had a term for this slightly tardy situation over the decades: "A day late and a dollar short."

These live broadcasts from all over the country gave us kids a close-up view of the world thousands of miles away, for the first time in history. That expanded our dreams, which in everyday life were usually limited to an old-school neighborhood that was repeated in the mid-20th century dozens of times over in Chicago.

Our lives revolved around the neighborhood, playing sports at Green Briar Park and summer trips to Camp Interlaken in northern Wisconsin. In 1950, at age nine, I counted Bobby Luckman, Bears quarterback Sid Luckman's son, as a fellow camper. Meanwhile, future NFL Hall-of-Famer Marv Levy, just starting his coaching career, worked at the camp as a counselor. On Parents Day, Sid Luckman visited. He taught me how to properly grip a football. I never forgot those camp days. A half-century later, when I had to make a business call to the Buffalo Bills, I got Levy on the phone and we sang the Camp Interlaken song together.

Back home on the far North Side though, with dozens of kids to pal around with, even with the depressed, by comparison, pre-war birthrate, life was pretty informal and unscripted. We had plenty of places to go in the pre-shopping mall era that did not require a car or a long fitness walk. West Rogers Park was equipped with the standard local features: a central shopping-district street (Devon Avenue); classically furnished movie theaters (the Nortown just a few doors north and the Cine on Devon); non-chain department stores (Crawford's and Abrams); multiple corner drug stores; and three-chair barber shops. There were also delis (Morry's and Roberts); a neighborhood bank (Devon Bank); a record store (Ken-Mac), hot-dog stands (25 cents apiece, 15 cents for a smaller one at Frank's); a pizzeria (Oddo's on Peterson Avenue); and a sporting goods store, where Cubs pitcher Johnny Klippstein worked in the off-season.

On the southern border of our "territory" was Green Park fieldhouse and its playing fields. Beyond that border, Peterson Avenue, was St. Hilary's Parish. Within our own domain was St. Timothy's, whose students I played ball with and hung out with in the proximity of Simon's Drugstore at Washtenaw and Devon.

From Day One, I did not possess those fears. Often while playing sports, I was called a "dirty Jew." I'd give the prejudiced name-caller a whack. Later, in my early 20s, I played unique-to-Chicago 16-inch softball at Boltwood Park in the directly north suburb of Evanston. I was called in for fighting by Park Director Jack Burmaster, famed for coaching Evanston Township High School's powerful basketball program. Burmaster said, "I don't know about you Jews? Why do you get so upset when someone calls you a dirty Jew? I don't get upset when someone calls me a dirty German." My response: "German is not a religion, it's a nationality. Jewish is a religion."

I did not start fights, but I could finish them if necessary. I grew to a good physical stature for my age—about 6-foot-1, 190 pounds. That in itself was a pretty good deterrence. I had a slick tongue, though, talking my way out of fights I did not think I could win. I had acquired a skill that was further honed for a later, more profitable outcome.

I was a happy-go-lucky guy and I didn't care about the consequences. I just developed as a middle-schooler who was far more cocksure than average, perhaps a reflection of Herb Zucker's persona, and boosted by my size. I could talk and play a good game, although Green Briar Park boss Ed Kelly—another lifelong friend and future Chicago Parks Commissioner—described me as "quietly tough" playing sports. The "little devil" quotient in me increased as I evolved into a teenager. I no doubt exasperated my parents at times and mystified my buddy Fizdale, who evolved into an opposite personality. Although at times I thought I could grab and possess whatever I wanted, get away with things in gray areas and take plenty of shortcuts, I was never mean-spirited nor sought to bully or dominate others.

Maybe the best description of me came from Fizdale, looking back from a more than six-decade vantage point.

"Steve was wild," he said. "My parents once were called into school because the school wanted to know why I wasn't a better influence on him. Steve acted out, pretended he was dumb 'til his father died (when he was 25).

"I never thought of him as a bad kid. He may have thought of himself that way. Some are class clowns with a competition to finish last in their class."

Maybe so in Fizdale's view. People said I was dumb, I don't know. I frequently did not go to class. When I did, I watched the clock for when it was over.

My father likely was an enabler. As a man who knew all the angles, he told me he could get me out of any trouble except murder. I rarely faced consequences for my actions. But Herb Zucker adored me so much that he likely shorted me on some necessary tough love. But his stance toward me was really put to the test in likely the most painful thing I ever did.

Just 15 days short of my 16th birthday and not yet possessing a driver's license, I appropriated my mother's 1956 Mercury convertible on August 6, 1956. Fortunately, that was the first car to have a safety steering wheel, which collapsed in a collision. That might have saved my life. Fizdale sat in the back seat, looking at record albums, and another friend was in front with me. I tried to whip a left turn onto Maplewood Avenue and failed. I hit a tree hit head-on. It landed all the way up to the windshield.

I busted my eye sockets and nose and broke my left wrist. I later found out I had a heart murmur, probably triggered by contact with the collapsed steering wheel. I still paid the price a half-lifetime later for that prank, undergoing open-heart surgery at 50. Fizdale hit the back of the front passenger seat, breaking his nose.

"My head went through the front seat," Fizdale said. "I thought Steve was dead. He had no nose. His nose was reconstructed."

Since I had no license, my friend Jimmy Phillips tried to slip me his license underneath the gurney at Edgewater Hospital. But my father called a friendly police lieutenant and the case was eventually dismissed in court. Apparently, the accident did not faze my parents. A month later, they purchased a 1956

Olds Rocket 88 convertible. I was gun-shy when I did get my license, not wanting ever to drive again. But Herb Zucker encouraged me to get behind the wheel. Amazingly, I did not have any period of penance for the reckless, illegal driving. Our apartment, now relocated a half mile southwest to 6133 N. Washtenaw, was loaded with friends from Senn High School in the weeks after I got out of the hospital. My face was a mess, but apparently the teenagers of 1956 did not care.

Off the road, I had sticky fingers. For whatever reason, I performed some minor shoplifting even though I did not lack for pocket change from my parents. I started at 6, stealing $20 from my father. I went to a card store at Campbell and Devon and asked for $20 in Easter cards, of all things. The proprietor called my father. Nearby, at the Ken-Mac record store, I swiped 33-1/3 albums. I've still got them. I stole small things. I was always looking to grab something. But I don't think the incidents were kleptomania. Perhaps it was just the thrill of getting away with it. I didn't worry about the consequences. To this day, I love the music of my youth, when rock 'n' roll began. One of my prized possessions now is a Frankie Lymon and the Teenagers record album.

Time finally ran out on me though with the law when I attended the University of Illinois in 1959. I got arrested at the Bailey and Himes sporting goods store on Green Street in Champaign. I walked in with a fraternity brother. I picked up a football, threw it to him, said "catch this" and he was about to keep going right out of the store, but he ran into a sales clerk and we were nailed.

We were jailed overnight. I remember the baloney sandwich I ate in the cell. Another fraternity brother contacted his father, a Cook County Republican judge. Meanwhile, my father called a friendly Republican ward committeeman. Republicans were contacted because that party dominated downstate Champaign County at the time. These Chicago connections reached out to the local GOP powerbrokers and the charges were dismissed. But that did not mean the arrest record was expunged. More than 40 years later, my wife Shelly received a GOES (Global Entry) card, enabling her to bypass customs lines coming back into the country from an overseas trip. I applied, but did not get the card due to the 1959 arrest. The FBI had it on its database. I eventually got the arrest expunged in Champaign and finally received the GOES card.

But how much of a truly bad boy was I? One day in our Washtenaw apartment, my buddy Paul Zeinfeld and I spied Herb Zucker's bottle of Crown Royal on the counter. We combined to drink the bottle halfway down. In a depraved way of covering our tracks, we refilled it to the top with our urine — the color was just right. Then we heard someone walking up the stairs — my father coming back with his business associates. One of them opened the Crown Royal, then spit it out. "This tastes like piss," he hollered. At that moment, we ran down the stairs yelling, "Because it is!" For that, I got in trouble.

One place where errant behavior would not have been tolerated though was the U.S. Marines Corps. For a brief moment in 1959, I thought of becoming a Leatherneck. Zeinfeld was in the Marine reserves. Another friend was on active duty and came in from Okinawa. He would get a five-day extension of his furlough if he recruited someone. I did all the tests and I told my parents, who went crazy. I told them I didn't want to go to school. But I was rejected anyway by the Marines, as I had the heart murmur, likely from the car accident.

I spent the summers of 1958 and 1959 in Houston, where Fizdale had moved for a few years. We had parties every night and I even had a Houston girlfriend while staying in that sweltering city. Just before I left Texas for my sophomore year at the University of Illinois, I rigged it to have many of the girls I had met in Houston send me love letters with photos, perfume and lipstick. I was receiving 10 to 20 letters a day, while my poor fraternity brothers were lucky to get one. My "brothers" never figured out it was a hoax which gave me the reputation as the great lover of the frat house.

When I was 21, we all followed a buddy down to Miami

Beach on his honeymoon. No, we were not *that* intrusive—he stayed at another hotel. We stayed at the Casablanca Hotel, interestingly owned by my future wife Shelly's uncle, Dan Lifter. The hotel lobby had its house parrot on display. At 4:00 p.m. daily, we'd convene and teach the parrot the seven bad words, and then some. The bird proved an adept mimic. We waited for an easy mark and sure enough, two older ladies came by one day.

"Oh, what a cute parrot. Polly, want a cracker?" they said. The parrot replied, "Go fuck yourself," with emphasis, to the women.

Then, in November 1960, just after John F. Kennedy's election to the presidency, we were sitting around the fraternity house at the University of Illinois when we got the idea of going to see Dean Martin at the Sands in Las Vegas. I picked up the phone and called the pit boss there and asked to speak to Dean Martin. The pit boss said who should I say is calling? I told him Joey Bishop, a star comedian Martin regularly ran with. Martin came to the phone and said, "Hi Joey buddy." I said this is not Joey. I told him that we were three college guys at the University of Illinois and that we wanted to drive to Las Vegas to see his show. He said "come on."

So we drove to Las Vegas, making one stop in St. Louis to see two buddies who were in pharmacy school there. They gave us some Dexedrine stimulant tablets. We gave them to Bobby Kushner, who was doing most of the driving, and he went all the way to Las Vegas, stopping only to get gas.

Upon arrival, we went to the Sands and found Martin and said "we made it." His show was sold out, but he arranged for a table just off the stage for the three of us. The show was the thrill of a lifetime for each of us. The next morning, one of the guys flew to the University of Colorado to see his girlfriend. Bobby and I were sitting in the Sands coffee shop when Martin came over to our table and asked, "How are you boys getting along?" We were in awe. He sat down and told us that his pal, Sammy Davis Jr., was getting married to Mai Britt that afternoon and that he wanted us to fly on his plane and come with him to the wedding. Believe it or not, we had to decline because we had to pick up our friend in Colorado and return to school.

Years later, Shelly and I were watching a movie about "The Rat Pack" of stars Martin ran with in those days in Vegas. That wedding story came up in the movie and it was set for May. I said to Shelly, "No, it was the last week of November." Sure enough, the date had been changed to late November.

On another road trip in 1962, I teamed with Zeinfeld to literally drive Route 66 in the same manner as stars Martin Milner and George Maharis of that year's popular CBS-TV show. We arrived in Las Vegas, where we lost almost all of our money. Then we went to El Cajon, California, to see Jimmy Phillips, he of the emergency license delivery when I was banged up due to the car accident. Phillips' sob story, he had fallen on hard times, stripped us of our last pennies. Somehow, we found our way to Lake Tahoe anyway. We got jobs as gambling shills and stayed with the pit boss. After a time we were offered bartender jobs at the Cal Neva Lodge, owned by Frank Sinatra. I had just been accepted at DePaul Law School. So I had a choice between the law and bartending. The latter might have seemed temporarily tempting, given the surroundings, but I believe I chose right; I think!

Law school had not been a given. Illinois eventually did not work out, academically or otherwise, for me. I probably attended two percent of classes, likely the only student on academic probation six semesters in a row. In my first year at Illinois, I lived in Lundgren Hall, also the residence of many athletes. Next door to me was Illini quarterback Mel Meyers, who became a good friend.

Fast forward exactly three decades later to 1988 when Chicago civil rights activist Reverend Jesse Jackson ran for president. Jackson referred in the *Chicago Tribune* to the fact that the first time he became aware of racial prejudice in the North was when he was a fabulous quarterback and he could not make the Illini's starting lineup due to his race. Two more decades forward, I spoke at Jackson's Operation Push with the reverend himself right next to me. I told the audience about their preacher. Everything said about his Illini football experience was true—except for the pertinent fact the starting quarterback at that time was Meyers. I kiddingly added the reason your preacher did not start was he stunk, not because he was black. Meyers hailed from Dallas and could not play major college football in the South—because he was black. At Illinois, Meyers simply beat out Jackson for the starting job.

Anyway, because of my academic performance, I had to transfer to Roosevelt University in downtown Chicago. There, I continued to "game" the system. I got ahold of a metal garbage can and hollowed out the bottom. When I'd see a fireplug, I'd place the can over the plug and park there. To this day, when my friends and grandchildren obtain a good parking space, they said they've pulled a "Zwock," my Fonzie-era nickname by which most called me from ages 12 to 29. When I couldn't hide the fireplug, I simply parked where I wanted. At Roosevelt, I accumulated 427 parking tickets. But I had arranged Indiana license plates, in those pre-computer days, so they never came after me as they'd do now with a boot.

But after I had amassed 90 total hours, two of my best buddies said they wanted to go to law school. Curious, I said I wanted to be a lawyer, too. A friend of my father was Dave Trager, who owned the Chicago Packers, *nee* Zephyrs, an expansion NBA team that is now the Washington Wizards. Trager introduced me to DePaul basketball coach Ray Meyer, who helped get me into law school in early 1963. Again, I short-cutted and kind of conned my way in. I did not take the standard LSAT tests to get into law school. People said I was dumb, and I thought maybe I was. But once I got into DePaul, I made up my mind I'd do it the right way. I finally learned how to study at 23.

One year behind me in law school was Rich Daley, oldest son of Chicago Mayor Richard J. Daley, then in the third of the five-plus terms he served. I met Rich in the DePaul lounge between classes. We quickly became friends, a relationship that was strengthened in a unique way in our start in the business a few years later, as I will soon explain.

I still had some schemes going while attempting to make sense of the turgid text of lawbooks — a student could not hip-fake his way to a law degree. All the while, Fizdale and I ran a "touting" service that supported gambling on college basketball teams. Fizdale had gotten the idea reading an article on how organized crime set sports odds in a magazine while in Henry's Barber Shop at 6312 N. Western Ave., below our 1940s West Rogers Park apartment.

We avoided the less-developed NBA of the era and stuck to colleges. Fizdale and I devised a formula for every team in the country. In setting the line, we had a formula and power ratings. Say we predicted DePaul 80, Toledo 76. We'd assign a five-point, home court advantage for Alumni Hall, a small gym. But we'd done our research. I'd call all around the country for information — newspapers, the schools themselves, anyone who could give us something "inside." But long-distance calls were expensive in that era, so I managed to charge the calls to third parties. Again, I usually dodged the bullet when trouble beckoned.

"As the season wore on, Steve did things like calling a sorority at Texas Tech to ask if any guy on the team broke up with his girlfriend," Fizdale said. "We adjusted the numbers on hunches, on if players' names sounded unique, unusual things like that."

The service grew to where we were clearing $500 to $1,000 a week. We only bet ourselves in one freak situation. In betting sheets, an Alabama-Mississippi game was listed as a night game. But in reality it was played during the day. I called a janitor at Alabama and asked him to do a play-by-play for me on the phone. In these pre-internet days, I thus knew the final score and bet accordingly, cleaning up. The bookie [I bet with] never caught it.

Chicago Mayor Richard J. Daley

But eventually, Fizdale bailed on our service and here's how.

"Bob Elson, the White Sox broadcaster, called us down to the press table at Chicago Stadium," Fizdale said. "He was interested in us, and he'd get us Sox season tickets. I'm horrified. If Bob Elson knows about us, more than three people know what we're doing. We're betting against the mob. Not long after that, I quit. We got in too deep."

That's why Fizdale and I were opposites who attracted. I

was afraid of very few things. Fizdale was, but I wasn't. I didn't know any better. And in an act related to our gambling tout, I snapped up a bunch of 1963 Final Four tickets for Freedom Hall in Louisville from someone at Loyola University, one of the participating teams, for $14 apiece. After driving to Louisville, I walked out of the Brown Hotel and went up to a guy looking for tickets. I told him I had better seats. Boom! Got arrested for scalping. In the lockup, I was given the one traditional phone call. Instead of arranging for bond, I called one of my clients to give him the picks. That was one of my first examples where "duty" called.

By the time I landed a job as an assistant Chicago corporation counsel — a city prosecutor — after my 1966 graduation from law school, I no longer was a tout. I simply did not have the time. I was burning the candle at both ends, dipping into the most glamorous aspect of Chicago nightlife. I went out at 10:00 p.m. many days and returned at dawn, hardly sleeping. On top of my city job, I squeezed in some outside law work.

Off-duty, I played hard. I had a client who was a bartender at the Playboy Mansion on north Dearborn Street and I subsequently got invited to all of Hugh Hefner's parties. Meanwhile, I also hung out at a nearby bar on Walton Street called the Stork Lounge, along with three buddies. All the Playboy Bunnies would come in after finishing work at the Playboy Club at 2:00 a.m.

It was heaven. We were all single. The Bunnies were gorgeous. One Bunny, Beverly, a Gary, Indiana, native, married Barry Crown of the billionaire philanthropist family. I later represented Beverly Crown, who became a champion bodybuilder in middle age. A lot of the girls like Beverly hailed from Indiana. All had come to Chicago for three month's training.

I also served in a wingman's role for Rich Daley, by now working in the corporation counsel's office with me. I introduced him to a Bunny or two, and he went out with them. However, his father — with his own rabbit's ears up for moral behavior for anyone in city government — soon caught wind of son Rich's nightlife. Apparently, Rich had been spotted with his bunny-girlfriend touring Lincoln Park Zoo. The elder Daley asked him how he met the Bunnies. Realizing Rich was on the spot, I pleaded with him to not give me up, lest my $6,300 annual city job go up in flames. Rich somehow kept his own counsel and never threw me under the bus.

Later on, Jack Kellman's father, who owned Globe Glass, proclaimed that we "bums" finally had to meet some Jewish girls. As a major donor to Jewish causes, he had enough pull. So we all became escorts for Jewish debutantes at the Israeli Ambassador's Ball and it was all formal dress. We had to learn to waltz. I had not grown up in the debutantes' world, to say the least. However, after the ball, like the Bunnies after hours, they could let their hair down and have a good time. They indeed enjoyed that in our company. I always compared our presence to having the legendary, hard-luck East Side Kids at the ball.

On those occasions when I did have a blind date, I would take them to the Redhead Bar, 367 E. Chicago. I'd tell the bartender, Billy, if I give you the "high" sign, he'd announce, "You got a call Steve, there's a riot," and give the girl cab fare home. It was my "out" if I was not clicking with the girl.

During the daytime, my devil-may-care personality crept into my nascent legal work. One day as a prosecutor, working the afternoon call, I went straight to court from Oak Street beach in my bathing suit. To see what I could get away with, I put on my shirt, tie and sports coat, but no pants over my bathing suit, as I arrived. The judge's bench was high, perhaps five feet, and with my back to him the whole time, he could not see anything but the back of my head. People in the courtroom were giggling as I prosecuted my caseload for the afternoon and the judge never knew what I put over — or under — on him. Hey, I did not do anything different than some TV sports anchors who, above the desk, were properly dressed in tie and suit coat, but below camera view wore shorts.

In spite of both my nocturnal and daytime rounds, my life

rapidly changed. I finally had to grow up, by necessity. My father was playing gin and listening to the Cubs on his transistor radio when he dropped dead at 54 in 1966. When the Cubs won it all 50 years later, I took that radio—still tuned to 720 AM, WGN's frequency—to the cemetery and brought a Cubs championship T-shirt. It was a way of connecting to my roots, of spanning to simpler times even though I had that devilish persona.

My father's sudden passing meant I was the senior Zucker male, head of the family. Life would indeed become serious business. And just in time for my corporation counsel's job. Only two years after Herb Zucker died, the son he allowed to run wild became an enforcer of laws, the adviser to platoons of police officers and a man to whom crucial negotiations were entrusted by the City of Chicago. I'd be at ground zero and would be a contributor to a world-shaking event that reverberated through today.

The real rest of my life had begun. I never had a bar mitzvah, but there was no question I was now a man, a certified adult who had to leave the wild-child behind in memories.

CHAPTER 4
SMACK DAB IN THE MIDDLE
OF A DEMOCRATIC NATIONAL
CONVENTION STORM

My lifelong friend, Rick Fizdale, had been talking me up to Jerry Rubin for months. As a city corporation counsel, I was a Chicago administration source for Fizdale, he of anti-Vietnam War sentiment himself, that he could bank on to tell the truth, to give Rubin, one of the two top anti-Vietnam War radical protesters, the straight story, and even bargain in good faith to move the city back from the brink of cracking down on protests Rubin helped lead.

After some cloak-and-dagger escapades in which Fizdale helped Rubin shake off much of his Chicago police surveillance, he persuaded Rubin to meet me at the southern end of Lincoln Park on Sunday, August 24, 1968, just as delegates and national TV personalities arrived in town for the Democratic National Convention. Other arrivals, not known to anyone but top government and law enforcement officials, were regular U.S. Army troops from Ft. Hood, Texas, bivouacking at Chicago's Clarendon Park, four miles north of my projected meeting place with Rubin. Everyone in authority feared serious trouble. Agitators like Rubin courted chaos and the country—already wounded by Vietnam, the assassinations of Martin Luther King and Bobby Kennedy and urban riots—could not really take another broadside.

Chicago was fast becoming an armed camp, to keep thousands of demonstrators away from the convention at the old International Amphitheater on the South Side and conventi⌐

headquarters at the Conrad Hilton Hotel—then billed as the world's largest hotel—at the south end of downtown. In the months leading up to the convention, projections of as many as 300,000 protesters streaming into Chicago stoked fears into Mayor Richard J. Daley's office and into even higher offices in Washington, D.C.

So with the blessings of my boss, Cook County Sheriff, Dick Elrod, and even more higher-ups, my goal was to tamp down tensions by any degree possible. Without enough friendly apartments or hotel rooms to house them, or not possessing the desire to pay for lodging, the protesters coming from every corner of the country desired to sleep in Chicago parks. They pushed against a firm city ordinance that had not been rigorously enforced in previous decades, such as during heat waves, when thousands fled their stifling tenements to attempt slumber on public-park softball diamonds and other open, cooler, breezier spaces.

I was given some wiggle room on behalf of the city if Rubin could offer the same. All the scouting reports told me that Rubin, the self-styled head of the "Yippie" [Youths in Protest] movement, a takeoff on the popular term "hippie" born in San Francisco earlier, was a pure agitator. But you never know the person until you take the measure of him one-on-one.

Fizdale, a serious, thoughtful anti-war activist, was also hopeful in bringing Rubin to see me in my role as a city corporation counsel. He did not want violence after two good men, Robert Kennedy and Martin Luther King Jr., who wanted to change the country for the better, were gunned down and hundreds of U.S. soldiers were dying weekly in Vietnam jungles 10,000 miles away. He knew the government would set up multiple lines of defense to protect the convention while the most militant of protesters would push back.

I met Rubin and Fizdale at the appointed time. But there would be no negotiation. Rubin went ballistic on me. He was irrational in my judgment. Just as advertised, he was confrontational too. Fizdale also remembers it clearly.

Steve in Lincoln Park during Democratic National Convention, 1968

"Rubin takes off on Steve: 'Zucker, you're a Jew…how could a Jew be a pig?'" he recalled. "It escalated. Other people heard Rubin yelling at Steve and joined in. It got scary. 'Fuck you, Zucker, fuck you, pig,' I heard. I got so pissed off with Rubin. I tried to broker this talk. But Rubin wanted images of police riots."

No chance of a deal. Reluctantly disappointing Fizdale, I walked away amid the chanting of a crowd shouting profanities. The only humorous aside of the incident was the protesters had a baby pig running for president under the Yippie party banner. When I reported back to Elrod, my boss, I told him the protesters are not looking to get along with us.

Rubin playing to the mob thwarted perhaps the last chance for even a semi-peaceful settlement to the fractious atmosphere. Everything went downhill quickly, as police drove the demonstrators from that same spot two nights later, engaging in what would be described as "unnecessary roughness," with media covering the confrontation. I was there, not liking what I saw. And on the climactic night of August 28, 1968, the same police I had advised on the law clashed with demonstrators outside the Hilton in what a witness, then WBBM-TV reporter Bill Kurtis, called the "tipping point" of the turbulent 1960s. Rubin, conveniently absent and watching on TV from afar during the main police-demonstrator battle, had sown the whirlwind, capturing just a short-term victory as demonstrators chanted "the whole world is watching" at the network cameras videotaping the melee.

But Rubin figured it wrong. He could have changed history, for the better, if he had been willing to bargain. He did not have the plurality of public opinion from what the cynical former President Richard M. Nixon called "the silent majority" on his side. Panicked, enough of the electorate chose a different direction two-and-a-half months later, ignoring their best interests and the lives of thousands of GIs. Rubin and his fellow agitator-in-crime Abbie Hoffman, lost in the long term. And history was changed for the worse, in my opinion, its reverberations still coursing through the world today.

I had a participatory role in all of it. In hindsight, I wish I could have been involved more positively in the impact on both sides. First off were the Chicago police who I advised. Next were demonstrators not under the spell of the Rubins of the world, who had what they considered a legitimate gripe at the U.S. Vietnam policy which I also actually supported at the time, but which history and the subsequent flow of events proved to be horribly off-kilter, as thousands needlessly died.

What did I sign up for, I wondered, when I landed a $6,300 annual job in Chicago's law department the previous January, less than two years out of law school?

Decades later, as a sports agent, many of my clients were surprised when they learned of my boots-on-the-ground background in one of the most raucous events of 20th century American history. I never served in the military. But I got my combat training, so to speak, in the parks and streets of Chicago throughout 1968. It would not cease through the turn of another calendar year. Only when I begged off to full-time private law practice would I leave "handling civil strife" as a job description.

The streets were getting active coming into the start of 1968, when I landed the city job through the intercession of politically connected 48th Ward Democratic Committeeman Robert Cherry. Gaining work through literal political connections was the age-old Chicago practice. Few looked askance at having what was then the politically correct term of *patronage* as your entrée into employment.

Living at 4250 Marine Drive in the Uptown neighborhood, miles southeast from my childhood home in West Rogers Park, I dabbled in private law practice after I got out of DePaul's College of Law. I also worked as a Democratic precinct captain, the backbone of the last major urban political machine under Daley.

I was friends with Steve Cherry, well-connected Chicago politician Robert Cherry's daughter. In mid-1967, Robert Cherry helped get me a job prosecuting cases in Traffic Court. But shreds of my old wild-child personality remained, such as the time I went to court in my bathing suit. After a few months Cherry mentioned an opening in the ordinance enforcement department in the city corporation counsel's office. He told me he could get me in with Elrod, then department supervisor and son of Machine 24th Ward power Arthur X. Elrod.

The assistant corporation counsel's job was a comedown from my original lofty goals, in the same manner as anyone has to sometimes scale back his or her dreams for practicality. Amid my rambunctious personality and actions of previous decades, I had a serious side with conviction. As I entered law school in early 1963, I had a grand plan of working in the U.S. Department of Justice for Attorney General Bobby Kennedy, who was then busy dueling the stubborn practitioners of discriminatory Jim Crow laws in the Deep South. In fact, at one point in March 1965, as Martin Luther King Jr. marched for voters' rights in Selma, Alabama, I had a brief notion to join the protesters there.

Our office was in a virtual cubbyhole next to Daley's office on

City Hall's fifth floor. We were a four-man operation. I took the job of Ken Sain, who was promoted into the mayor's office. Very quickly, I learned the routines. Our crew would be out on the streets, advising police on how to enforce city laws and informing demonstrators, as the proverbial "good cops," on what they could and could not do in exercising their First Amendment rights. The job was crucial as the U.S. Supreme Court was busy in this era codifying the rights of suspects in criminal matters along with other cases that prevented police from their former one-stop-shop roles as judge and jury on the street.

When not out on assignment, we waited around the office like firemen on call. Both prosecutors and police assigned to us engaged in high-stakes gin rummy games in the office. At one point, Elrod proclaimed no more gambling in the office and the smart-aleck in me responded by rolling a couple of dice across his desk.

A "wink-wink" attitude from the department brass also applied to outside legal work. I managed to carry on a private practice that helped maintain my upscale-styled appearance. I preferred European suits to off-the-rack apparel from now-defunct Robert Hall's stores, so these supplements to my $6,300 salary helped keep me properly clothed and helped fund an around-the-world vacation as well.

But my idle time in the office quickly faded away. I literally had to hit the ground running as 1968 events began unraveling American society's previously calm and orderly manner. The year proved perhaps the most eventful in post-World War II history — and for all the wrong reasons.

I was on the job almost non-stop the weekend of April 5–7. During the dinner hour on April 4, Dr. King Jr. was assassinated by James Earl Ray at a Memphis motel. Despite the rise of black militancy due to rampant discrimination and poverty, the Nobel Prize-winning King was the one civil-rights leader who could still hold the center. His violent death was aptly described as a "crucifixion of the very finest kind of man this country has produced," according to John McDermott, director of the Catholic Interracial Council. Despite an appeal for calm by President Lyndon Johnson and top black leaders, the nation's cities began to go up in flames. Civil disorders immediately broke out in New York, Washington, D.C., Houston, Boston, Newark and other major cities.

While 4,000 regular Army troops tried to damp down the violence in the nation's capital, just blocks from the White House, Chicago may have gotten hit even harder, as riots began in earnest on April 5. A two-mile stretch of West Madison Street became engulfed in flames, the riot spreading throughout the West Side, as roughly half the city's firefighting crews, totaling 2,000 men, dodged rioting snipers and tried to put out the conflagration. Suburban fire departments helped out their city brethren as looters ran rampant.

Some 3,000 Illinois National Guardsmen with fixed bayonets patrolled the streets to back up beleaguered Chicago police, who had all furloughs canceled as every able-bodied officer went on duty. The south side, the city area heavily populated by African-Americans, did not go up for grabs as much, partly because of warnings sent out from Jeff Fort, a sort of black Al Capone as head of the Black P. Stone Nation megagang. South side shopkeepers placed signs on their storefronts from Fort warning of retaliation for any looting.

I took to the streets in a squad car with Sgt. Kevin O'Malley. He handed me a .38 revolver, the only time in my city attorney's career I carried a gun. I did not know how to use the firearm and thankfully did not have to find out if I could. O'Malley also issued me a police blue-and-white riot helmet. There were reports of rioters pulling white passengers off CTA buses. We took fire from the direction of the Cabrini Green public housing project on the city's near north side. And looking west on Roosevelt Road from police headquarters at 11th and State Streets, you could see nothing but smoke and flames in the distance.

Traveling to the south side at 63rd and Halsted Streets, I briefed Earl Strayhorn, a top commander in the National

Guard, who was traveling in an Army tank. Strayhorn eventually became a top Cook County judge. I feel we saved lives and property. I'd tell people on the street to please go home or they'd be arrested. I think the majority listened. The toll of lives and property could have been much worse, otherwise.

King's death was simply the match that lit a smoldering torch. The inner city's anger was pent-up over what its residents felt were decades of treatment as second-class citizens. I understood their anger. The city had been a racial tinderbox for years. King had marched for open housing in the city's all-white Marquette Park area in the summer of 1966. Carefully guarded by two lines of police, King was hit by a rock from the assembled seething mob of neighborhood residents. He came away uninjured, but remarked he was more fearful than he had been in any of his marches in the Deep South. The attending police were scared and so was Elrod, working at the scene.

The King riots were by far the worst of three Chicago inner-city disorders that had previously broken out in 1965 and 1966. One riot was touched off when the rear end of a seemingly out-of-control speeding fire truck struck and killed an African-American female who was simply standing on a street corner. For every move forward in racial progress, we seemed to take a corresponding step backward.

We did arrest a number of people in the King riots, charging them with mob action and criminal damage to property. We charged many with mob action and all with disorderly conduct, the latter of which gave us jurisdiction. Most were first offenders and received probation.

But the fires had hardly been put out—with much of the burned-out west side of the city not rebuilt for decades—when I had to handle my first major anti-war demonstration; a 5,000 protester-strong Peace Day rally armed with a Chicago Park District permit for Grant Park on April 27, 1968. That part of the rally began peacefully, with media accounts telling of demonstrators plucking dandelions and lilacs to adorn their hair and fashion necklaces. However, when neither the Park

District nor the demonstrators could rig up a sound system so all the rally attendees could hear, the protesters began to march to the Civic Center Plaza, four blocks west. The marchers on the sidewalk were lawful so long as they did not block traffic or obstruct people moving in and out of buildings.

But when they did, First District Commander James Riordan told the protesters via megaphone they had to break up the march. I was with Riordan and his officers as many of the marchers tried to break through ropes surrounding the then-new, elite Picasso Statue in what is now Daley Plaza. The city had picked that day to caulk the area but that's when a melee began. Riordan was cut on the head by a protest sign and needed quick treatment at nearby Henrotin Hospital. Corporation counsels also were in the line of fire. My colleague Larry Chambers was beaned in the head by a sign as some 50 were arrested and 15 injured.

In the same fractious period, a more serious outcome was avoided when other marchers tried to enter the Chicago Avenue Armory in the Streeterville neighborhood, adjacent to downtown, east of Michigan Avenue. The protesters stopped at Chicago Avenue and St. Clair Street. Army personnel actually came out to block their attempt to enter. They were 100 feet away. Hundreds surged forward, so a police lieutenant ordered tear gas to be deployed, but the wind blew the wrong way as the gas "nailed me." My eyes burned. It was horrible—seemingly the byword of the era.

But I wished every demonstration to which I was assigned had been as seemingly innocent with a humorous aside as on May 9 at downtown Roosevelt University, where I had finished my undergraduate studies only six years previously. A gaggle of students staged a sit-in at school offices. A flute player serenaded me in a photo in the Chicago Daily News, which tagged the caption, "Music to go to jail by." Despite the pleas of Roosevelt University President Rolf Weil as Elrod and I looked on, the protesters refused to move. Sixteen were camped out in the area, taking it over as 50 more staged a diversionary disturbance at the

Steve at sit-in, Roosevelt University, Chicago

opposite end of the corridor. Thirteen were arrested.

Less than a month after that relatively quaint sit-in, part of my heart was ripped out when Bobby Kennedy was fatally wounded by Sirhan Sirhan moments after celebrating his California Democratic presidential primary win in Los Angeles. Bobby Kennedy was a great man. His assassination destroyed a lot of hope about ending the Vietnam War. He truly cared about people.

African-Americans really believed in Bobby Kennedy, even more so than his late brother, John, who I believe was a comparatively latecomer to promoting civil and economic rights. Bobby Kennedy's memorable ad libbed speech announcing King's death to a stunned crowd in Indianapolis' inner city on April 5 was credited with heading off disorders in Indiana's state capital. The outcome of the forthcoming convention and its effect on the entire world was dramatically changed by Bobby's absence. I believe he would have won the nomination and the November election. He is the man I most admired in my personal "Hall of Fame." Bobby Kennedy's loss stings to this day.

The post-assassination reality left me with the memory of preparing for the onslaught of protests for the convention as the summer of 1968 progressed.

Daley had wanted the convention in Chicago. The city had frequently hosted both Democratic and Republican conventions at the old Chicago Stadium arena, but missed out on both gatherings in 1964, when they were held in Atlantic City and San Francisco, respectively. In 1968, the mayor thought he could control the situation in which the entire process would run smoothly. But the event had to be housed in a substantially inferior facility — the old International Amphitheater, near the declining, industrial Stock Yards neighborhood four miles southwest of downtown.

When projecting ahead to 1968, Daley had hoped to stage the convention at the original showcase lakefront McCormick Place, which was destroyed in a January 1967 fire. In spite of the loss of the much newer building, the Democratic National Committee awarded Chicago the convention on October 8, 1967. At the time, incumbent President Lyndon Johnson appeared headed for nomination for a second term before the flow of events took everything in a radically different direction.

Original projections had as many as 300,000 protesters converging on the city. But an April ruling by U.S. District Judge Richard Austin backed the city ordinance against the visitors sleeping in the parks. Austin's ruling, along with the police reaction and arrests during the April 27 Peace Day, no doubt kept away tens of thousands. Around the same time, I relayed the city's position closing the parks at night to Fizdale, my old friend and a protester himself who had contact with the top anti-war radicals in New York.

"I was visiting Arthur, a friend in New York," recalled Fizdale. "We went to Abbie Hoffman's apartment in Greenwich Village. I met Rubin, Timothy Leary, Phil Ochs and Paul Krasner. They did not believe my story that I had a friend in the city law department who knew the policy on the parks."

Rubin came anyway to Chicago like the proverbial moth attracted by a light. In this case, it was the red lights of TV cameras. We got police "Red Squad" reports daily on the activities of anti-war leaders. They were under heavy surveillance.

"A few days before the convention, I was walking south on Clark Street," recalled Fizdale. "Rubin was going the other way, followed by a couple of cops. Jerry said he was staying at a place on Armitage and Mohawk. I lived around the corner. He complained there are so many police cars in the area. I said maybe you can stay with me.

"We needed a way of escaping (surveillance). I take Rubin up on the roof, then we use the fire escape to go to the alley. We cut through a yard and went into my apartment. Jerry said, 'This is all great.' I told him about Steve, and said I'd call him and maybe we can cut a deal.

"So I called Steve and told him I heard you're looking for Rubin. His answer: 'How do you know?' I tell him maybe I can help you find him. I ask him to reduce the number of police cars watching from 15 to three. Steve calls me back 45 minutes later and says Rubin has a deal. I tell him Rubin was at my house. We arranged a meeting for Steve and Rubin to meet. He's your best shot to negotiate to where you can avoid a lot of trouble."

But with Rubin and other radical leaders in town, I figured I'd be in for the busiest week of my life. While having dinner with my mother and aunt at the Singapore restaurant on Saturday night, August 25, I told them I wouldn't be home for a while. My mother expressed concern for my safety. Her fears did not prove unfounded, given what I'd learn the next day.

I relayed the Rubin meeting plan to Elrod and he granted me full authority to negotiate. The chain of command above Elrod was open to de-escalating the situation with the protesters. Daley certainly did not want trouble. He was open to any reasonable tactic to calm the waters. Ed Kelly, my old coach at Green Briar Park [and later Parks Commissioner], would have been a conduit for any successful talks with Rubin. As the convention was about to open, Kelly literally slept in his parks superintendent office across the street from the Field Museum near downtown. He was busy moving both regular Army troops and National Guard units to staging positions at assorted parks. Kept secret at the time from the public and media was the stationing of Vietnam-veteran troops from Ft. Hood at Clarendon Park, near my Uptown [neighborhood] home and a short drive from Lincoln Park.

"I followed Steve and was very supportive," said Kelly. "If Steve came over to me (with a successful deal to not spark violence), I would have gone to the mayor. It's possible he could have granted a one-time exemption to let them sleep in the park."

Kelly placed huge importance on peace talks with the demonstrators. My meeting with Rubin was secret, so the media at the time would have chomped at the bit to learn the news. "It would have been a scoop," said Bill Kurtis, then a young street reporter for CBS-owned WBBM-TV.

But Rubin truly did not comprehend the hornet's nest he stirred by setting me up. Only after he verbally ambushed me as we met in near-downtown Lincoln Park did Fizdale realize he'd been had too.

"Rubin wanted it to get out of control," Fizdale said. "(Abbie) Hoffman and Rubin were close friends. They understood 'sound bite' before the word became popular, like the idea dumping (hallucinogenic) LSD into Lake Michigan and everyone in the city would get high. That couldn't happen given the size of the lake and sheer amount of water coming into the city. But that was guaranteed to get on TV. They just had to say stuff, so they could mobilize other followers."

While I was rightfully angry at the cynical Rubin, I felt for legitimate protesters who simply wanted to exercise their constitutional rights to free speech and free assembly in Chicago. There were thousands, but they couldn't be heard as loud as playing-to-camera performers like Rubin and Hoffman. Media at the time often used "hippies" as a blanket term to describe all demonstrators, and I believe that was wrong.

"Hippie" implied counter-culture youth — immersed in sex, drugs and rock 'n' roll — as popularly portrayed from 1967's "Summer of Love" in San Francisco. I found so many examples of serious students, older anti-war protesters and people committed to opening up debate and change. I talked with many of these activists one-on-one in the parks and other places to which I was assigned. But since these people were not as theatrical as the Rubin-Hoffman leaders and their hard-core followers, they didn't provide for "sexy" broadcast images and sound bites.

Remember, King himself had come out against the war via many of his speeches. He was not just a one-note civil rights leader. In the spirit of such intellectual depth, a much more reasonable anti-war activist was Rennie Davis, with whom I could negotiate. I respected Davis, project director for the National Mobilization Committee to End the War in Vietnam. I respected him for his persona and legitimacy over what I considered to be the cartoonish Rubin and Hoffman. If Davis had possessed even more sway over the thousands who came to Chicago, I believe we would not have had events play out the way they did.

Although I had hopes of negotiating, Rubin indeed played to form as the pre-convention intelligence had projected. After the convention, the city quickly put out a booklet, "The Strategy of Confrontation," describing and analyzing the events. Shortly after the convention was awarded to Chicago, *The Village Voice* [newspaper out of New York] quoted Rubin on his plans for Chicago: "Bring pot, fake delegates' cards, smoke bombs, costumes and blood to throw and all kinds of interesting props. Also football helmets."

Even more mainstream anti-war leaders like Dave Dellinger and the late activist-turned-politician Tom Hayden, publicly spoke of confrontation, promising tactics of "prolonged direct action to put heat on the government and its political party." *Barron's* magazine defined New Left "direct action" as including "street barricading, fire bombing, seizure of buildings and massive confrontations with the police." Public drills of guerilla and assault tactics were witnessed by media. Stores near the upscale Lincoln Park neighborhood reported an unusual amount of sales of caustic materials, including oven cleaners paid for with $100 bills to counteract police-employed mace. Demonstrators were encouraged to throw handmade projectiles at police. Wildest reports filtering into police included assassination plots against Daley, presumptive Democratic nominee Hubert H. Humphrey and anti-war candidate Eugene McCarthy, and even a plan to murder a young female supporter of McCarthy and blame it on the Minnesota senator.

The only good thing to come out of further agitating demonstrators was no encouragement to possess firearms. Otherwise, there could have been true carnage. But remember, this was 1968—a far-less gun-crazed era than we have now, when police need high-caliber weapons to match those of street gangs and others with illicit intent. Mass murderers, meanwhile, employ military-style automatic weapons for lethal effect.

Most of the more outlandish reports never panned out. But the plans for confrontation only intensified after my failed meeting with Rubin. The protestors simply camped out in the southern end of Lincoln Park with no intention of leaving at the 11:00 p.m. closing time.

"It was building tension which we thought would lead to violence," said CBS' Kurtis. "There wasn't a march every night that didn't have violence to it. It's almost as if someone had planned it that way. I remember thinking I have to cover this—the streets were where the action was."

Three straight nights of demonstrator-police clashes at the park began on August 25, only getting worse each night as police tried to clear the park after 11:00 p.m. All the while, orderly efforts to protest were accommodated. On Monday, August 26, a line of marchers was permitted to walk on the west sidewalk of Michigan Avenue, right next to the Conrad Hilton Hotel convention headquarters.

But by now, many police officers were fed up with the perceived pro-demonstrators news coverage, an attitude picked up on by Kurtis and his colleagues.

"There was that feeling media was on the yippies' side," Kurtis said. "Many police felt we had fueled the fire and tension and telling the story of the outside agitators."

Kurtis and his WBBM camera crew were close by us as some 2,500 demonstrators set up barricades to slow the police advance into Lincoln Park late on Monday, August 26. The tear-gas discharge blew back in the faces of police, newsmen and city officials. None of us had masks. Regretfully, and against orders from high police command and the corporation counsels on the street, police took out their frustrations on some media members. Four reporters, a still photographer and a film cameraman reported being struck by police, prompting Deputy Superintendent James Rochford to issue a written order of no contact between police and the media.

But by now we saw we were having serious problems. In retrospect, it proved to be not the smartest decision to continue closing the parks with the sheer number of demonstrators determined to camp out. Thus the agitation and conflict only increased as the third straight night of park-clearing was attempted late on Tuesday, August 27.

As the police tried to push the demonstrators out of the park past the intersection of North Avenue and LaSalle Street, toward the downtown-adjacent Old Town neighborhood, more media members were caught between protesters and police. I tried to control it as best as possible, informing as many police as possible they were in violation of orders and the law. The city was by now angry at any rogue officers. But the action was moving too quickly to dampen down white-hot, street-cop emotions. Police were outnumbered and demonstrators were intent on egging on police by throwing rocks and bags of excrement a them.

"There was a summit meeting between the media and Rochford," Kurtis noted at the time. "He was told, 'Your guys

Steve with Chicago Police Superintendent James Conlisk, 1968

are going after the media.' There was a 'treaty' to not do it anymore."

Chicago Police Superintendent, James Conlisk, and his top command structure indeed attempted to stop the police-media conflict as the hours wore on. Yet, events were spiraling beyond any tightly controlled battle plan by the authorities. The coup de grace was about to take place in my long day's journey into night on what would be a fateful Wednesday, August 28, the day that I believe changed the course of history.

In a pre-convention court hearing, the anti-war groups were given a number of options for rallies and marches that would have been granted city permits. The only one accepted by the protesters was an afternoon rally at the Grant Park band shell on August 28. The groups desired rallies much closer to the actual convention hall. Of course, that was not acceptable to the city, which, given the war-like atmosphere, wanted no protesters within hailing distance of the convention-hosting Amphitheater.

The rally at the band shell got underway as scheduled in mid-afternoon. I worked with attending police, who faced a barrage of verbal assaults, the popular "pig" insult of the times along with the usual profanities. But I cautioned them to hold back. They could do nothing physically and could not make arrests. As vile as their language, the protesters were protected by free speech in the First Amendment.

But one act in the rally went beyond the pale. Around 3:00 p.m. on August 28, one protester tore down the American flag at the band shell, replacing it with a red flag. Others joined in tearing and stomping on the flag—perhaps going beyond the protections of free speech. Angered to no end, I told the head police official on the scene to make the arrests. Other police were called in to augment the original squad tending to the flag incident. One officer was bitten by a female protester.

The battle over the flag sparked a protesters' mass reaction. Rally attendees turned over the band shell benches, some trying to use them as barricades against police and they began running down the adjacent Lake Shore Drive main thoroughfare, blocking traffic. Police chased them north. The protesters could not cross back west to Michigan Avenue via Balbo Drive or Congress Parkway, which were blocked by police and National Guardsmen. The demonstrators finally found an open street westward on Jackson Boulevard and turned to run toward Michigan Avenue.

Meanwhile, another protester put up a Vietcong or North Vietnamese flag on the General Logan statue in Grant Park. I told the police to pull the protester and flag down. He broke his arm. At the time, I felt I made the right decision. We were at war and our enemies used that flag. In the superb 2017 Ken Burns' documentary on Vietnam, I spotted a quick clip of myself leading a group of police toward that flag on the statue.

My actions might have agitated the crowd more than might have happened if the flag protesters went undisturbed. At the time, the Supreme Court had not yet ruled burning the American flag was a First Amendment-covered action. I just felt I did my patriotic duty. But as I learned within a couple of years, that war had to end. I believe we were not in it to win and we suffered 58,000 dead as a result. To what end? What I experienced and did, though, had to be put in the context of the times and the heat of the moment.

As the demonstrators scattered and then re-congregated on Michigan Avenue, tensions built further. The mass of people was blocked by police, backed by the National Guard, from moving south of the Conrad Hilton to prevent any march on the Amphitheater, where Vice-President Humphrey prepared to accept the Democratic nomination for president. Then a fateful event not directly part of the anti-war movement helped trigger the one searing scene from the convention that panicked much of Middle America.

A Poor People's mule train directed by Hosea Williams, under the auspices of the Southern Christian Leadership Conference, proceeded slowly southward on Michigan Avenue to the Hilton and the police line around 8:00 p.m. A mass of demonstrators gathered behind the three-wagon mule train, which had been given permission to continue past the hotel on Michigan. After it proceeded, the train eventually stopped a block south, where it was met by the Reverend Ralph David Abernathy, a longtime Southern Christian Leadership Conference associate of Martin Luther King. Surveying the nearby tinderbox situation as he prepared to give a speech, Abernathy canceled his plans and ordered the mule train out of the area. Under police escort, it returned to its starting point on what was known as the city's near west side.

What happened next was literally a chain reaction of protester anger with assaults on the police and miscommunication by a key police commander on the scene.

To make room for the mule train and its 100 participants to proceed, protesters were pushed aside and back. Fizdale, on the scene to exercise his legitimate right to protest, noticed an unfortunate ripple effect on the crowd as it was forced west to another police line guarding the Hilton on the Wabash Avenue side. Watching from atop a car at the corner of Balbo and Michigan near the hotel, Kurtis also noticed a mass movement of people in different directions triggered by the mule train.

"I thought there was indeed a surge at that time," he said. "Demonstrators thought they were going to be allowed through (in the direction of the Amphitheater). They started following the wagon. It looked as though demonstrators were trying to break through. I thought the cops had to do something."

These police, directed by an area commander, believed they were being attacked by the protesters. They were not in radio coordination with the Michigan Avenue-stationed fellow area commander. In a surprise for us corporation counsels on Michigan Avenue, the Wabash commander had his line push the protesters eastward toward Michigan Avenue—right into the main line of officers.

The *Chicago Tribune* deadline report assembled minutes after the clash confirmed the misdirection of police lines, which we would have prevented given better communication ability with the spread-out commanders: "Some observers said the protesters were caught between two groups of police which, instead of pushing them back into Grant Park, were squeezing the demonstrators between police lines. Neither of the police groups was aware of what the other was doing," the report stated.

The battle commenced. Police made contact with the mass of protesters in the street in an attempt to move them back into Grant Park. Bottles, rocks and other small, sharp objects were supplemented by what the *Tribune* described as office staplers and wooden saw-horse barricades. Ashtrays and water were dumped out of windows in the Hilton, with one allegedly traced to Eugene McCarthy's 15th-floor suite.

Suddenly, police used their nightsticks on individual demonstrators and dragged them into waiting squad cars. The dragging process came across as the worst to onlookers. In the chaos, several people were pushed through plate-glass windows on the ground floor of the Hilton. Demonstrators who sought refuge inside the hotel were chased back outside.

Meanwhile, some of the officers in the outer police line

inadvertently dispersed. Some demonstrators ran west on Balbo and then turned either north or south on intersecting alleys and streets. Police left their posts to chase these protesters. That was absolutely the wrong tactic for which we all trained. Our goal was to get as many people off the streets as possible. If they ran away without assaulting police or innocent bystanders, so much the better. However, police in pursuit only diminished the assembled total force, which turned out to be not enough for the task at hand.

The police had really stumbled into a new era in handling demonstrators.

"The cops really had no extensive training in crowd control," said Kurtis. "They were just a bunch of cops on a line. They were ad libbing it. They stayed in a line, then Rochford must of have said clear the intersection. They charged."

The image of the cops smacking up against a small portion of the thousands of assembled demonstrators might not have had the impact nationwide at another time and place. The daytime protests were caught on film, edited and shown on newscasts hours later. But in prime time, studio-size video cameras placed on the marquee of the hotel had an elevated view of the intersection. They could not transmit live video to the networks with the big mobile units kept off the street due to a concurrent taxi strike. Noticing the cameras, demonstrators beyond the reach of the charging police batons chanted, "The whole world is watching," five words that have reverberated through the decades and into a new millennium.

Kurtis said the tape of the melee was given to network motorcycle couriers dressed like police so they could zoom through the defensive lines. The tape was rushed to the main control trucks at the Amphitheater and put on the air unedited.

"The producer called Walter Cronkite and said all hell has broken loose," said Kurtis. "We don't have time to screen it."

No reporters' narration was featured to put the chaos into context—the mule train, the demonstrators squeezed between uncoordinated police lines, the debris thrown at police that could not be picked up by heavy cameras airing scenes only their accompanying lights could illuminate after dark. CBS' Cronkite simply ad libbed a description of the video, minus interaction with any colleague on the scene.

Trying to restore some order in the middle of the melee, I thought America as we knew it was ending. Imagine what the millions of viewers at home believed, watching the same scenes of disorder. In most cities it was still a three-channel TV universe. After eight full months, that year of events both foreign and domestic seemed to be spiraling out of control.

"People in another part of the country, far from the convention, are saying the revolution is here," Kurtis said. "It was the impact of those images, the cops' blue helmets and the protesters."

The video views proved to be worse than the list of casualties or arrests. This was no Charlottesville of 2018. No one was seriously injured or maimed for life. Not a shot was fired or multiple people run over by a careening vehicle. Almost all the protesters arrested had their cases dismissed. The police involved did not show up in court and the squad-car drivers could not serve as witnesses.

Meanwhile, master agitator Rubin and comrade-in-anarchy Hoffman were nowhere to be found around Balbo and Michigan. "Rubin was back at my apartment watching it all on TV," said Fizdale.

Chicago Tribune "Tower Ticker" columnist Bob Wiedrich immediately lit up the Yippies: "When the moment of truth has arrived and the tear gas shells have begun to fly, these two courageous leaders have just melted away to plot for another day. Obviously, lumps are only to be taken by the rank and file.

"We do not wish, however, to dilute the heroics of these activists. Why, do you know that Abbie yesterday was brave enough to paint an obscene four-letter word on his brow and walk through the near north side so even little kids could enrich their vocabularies? Yes sir folks! That takes guts, real guts! Take a bow, fellas!"

Meanwhile, Rubin and Hoffman stayed far out of harm's way, but the more-respectable Rennie Davis was injured earlier on August 28 when benches began flying and tear gas began wafting at the Grant Park band shell.

More media were caught in the cops' crosshairs even after two days of orders to cease and desist contact with reporters and camera operators. Kurtis gingerly attempted to get through the intersection after the worst of the disorder had passed. He saw what he believed was another courier kitty corner on the east side of Michigan Avenue.

"I had some film I wanted to get back to the station," Kurtis said. "I was dressed in a sport coat and tie. They must have thought I was a corporation counsel, so the police did not stop me. When I got to the guy on the motorcycle, I found out he was a real cop. So I had to retrace my steps back across Michigan Avenue."

After the melee fully died down and the arrested had been removed to police stations, more demonstrators gathered on Michigan Avenue as midnight ticked by. Someone up high finally realized that letting the assembled stay in Grant Park past the 11:00 p.m. curfew was a temporary—but wise—move. Even with the August 25 ambush by Rubin, I believe some of the confrontations with demonstrators might have burned themselves out with the visitors mellowing in the park through the wee hours. Obviously, the brass also would have had to turn their noses the other way in enforcing anti-marijuana laws.

Even with the National Guard on hand, no one was spoiling for more fights. Police informed the demonstrators they would not be interfered with if they stayed in the park and did not block Michigan Avenue. That announcement was greeted with cheers and no further violence occurred the rest of the night.

My estimate was that about one percent of the police actually acted against training and tactical orders in roughing up demonstrators and covering media. There could have been a few rogue officers who were multiple offenders in aiming their ire at media. Even police spokesman Frank Sullivan said at the time he could not deny "somebody swung a club more than he should."

Joe Lefevour, head of the Chicago lodge of the Fraternal Order of Police, saw the same thing I did as I talked to protesters who were not under the immediate sway of Rubin and his hit-and-run colleagues. Lefevour branded the majority of young demonstrators in Grant and Lincoln Parks as "orderly...They obeyed our orders and joked with us. But then their leaders work them up to a fever pitch and disappear, leaving the kids to take the consequences...Maybe some police did get a little carried away. Maybe I would, and maybe you would, too."

Added Parks Commissioner Kelly, getting first-hand reports of all the humanity in the parks: "A lot of young kids were down there not knowing what to do."

While cautioning against violence, the Catholic Interracial Council's Marie McDermott also admitted police were overly provoked by protesters, "Some of whom do not share our commitment to nonviolent methods."

But one more spasm of confrontation was on the docket. On Thursday night, August 29, another attempted march to the Amphitheater was stopped at 16th and Michigan. At first, Sargent Kevin O'Malley and I were the only officials there. We called for help. The National Guard showed up and blocked the forward path of the marchers. They agreed to turn around to Grant Park and were not arrested. Later, more guardsmen lobbed tear gas at crowds to get them off Michigan Avenue near the Hilton. The crowds retreated into Grant Park, but the guardsmen and police did not follow them. Again, the policy of letting the protesters temporarily have the parks morning, noon, night and overnight proved too little, too late.

Once the conventioneers and protesters departed Chicago, the city staffers had no break or extra combat pay coming. Higher-ups had us quickly produce "The Strategy of Confrontation" booklet for release in one week. But that account still came out two months before the presidential election.

My addendum to "The Strategy of Confrontation" nearly five decades later is sharp, and made even more so by the current events and presidential controversies of 2017–18. Simply put, if the radical leaders had agreed not to push the demonstrators into clashes with police, and the convention had not been almost a sideshow to the events on the street, then I believe Humphrey would have been elected president—not Nixon—and Humphrey would have served two terms. The Vietnam War would have been ended sooner, no Watergate scandal would have ensued and a succession of what I considered weak presidents would not have taken office later in the 1970s.

Panicking an already-jittery pubic were the color images of the police and protesters clashing in front of the Hilton, combined with convention video of Senator Abraham Ribicoff (D-Connecticut), decrying "gestapo tactics in the streets of Chicago," plus Daley's inaudible shout-backs to Ribicoff and Cronkite proclaiming a "bunch of thugs" were causing scuffles on the Amphitheater floor with CBS reporters Mike Wallace and Dan Rather.

"No question that hurt Humphrey," said Kelly, one of the top slate-making officials in the Illinois Democratic Party and anywhere in the country, for that matter.

Meanwhile, Nixon loudly promised "law and order" along with a never-detailed end-of-war panacea in his campaign. He was not called Tricky Dick for nothing as his advisers pursued a "Southern Strategy." Many voters bought these messages after the convention, while others were siphoned away by the even more right-wing and racist appeal of third-party candidate George C. Wallace. Though the convention chaos gave Nixon a big boost in the polls, the race began tightening in October even though I believe Humphrey did not run a strong campaign. Without chaos at the convention, I believe Nixon would not have had the jump in the polls and Humphrey would have had enough support to win, especially with any progress toward Vietnam peace.

"A definite possibility," Kurtis opined of a Humphrey victory.

The late Bobby Kennedy likely would have ended the war relatively quickly had he lived, been nominated and elected, running against Nixon. But I believe Humphrey, a lifelong liberal, would not have been far behind that pace if he had been elected.

Meanwhile, the war raged on and Nixon's platitudes kept promising "peace with honor." Rubin had to confine his theatrics to a federal courtroom as a defendant in the famed conspiracy "Chicago 7" trial, charged with inciting the convention disorders. Eventually, Rubin and five other defendants were convicted of inciting, but won on appeal.

Clean legally, Rubin was now a clown without a circus. He likely helped slow down the war but I believed should have been, at the latest, a 1970-vintage ending. The decades passed, social problems still needed be solved and he was nowhere to be found to argue for a better world.

But so much for "up the revolution" as Rubin became a capitalist, working briefly for the Wall Street firm of John Muir and Company. He later marketed himself as a networking expert, attracting "yuppies" instead of promoting "yippies."

He died at 56 in 1994 doing one of the most dangerous things in his life—jaywalking. Dashing across busy Wilshire Boulevard in the Westwood neighborhood of Los Angeles, he was hit by a car, never regaining consciousness and passing away shortly afterward.

What a waste.

I tried.

CHAPTER 5
I DIDN'T WIN EVERY COURT CASE, BUT...

"My name is Steve Zucker. I am your lawyer."
Tipped off by friendly barkeeper Terry Cohen to the forthcoming carnival, I was waiting on the ground floor of the John Hancock Center with an offer Dan Goodwin, otherwise known as "Spider Dan," could hardly refuse, midday on November 11, 1981.

"Spider Dan" had enthralled an entire city of Chicago by scaling the 100-story building all morning, thwarting Chicago Fire Department attempts to stop him from continuing his climb but eventually winning then-Mayor Jane Byrne's approval to let him go all the way to the top rather than risk the "optics" of a such an attempt leading to his fall.

Byrne and an angry Police Superintendent Richard Brzeczek spoke to "Spider Dan" through broken-out windows. Diners in the Hancock's 95th floor restaurant went almost nose-to-nose against the window with Goodwin, who gave them a thumbs-up as he inched his way skyward. But what goes up must come down and I wanted to make sure when the committed climber — adorned in a Spiderman-decorated wet suit and makeshift gear — reached terra firma that he'd face nothing more than a legal slap on the wrist.

The Goodwin event practically gave me a sneak preview of the rest of my career, the bread and circuses of the 1985 Bears and other public figures just a few calendar turns into the future.

However, the human fly gave me a refreshing break from the often grim task of turning guilty legal cases into much lesser charges or acquittals as a criminal defense attorney. My busy schedule of negotiating with prosecutors and judges had put food on the table and a nice home over the heads of my growing family throughout the 1970s. I was good at that often-unenviable task, but somehow it would not last into middle age. More colorful clients like Goodwin, as well as Larry Flynt, the publisher of lusty *Hustler* magazine, and White Sox outfielder Ron LeFlore, known well for his off-field transgressions, would provide new directions in the early 1980s from my circuits through the courts.

I had some of my legal and political talents to use to handle "Spider Dan" Goodwin, who didn't put his neck at risk for just a mere publicity stunt. He had witnessed the fatal 1980 fire at the MGM Grand Hotel in Las Vegas nearly one year previously. Some 85 people died, mostly of smoke inhalation and without a ready way to be rescued. Goodwin had climbed a series of super-tall buildings, including the then-Sears Tower (now Willis Tower), to demonstrate to public safety departments what he believed to be groundbreaking rescue equipment.

Goodwin had been fed by popular local restaurateur and my friend, Terry Cohen, at his Alexander's restaurant at 4:00 a.m. to prep for his Hancock climb. Goodwin made it a point to climb only on holidays to maximize media publicity for his vertical prowess. As he ate, Goodwin asked Cohen for an attorney, as he knew he'd face legal flack. I told Cohen to tell Goodwin to call me when he reached the top.

A friend of Goodwin alerted the media as he ascended just out of reach from the ground. At the 20th floor, firefighters lowered a window-washing scaffold to block his path, but Goodwin simply swung around the apparatus and continued. Fire Commissioner William Blair ordered the prospectively dangerous spraying of Goodwin with water by his men around the 36th floor, but top city officials stepped in thereafter and tried to dissuade Goodwin from going further. Firemen even held fishing-type pike poles above him to block his path.

But with a gathering mob of thousands at ground level cheering him on and the bad optics of the city trying to reel

"Spider Dan" climbing a tree in our backyard

him in, Byrne decided to let him finish his ascent. He was even given gloves, warm clothes and a signaling device, while firemen and cops would monitor him floor-by-floor in case he ran into trouble. Later, firemen quoted in the media said they were "embarrassed" and "ashamed" by their department's "bush-league" actions and worried that they tried to kill Goodwin with the dousing and improvised barricades.

I worked my way inside police lines as I knew people from my 13 previous years as a city prosecutor-turned-defense lawyer. The crowd, which several times had chanted, "Let him climb! Let him climb!" spilled out onto Chestnut Street as he came back to earth. A woman ran up to kiss him as police led him away with me following closely.

Some of the assembled already had made money off Goodwin. Vendors sold snacks and coffee to the crowd while the Hancock bar quickly offered a $1 Spider Man Special cocktail, a crème de menthe-vodka mix.

Goodwin would have to answer the next day to Circuit Court Judge Harold Siegan, who previously had issued an injunction against the climb. Goodwin was charged with contempt of court. The courtroom was jammed. I had never seen so many reporters in my life—of course, I had not yet worked a Super Bowl. Goodwin was mobbed by autograph seekers, which upset Siegan.

The judge set Goodwin's bond at $100,000. I offered to put my house up for that bond, even though I had known Goodwin for less than 24 hours, but when my wife Shelly heard about the bond offer on TV, she called her father, Herbert Young, a friend of Siegan's. Young contacted Siegan, who changed the bond to a personal recognizance bond, requiring no money or property to be put up. Oddly enough though, we never went back to court.

Goodwin went on with his vertical journeys for his advocacy of high-rise safety equipment. Soon after, we contracted with Japanese TV to climb the 74-story Parc Torres in Caracas, then the tallest building in South America. I flew down with Goodwin. And so I went on my first publicity tour and it got me thinking about vistas beyond my present legal practice. I struck out though in my first attempt to link Goodwin with show business.

Even Marvel Comics turned down an idea for Goodwin to formally associate himself with their trademarked Spiderman character. And so, almost amazingly, Goodwin was still at it at age 58 in 2014, climbing the Telephonica Building in Santiago, Chile, for comic book-legend Stan Lee's *SuperHuman* TV series.

If Goodwin subliminally suggested a new path for me, events in 1970 established the career persona that would come in handy the rest of the way.

I returned from my own mandated three-month leave of absence to attend to the trial of radical Weatherman Brian Flanagan. I had circulated a false story about the disabling injury of Dick Elrod, my mentor, to help Elrod's political aspirations. Obviously, given the thread of events, I was not fated to last much longer in my city assistant corporation counsel's practice. I hung out my shingle full time as a criminal defense attorney, drawing from the relationships I already had made in the local court system.

But the most important event before I embarked on a new career was marrying Shelly. I met then-Shelly Scher at a May 3, 1970 party hosted by three women we had known. We had immediate chemistry.

We got engaged on July 11, 1970, and I gave her a wedding ring on August 21, my 30th birthday. Rich Daley, among others, was at the birthday party at her parents' house. I was on schedule. My late father, Herb Zucker, had told me 30 was the ideal age to get married. And I had to earn some real money in private practice rather than prosecute demonstrators and rioters for a city salary, while moonlighting with some other legal work.

Shelly would soon find out marrying me was not setting her up for a sedate life. A month before our wedding on December 29, 1970, I took her to a movie at the Three Penny Cinema. But something looked odd, and off. The guy in the ticket window wore a necklace with human teeth. The ticket-taker and usher looked familiar. Six months later, a public defender asked me if I had been at the Three Penny Cinema. The "staffers" actually turned out to be members of The Young Lords gang, which I had prosecuted while in the corporation counsel's office. I believe they may have had a contract out on me and possibly intended to kill me that night—somehow having scouted my movements. But for some still-unknown reason, they did not follow through on the contract.

Anyway, we planned to get away from such troubles on our honeymoon in London, Paris, and St. Moritz in Switzerland. We got as far as London and stayed a couple of chilly weeks. Between a persistent fog and an Air France strike, we were stuck and could not go to the continent. Finally, when we were able to get out of London, we opted for what we thought was the warm-weather spot of Bermuda.

But while boarding the plane at Heathrow Airport, the flight crew announced the temperature in Hamilton, Bermuda's capital, was just 52. That's no sunny mid-winter vacation. I pulled my old self-named "Zwock" sleight-of-hand (a play on my name), proclaiming Shelly was deathly ill. We got off the plane, had an ambulance take Shelly to a quarantine area and in the process I dumped her prescribed medicine down the toilet. We pulled a switch and got on a plane for Acapulco, where it was appropriately hot and humid. Our luggage, however, went on to Bermuda. Shelly finally stopped me when I said I wanted to continue on to Hong Kong. I loved going 'round the world, but marriage slapped some limits on those desires.

Coming back to Chicago, I set up my law practice, leasing space from a friend at 111 E. Wacker Drive. Initially I had a secretary, but quickly it built into one of the biggest criminal defense practices in the State of Illinois. I hired other attorneys to work with me. I loved the action and the give-and-take with others in the system. I did not consider any other kind of law practice.

The judicial system of the early 1970s was different from today, with a lot of holdovers in longtime attorney-prosecutor-judge relationships.

Three prosecutors worked in every courtroom. Most were men. All these guys would be in office in a few years to learn to try cases before they'd go into private practice. They'd talk to you. These days though, the system features many lifetime prosecutors. The old boys' network is gone.

Back then, you could develop good relationships with judges. You knew which judges to try to get your cases in front of for which offenses. I tried to steer my cases to the Daley Center in the city-central Loop instead of the old courthouse on the south side at 26th and California. Out of four judges stationed at the Daley Center, I thought two were unbelievably great and I'd always do my utmost to have all my cases over there. I knew them, and they knew me. I knew I'd get a fair trial.

As leftovers from the longtime system later changed by reforms, a few judges were, say, wayward. One judge at 26th and California was nicknamed "Pay or Die." He handled only major cases, including lots of murders. He allegedly charged $10,000 to "take care" of the case. His clerk allegedly collected the hefty bribe and the accused murderer would walk. If not, he'd allegedly be sentenced to death. "Pay or Die" eventually was caught, indicted and sent to prison, along with his clerk.

I felt I had an advantage in most courtrooms. After Elrod was elected Cook County Sheriff, a huge portrait of him hung in every courtroom. Word got around I was formerly Elrod's right-hand man in the corporation counsel's office.

The law in Chicago was certainly not right out of the old, classic *Perry Mason* criminal-defense lawyer series. Most of the trials were done by public defenders to give them experience. They represented murderers without money to pay for a private attorney. I didn't have time for trials. But in the process of negotiating a case, the state's attorney's office needed to know you'd be willing to try the case and win. You really had to know the case to reach a non-jury outcome.

Almost everyone I represented in my career was guilty. I had learned about the guilty percentage from my career as a prosecutor. I had to find a way to win the case or negotiate it. The key was bargaining down the charge and avoiding jail time. In those days, prosecutors and judges were rated on how many guilty convictions they recorded, no matter what the charge. With my negotiating skills, I felt my best chance was working with the prosecutors and judges I knew and not the jury members who I didn't. They were 12 strangers and thus you had to take your chances on the verdicts. The chances of a jury acquittal were 50-50.

I tried to talk to prosecutors and judges with a smile on my face, in a conciliatory manner. To be sure, I knew the nuances of the law from my days at DePaul. But I was really self-taught, learning so much in practice after law school. When I read something, I retained the information. I can sit down and talk about almost any case and know the answers. I took after my father to possess as foolproof a memory as possible. I was always an angle guy and my experience on the streets as a prosecutor helped me all my life.

I had learned to negotiate in my city prosecutor's job. It's a must. Without plea bargaining, the system would fall apart, so the first order of business was insisting my clients tell me the truth and I just had a way of getting clients to open up to me. I put all I had into every case, getting to know the person really well. But I always remembered that I was selling myself.

The toughest thing for me by far was to represent an innocent person. That's *pressure*.

I had some tough cases involving tragedies, but I was never conflicted. I'd sit down at the dinner table with my wife and four kids to tell them why I did what I did. First, I told them the crime rate is up. Just as importantly, everybody is entitled to an attorney, a concept solidified by the 1961 U.S. vs. Wainwright case that went before the U.S. Supreme Court.

I handled a lot of drug cases, where the defense attorneys look for technicalities and motions to suppress evidence. Some really tough cases included a murder that stuck out when a guy's wife left him. When the couple was briefly reunited, they were sitting in a car when the man gave his wife a beautifully wrapped gift. He told her that he loved her and asked her to take him back. She said "no" but started to open the gift anyway. Inside the gift box was a butcher knife which the man grabbed and allegedly stabbed her — a fatal 27 times.

Of course, a criminal defense attorney has some personally harrowing times. Years before restaurateur friend Terry Cohen tipped me off to Spider Dan Goodman, he owned The Den, another dining establishment, on Walton and Rush Streets. Subsequently, and partially through Cohen, I became known as the "Rush Street Lawyer." He introduced me to his hatcheck girl, whose husband ran a motorcycle gang. I would represent a number of these gangs.

One group had cases with me for six years, but none went to jail. One day I represented 72 at one time on a misdemeanor charge at the Branch 43 court on the near west side. However, the court did not have a metal detector and standing at the top of the stairs, the gang members dropped 30 to 40 knives and guns in my briefcase for fear of being stopped and frisked. But even with their wild image, I liked representing them. One time they invited me to their hangout and I spoke there.

Many years later I worked a rape case involving two members of another motorcycle gang. The case was assigned to a judge I did not know and I was justifiably worried.

I partnered with an attorney with whom I had once prosecuted cases but he did not show up at court. The state put on its case and I said to myself, "Oh, my God, I'm going to lose"—not only the case, but personally. During a recess, I went to the bank and got the gang's legal fees as a refund. The gang asked where my partner was and later that day they allegedly went up to his office and threatened to kill him and me along with our wives and kids. I was scared to death but the other attorney vowed he was not scared of anything.

After they left, he said, "Fuck them," and reached into a drawer, which contained a gun, which he said would provide us some "insurance." He picked up the phone to call his uncle, who apparently was in the "Mob." And so, three weeks later, one of the two guys charged in the rape case was found shot in the head, gangland-style. Did the gang threaten the wrong guy, who obviously had connections?

Normally, I did not fear for my safety and my family's. As a precaution, though, my home phone number was not listed. I never had a client over at the house and if the defendant was a violent guy, I was very careful to never tell him anything on which I could not deliver.

My reputation working challenging cases apparently had circulated into the sports industry when I was asked to represent White Sox outfielder Ron LeFlore after he had been charged with possession of drugs and unregistered firearms when police searched his apartment on September 30, 1982.

LeFlore, of course, had been the subject of uplifting stories after he was signed by the Detroit Tigers out of prison in Michigan in 1973. LeVar Burton, who had starred in the celebrated

ABC-TV *Roots* mini-series in 1977, portrayed LeFlore in a made-for-TV movie on CBS the following year. The speedster developed into one of Major League Baseball's top leadoff men with the Tigers and Montreal Expos. Between 1978–80 he stole 243 bases, including a National League-leading 97 with the Expos in 1980.

White Sox owners Jerry Reinsdorf and Eddie Einhorn built up predecessor Bill Veeck's cash-strapped franchise quickly. They hired LeFlore, future Hall-of-Fame catcher Carlton Fisk and slugger Greg Luzinski in 1981. Under manager Tony La Russa, the Sox developed into a contender, eventually winning the American League West by 20 games in 1983 in their "Winning Ugly" season. But LeFlore was fated not to be a part of it.

He ran afoul of management with three suspensions during 1982. He sat for three games for arriving late for a July 18 game in Milwaukee. Two weeks later, he was benched again for not joining the Sox for the then-annual exhibition game during the Hall-of-Fame ceremonies in Cooperstown, N.Y. LeFlore was reinstated when he explained he had joined his wife, enduring a difficult pregnancy at the time.

But the coup de grace took place near season's end on September 30. Operating on a tip, Chicago narcotics officers entered LeFlore's apartment and found 5.5 grams of Quaaludes and 5.7 grams of amphetamines. Also discovered was a pair of .25 caliber pistols.

The case eventually came to a bench trial in front of Judge Thomas Cawley on June 14, 1983. I had known Cawley years earlier when he was chief public defender. Based on strategy in the handling of previous drug cases, I argued that LeFlore did not have exclusive control of his apartment when he went on Sox road trips and the drugs and guns could not be proved as his property beyond a reasonable doubt. With Sox attorneys from the team firm of Katt and Muchin in the courtroom, Cawley said LeFlore was not responsible for the Quaaludes and guns and he was acquitted.

"I feel like a million pounds were taken off my back,"

LeFlore said as he embraced me. He stayed in touch over the coming years as he unsuccessfully tried to make a comeback in baseball.

LeFlore was my second celebrity client. I added a third six months later. His case changed my life—but not for the reasons you'd think.

Larry Flynt, publisher of the lusty *Hustler* men's magazine was arrested at O'Hare Airport on December 3, 1983, on bond forfeiture charges. Involved in a federal case in Los Angeles, the controversial Flynt had been prohibited from leaving Los Angeles County. A paraplegic and a wheelchair-confined man since a 1978 shooting, Flynt had been charged with desecrating the American flag by wearing it as a diaper in court. His bond had been set at $10,000.

When he appeared on December 4 before U.S. Magistrate Olga Jurco, he went to so far as to twice deny he even was Larry Flynt. Declining a court-appointed attorney, he was returned to federal custody at the Metropolitan Correctional Facility. I visited him in jail around 3:00 a.m. and I thought I had gone down the rabbit hole. Few people as unhinged as Flynt ever crossed my path.

Among other claims, he suggested the KAL Korean jetliner shot down by a Soviet fighter jet nearly 3½ months prior was the handiwork of Al Capone (then dead 34 years) and Richard M. Nixon, living together in China. Flynt said he gave $400,000 to FALN, the Puerto Rican terrorist organization. Topping them all was his claim he had tapes of President Ronald Reagan and department-store magnate Alfred Bloomingdale with two hookers. When Flynt's entourage asked me if I wanted to see the tapes, I firmly declined.

I was confused to the point of asking myself, what was I getting into?

The next two days proved that it was far more than I had bargained for.

On December 5, contempt charges were lodged against Flynt, who screamed obscenities and threw a small Soviet flag at the bench. I thought I could take control, but you could not control Flynt.

He finally topped himself on December 6 with Federal Judge Frank McGarr presiding. Flynt spit at and yelled more obscenities at McGarr when the judge ordered his silence. "You fascist mother fucker," Flynt yelled. He then whipped off the blanket covering his wheelchair, revealing that he was naked from the waist down.

That very moment was my tipping point. I never wished to be a criminal defense attorney again.

Never had I seen a defendant behave like that. I could have gotten into trouble. But Judge William J. Bauer, supervising the federal court in Chicago, and I both served on the DePaul Law School Dean's Advisory Board, but I needed 15 years before I convinced Bauer I was not behind the Flynt outbursts. Bauer had always thought I had set up the court.

Once Flynt returned in a few days to Los Angeles after McGarr ordered him to serve 60 days in federal prison for contempt, the court tried to make official what I had noticed. He was ordered to undergo psychiatric tests at the request of federal prosecutors, who called him a "lunatic" and a "degenerate" with a history of mental illness.

And after all of that tumult, Flynt tried to pull what Donald Trump is allegedly known for and remains somewhat famous for—he did not pay me. For six months, I hounded him for the fees.

But enough was enough for me, so at that point, after 13 years full time, I walked away from my criminal-defense practice. I had made a lot of money in that time, but I was prepared to walk away. I didn't think of money then.

Within one month, I began my newest and highest-profile incarnation. I met Bears quarterback Jim McMahon, who would later ask me to be his attorney.

But never say never. Oddly enough, after my official retirement as a sports agent, I still dabbled in criminal law. I could not get away from it no matter how much I tried, taking cases here and there. I relied on my knowledge of negotiation and even as I tried to chill out in "retirement" in the balmy winters in Palm Springs, I kept getting requests from back in Chicago for representation.

But mere toe-dips in my old job were all I could handle and I certainly I would not like to be a full-time criminal lawyer starting out today. The system is totally different than when I started, without the old-boy network and featuring career prosecutors who don't have any aspirations of being a private attorney. In my opinion, they don't care enough and have orders not to reduce sentences. I got out just in time.

But that is one reason why prisons are overcrowded. For major crimes, you serve 85 percent of the sentence. Many sentences feature mandatory minimums, such as for crimes of delivery of a moderate amount of drugs. Judges are afraid of saying "not guilty" because they could get heat from their chief-judge supervisors and the voting public. Guilty verdicts keep the wolves away from the door.

And even negotiating attempts at damping down on violent crime have been rolled back. Rich Daley had a council of gang members, and one of my clients was gang leader Gator Bradley. The council worked at communication with the city but when Rahm Emanuel became mayor, he prioritized putting those same guys in jail and with that, the gang structure fractured with its leadership gone. But they remain one of Chicago' largest menaces.

Meanwhile, the way judges ascend to the bench must be altered. They have been elected forever. But, eventually, merit selection of judges has to take over.

In any field, change is inevitable and necessary. My life has been one of continual changes. I would not alter its outcomes or its highs and lows, even though I represented a couple of saints and a lot of sinners.

CHAPTER 6
Da Bears

No wonder many fans thought I was a Bears employee and spokesman. Within a couple of years after the Super Bowl XX championship, I represented a platoon of starters.

With Jim McMahon's recommendations and that of several teammates, these Bears with championship rings came into my fledgling Zucker Sports Management fold. Offensive linemen Jay Hilgenberg and Mark Bortz joined up, although I just missed landing Jimbo Covert, the top-rated blocker of them all, after he was the No. 1 pick in 1983 — one of the Bears' all-time best drafts.

Also coming aboard were linebacker Otis Wilson, defensive lineman Steve McMichael and defensive backs Dave Duerson and Shaun Gayle. A business savvy alum of Notre Dame, Duerson was the only client I eventually considered employing in my business. Though a backup, Gayle already had a hero's mantle, having returned a blocked Sean Landeta punt from the playoff victory against the New York Giants in 1986.

A favorite McMahon receiving target, Dennis McKinnon, also came into the fold. The baby of them all, Kevin Butler, the Bears' most reliable kicker until Robbie Gould, also became a long-term client. I did not do the contracts of future Hall-of-Famer Richard Dent. But I handled his appeal of violating the NFL's drug policy in 1987 as his attorney.

While the majority of my clients had changed agents, hired me and got new contracts without an excess of hassle through my chats with Bears' executives Jerry Vainisi and Ted Phillips, Hilgenberg's attempt to become the second $1 million NFL center in 1992 represented one of my most challenging negotiations ever. "Hilgy" would have to leave the Bears, with whom he wanted to play out his career, to get what I felt was deserved, a definitely desired seven-figure payday.

Hilgy played out his contract in 1991, his 11th Bears season. He was semi-royalty in the NFL. His uncle was Wally Hilgenberg, a noted All-Pro Minnesota Vikings linebacker from 1964 to 1979. Among my selling points: Jay Hilgenberg was a two-time, first-team All-Pro who had made seven consecutive Pro Bowl teams through 1991; he was from Iowa City, a region most Midwesterners believed to be within the radius of the team's core fan base. He should have been a Bears lifer.

After all his career accomplishments, Hilgenberg wanted to be the first center to cross the $1 million barrier. He desired to pass Bruce Mathews of the Houston Oilers as the highest-paid center in the NFL. Salaries were starting to take off in the early 1990s from their very modest levels of the Super Bowl XX era because of the influx of ever-increasing TV rights' fees. But in the Bears' view, our request for $1 million was way too much money. They did not want to pass the $800,000 mark.

Contract talks, lasting all summer, were hot and heavy. I first dueled with chief Bears negotiator Phillips, with whom I had a long-standing good relationship. Later joining the negotiations was the hard-nosed Bill Tobin, the general manager-without-title working under Michael McCaskey, who could have been called executive general manager. The latter, officially titled the Bears president, soon made it a threesome at the bargaining table. They would not budge until I stopped mentioning the $1 million desired goal.

With the apparent stalemate, I back-channeled separate talks with Cleveland Browns owner Art Modell, asking him if he'd like an All-Pro center. Modell agreed to give Hilgenberg $1 million.

I went back to the Bears. Tobin said, "OK, I'm making him a free agent for 24 hours, time to shit or get off the pot." McCaskey later claimed that Hilgenberg was not given the Bears' offer, but he was caught in a lie to the public — Hilgenberg was also in the negotiating room.

But the Bears did not know of Modell's intentions. Soon after Tobin's intemperate remark, I had a deal with the Browns. The Bears officially dispatched him via a trade to Cleveland.

"We would have liked to have had him finish out his career in Chicago, but it was his choice," McCaskey told the *Chicago Tribune*. But the choice was mutual. They had their own hard salary cap they chose to enforce, a big-market franchise with immense popularity and revenue potential playing down to middle-market status, while avoiding cutting into the dividends of many family heirs, in my opinion. In my experience, the two hardest teams to get money out of were the Bears and the Cincinnati Bengals.

Hilgenberg played just one more season, as a Brown, but achieved his goal. And money turned out to be not the only motivation to bolt to Cleveland, not exactly the nation's garden spot, with much more lake-effect snow than Chicago. He liked the Browns' new training base compared to the more-cramped Halas Hall, by comparison at that time.

"What struck me is when I walked from the indoor facility through the weight room to the locker room, I thought, 'All on the same level?'" he told the *Chicago Tribune*.

By 1992, the Bears lagged behind most cold-weather teams in indoor practice facilities. At the time, they tucked into an air-supported bubble north of their home base of Lake Forest, Illinois. The bubble leaked.

"We had to walk through slush, drive 15 minutes north and get rained on," Hilgenberg told the *Tribune*.

The Bears were miffed by the fractious contract talks, to say the least. In an interview on a team-controlled pre-season telecast on NBC-owned WMAQ-TV (now NBC Chicago), McCaskey mandated that sports anchor Mark Giangreco interview him on the sidelines. He proceeded to blast me live and in color.

"Giangreco was basically a functionary of McCaskey and guided the conversation along a path critical only of Steve," said longtime Chicago sportscaster Tom Shaer. "I later saw Steve, who privately said to me, 'I always tried to be fair and cooperative with Mark. I was surprised he did that to me.' But Steve never complained publicly."

Talk-show hosts, particularly all sports-talk *The Score*'s Mike North, took my side. It was not hard to beat McCaskey at that point in the court of public opinion with just one playoff victory since Super Bowl XX.

Early in my agent's career, I believed I won more friends than not among the pen-and-mic crowd. Conveying the players' and even the increasingly more-inaccessible Bears management side of contract talks to media became part of my daily job early in my agent career

"I always found Steve Zucker to be accessible and understanding of the media's need for information," said Shaer, who worked for WGN and WBBM Radio before he was the first voice heard on *The Score* when it powered up its transmitter on January 2, 1992. He also served as a sports anchor on NBC-owned WMAQ-TV and Fox-run WFLD-TV.

"He was very professional, always returned calls and did his best to help—without disclosing confidential things or putting the Bears or others in a bad position," Shaer said.

"Of course, Steve also understood that we were the same media which could publicize his clients, their endorsements and him as an agent. It was a win-win but, unlike other agents, Steve realized the media didn't work for him and could not possibly be 100 percent positive when controversies arose. Steve was the anti-Scott Boras or Drew Rosenhaus, agents known for their hardline stances.

Being open about the Hilgenberg contract process, even with the barbs from the Bears' executive suite, helped me a lot. That's how agents are measured: getting your players paid. I prided myself on such successful contract talks. Once the $1 million barrier for centers was breached in the Hilgenberg case, salaries went up while true free agency was finally introduced to the NFL, nearly a generation after it came to baseball.

Even with the realization the Bears would pay at levels lower than teams in smaller NFL markets, I won't soon forget my stable of "Halas' men," as newspapers sometimes referred to Chicago players.

After McMahon, my second client—and an all-time favorite—was receiver Ken Margerum. He was a true free spirit. Margerum taught a windsurfing class at Stanford. He had some 400 students sign up and he had to turn away even more. It isn't hard to relate to a California surfer type who still puts on the pads and helmet.

But even with the Bears' frequent stinginess, I managed to get blood out of stones for clients. Guard Mark Bortz made a very modest salary as an All-Pro in 1985. I managed to triple Bortz's salary for his next contract. Later, I finagled a decent payday for offensive line mate Keith Van Horne, too.

By the time of the tumultuous events of 1987, such as the firing of negotiation friendly General Manager Jerry Vainisi and the drafting of quarterback Jim Harbaugh, I had begun building up Zucker Sports Management. We started in small quarters in an office park west of the Old Orchard shopping center in north suburban Skokie, Illinois. I also shared offices with baseball-oriented agent Alan Nero. Eventually we expanded into a sizable suite of offices in Northbrook, about seven miles farther north.

Kathe Clements, wife of former Notre Dame star Tom Clements, became a trusted assistant at the start of the company. She was talented enough to become an agent in her own right. Nancy Mitchell and Bonnie Rucks were savvy marketing people who helped with personal appearances. In the years after Super Bowl XX, Bears were in demand all over the Chicago market. A $3,000 fee, a nice supplement to a then-modest NFL salary, was typical for a garden-variety event or speaking appearance.

But within the Bears' stable, there was a kind of caste system. McMahon, of course, was invited to practically everything, including fans' personal events. Of course the money invariably wasn't enough and the time commitment too much. Being a homebody away from the Bears, McMahon turned down almost all these offers.

Thus the African-American McKinnon became the afore-mentioned "Bar Mitzvah King" of the Bears. McKinnon would show up for an hour or so for a fee in the low thousands. He'd sign autographs and take pictures on the bar mitzvah parties, most often held on Saturday nights. Other Bears in my agency ran the gamut of personal appearances, postgame and morning-show broadcast deals, local ads, posters and photo shoots.

Given the wide net McMahon had helped me cast over many of his teammates, you may wonder why I also did not land commercial-heavy coach Mike Ditka, given the success of McMahon's endorsement portfolio coming off the Super Bowl XX title. I already had a decent rapport with "Iron Mike" as a go-between with McMahon earlier in his career.

The stark fact is I could not have represented Ditka. That would have been a conflict of interest as an agent working for both players and their coach. At times, Ditka and McMahon appeared to be rivals for endorsements as the Bears' commercial leaders. But they really existed in different realms. Ditka was as busy as humanly possible with both local and national deals with his lunch-pail "Grabowski" image, furthered by *Saturday Night Live* skits, while McMahon was more selective. "Iron Mike" far outlasted McMahon as an endorser and active personality, gobbling up football TV analyst work at CBS and ESPN.

I can't knock Ditka for making a lot of money. Who can argue with what he has done? You can make a strong argument he was overexposed. Having Ditka hawking products and services at every turn was fine for him. He got what he wanted. Ditka was a good businessman, but McMahon didn't care about that kind of volume. I did the best job I could for McMahon while Ditka did the best job he could do for himself.

But squeezed out of his alliance with former General Manager Jerry Vainisi, Ditka bit his lip for his final six seasons in

Chicago. He wanted to remain coach of the Bears, and he would garner the extra income. People respected what he said. He is in many ways still the face of the Bears and the franchise owes a lot to him.

The Bears also benefited for the more than half-decade of service from Duerson. He was a finance major at Notre Dame, where you cannot skate through academically as a football player. Dave was a leader, a gentleman, great in the locker room and a terrific strong safety. He would have earned a starting job anyway, but got a break by taking Todd Bell's secondary spot due to the latter's 1985 season holdout. He was perfect for the Bears, possessing a great relationship with defensive coordinator Buddy Ryan. When Duerson's Bears days were done, I helped relocate him to the Super Bowl-winning New York Giants and then the Arizona Cardinals to carve out a decade-long career.

Duerson passed up a chance to work as an agent with me. Instead, he made a name for himself running a Kenosha, Wisconsin-based meat business that had McDonalds as a major client. Later, he went on the board of the NFL Players Association, inserting himself in issues involving the budding controversy over long-term debilitating injuries from head trauma. Duerson was portrayed inaccurately, I believe, in *Concussion*, the Will Smith movie with a strangely short-lived run in theaters in 2015. His 2011 suicide, in which he shot himself in the heart to preserve his brain for postmortem CTE study, came as a shock, and still is very disturbing today when I think of a life cut too short following years in a brutal game.

Long before players had to face the post-career consequences of Chronic Traumatic Encephalopathy, or CTE, I would obtain a Lloyd's of London insurance policy on each one as a hedge with the constant specter of career-threatening injuries. Lloyd's came in really handy when the policy kicked in for Wilson three days before career-ending knee surgery after he had moved on to the Oakland Raiders. Wilson was injured in a pre-season game. We asked Lloyd's to bind him for one game, but it lasted for seven games. He got $700,000 tax-free.

I also helped several Bears extend their careers when they were backed into a corner.

After 11 productive seasons as a starting defensive tackle, the colorful Steve "Mongo" McMichael seemed headed for the scrap heap in 1993 under Ditka successor Dave Wannstedt. I always recommended against leaving a team via free agency, as the grass wasn't always greener on the other side. But as with others, the Bears simply would not pay him at his veteran's market value of $1 million. In an uncommon move, I took McMichael to the Green Bay Packers for his final season.

Unlike McMahon, McMichael was wild and crazy both on and off the field. Handling TV analyst gigs post-career, Mongo, so named for his role in Mel Brooks' *Blazing Saddles*, cut off the tie of WLS-TV sportscaster Giangreco during their live segment together, among other eye-opening actions.

I was particularly satisfied with getting additional years of NFL paychecks for Al Harris. Inactive during the entire 1985 season due to a holdout in a contract squabble with General Manager Vainisi, Harris, a former four-year starting linebacker, joined me when he came back in 1986. I felt he hired the right guy. I managed to get him back with Vainisi, who had held the line on his '85 contract and put him on the sidelines. I sweet-talked the Bears. The new deal putting Harris back on the roster happened pretty quickly. Having sat out a full season amid a contract impasse, most teams wouldn't have taken Harris back. But he got in another three seasons in the regular Bears defensive rotation and two more years on the Philadelphia Eagles after that.

Probably the most fit Bear, pound-for-pound, that I ever represented was defensive end Alonzo Spellman. He was the third first-round draft pick I ever represented, this time in 1992 out of Ohio State. Spellman was a 20-year old with the best physique I ever saw, 6-foot-4, 287 pounds of rippling muscle. He was impressive when he took off his shirt, probably possessing the best body I've seen in the NFL. He was extremely fast for a defensive end.

Spellman played in the collegiate All-American Bowl in Tampa, and then I signed him. I met him with his mother at a diner in his native New Jersey. I liked this gentle giant a lot. He had a wonderful mother and family. The Bears were happy to have him. Spellman recorded 30 sacks in his first five seasons as a Bear.

But he had an underlying problem later diagnosed as bipolar disorder. He came apart in 1997, when he had a standoff with police after he refused to leave his publicist Nancy Mitchell's north suburban home for eight hours. The Bears would wind up waiving him and he was out of the NFL for a season. But I was able to help get him two more jobs. Spellman had two good seasons as a defensive tackle with the Dallas Cowboys in 1999 and 2000. In 2001, he moved on to the Detroit Lions, who cut him in late October. I keep wondering what his potential would have been if he had been as healthy of mind to go along with body.

At the same time though, I acquired Bears cornerback Donnell Woolford as a client. We missed connecting in 1989 because I already represented Deion Sanders, and both played cornerback. But eventually, Woolford asked for my services. Woolford had a productive seven seasons with the Bears, including a Pro Bowl selection in 1993. A memorable moment was when Woolford got engaged at the Bub City eatery. In the middle of the restaurant, he dropped to his knees to propose.

Succeeding Ditka as coach in 1993, Dave Wannstedt called me to proclaim Spellman and Woolford were his two best players. But I never developed the relationship with the ex-Cowboys defensive coordinator that I did with Ditka. In the usual palace intrigue at Halas Hall, Wannstedt eventually fell out of favor with his players after a promising start and the Bears were in the dumper by the late 1990s. Wannstedt was fired after six seasons and moved on to be an assistant and then head coach with the Miami Dolphins. He has kept a high profile, though, as a broadcast analyst.

The peak of my Bears involvement by now had long passed. But I had one little behind-the-scenes task left. By now, the Bears had trouble acquiring public financing for rebuilding Soldier Field. So I called up Phillips, with whom I had done contracts for the better part of a decade. In that time, amid his constant interruptions to check contract terms with McCaskey, we had a good relationship. I suggested that I be the point person for the Bears in the stadium deal. Richard M. Daley, now a third-term mayor, simply could not stand McCaskey. I called Rich up, having known him for three decades since our corporation counsel days together. I told him that in Phillips he'd be talking to a good guy. When McCaskey was promoted to Bears chairman and Phillips succeeded him as president, the Soldier Field deal finally got done.

But it turned out to be the wrong deal. The two parties should have built a domed stadium, I believe. Chicago, as a cold-weather city, needed a domed or retractable-roof stadium to net a Super Bowl. Chicago has so much to offer and several NFL Drafts hosted by the city have proven that point. All the league needed was assurance the game would not be played in a snowstorm or zero cold. Bears weather is a nice image for rough, tough regular-season football, but not for this league's showcase event.

However, in spite of the Hilgenberg talks and McMahon's departure in a 1989 trade to the San Diego Chargers, I can look back with satisfaction about the Bears experience. I had so many players and tried to make sure they stayed with the Bears. I was able to enjoy everything about that championship and playoff appearance-consistent run. I felt I was a part of it, having been up at Halas Hall in the locker room every Wednesday, saying "good game" to all 45 players coming off the field after the final gun. I still have the T-shirt from the 1987 strike labeled, "We shall return."

The good far outweighed the bad, a lot of the latter coming at the end. Bottom line, the Bears could be the franchise showcase team of the NFL if they'd only let a Theo Epstein-like guy run the entire football operation like he has in achieving the Cubs championship.

Yet that's an action above my pay grade and for another family of which I am not a part.

CHAPTER 7
THE SUPER BOWL OF DISTRACTIONS

The Bears' Super Bowl XX story should have been exclusively about an unprecedented defensive performance
and Walter Payton, one of the greatest players in NFL history, getting his first chance to win a championship.

Nothing doing. I represented Jim McMahon. So naturally
we generated storylines that complemented, if not shared, the
main angle in the run-up to the Bears' 46-10 thrashing of the
New England Patriots. McMahon literally became a pain in
the ass to the Bears.

Having earned home-field advantage in the divisional and
NFC title games at Soldier Field, the Bears' defense rose and
hometown, Windy City omens rose to the level of Bears' fans'
ecstasy. First, New York Giants' punter Sean Landeta's whiff
on a punt in the nasty Chicago wind rolled right into the Bears'
Shaun Gayle's hands (soon a client), who returned it for a
touchdown, making it look like divine intervention, Windy
City style, pointing straight to a Chicago title after a 21-0
victory. McMahon added two touchdown passes to favorite
target Dennis McKinnon. One week later, snowflakes swirled
as the defense humbled Los Angeles Rams quarterback, Dieter
Brock, ensuring that the heavens were aligned just right for the
Bears. They completed a 24-0 victory, 22 years into a championship drought.

Media outlets, though, had to attend to defensive coordinator Buddy Ryan's record-breaking unit like an all-out blitz
of their own. Someone else had to cover the main story as
well—the Bears were Super Bowl bound for the first time.
Other reporters zeroed in on Ryan's "46" defense—named

for the unique position of safety Doug Plank, No. 46 in your program—amassing yet another shutout, its fourth between the regular season and playoffs. Such blankings just weren't possible in the modern NFL—or were they? A few reporters gathered comments from the humbled opponents.

And of course, a few more had to be deployed on the charismatic McMahon. He couldn't help attracting the attention of the public and NFL Commissioner Pete Rozelle. He started out relatively innocently with his headbands. Sporting the commissioner's name on one in a game, in protest of the commissioner disapproving of his wearing an Adidas-adorned headband during the regular season, did not sit well with the commissioner and his office. And once that issue was settled, McMahon threw the city of New Orleans and the entire sports world into an uproar with supposed Bourbon Street shenanigans as the NFL banged its publicity drum for the Super Bowl itself.

Players, by league mandate, had been forever banned for promoting any companies on their uniforms or other game gear. So McMahon had received flak from the NFL for the Adidas headband. But only after he wore the headband in the Giants playoff game did he formally get notification from the NFL to cut it out. He got a letter and a $5,000 fine. I acted quickly, calling Adidas and getting a $25,000 deal, absorbing the fine. Adidas also paid for a postseason trip to Europe for the foursome of Jim and Nancy McMahon, and Shelly and me.

In his own special way, McMahon decided to poke fun at the originator of the fine. While some players went through their routine prep before the Rams game, McMahon busied himself scrawling "Rozelle" on another headband he'd wear in action. Walter Payton did the same in sympathy with his teammate. Rozelle could not miss his name anytime the two were on the field or standing with helmets off on the sideline.

"I guess the networks don't like us giving publicity to these companies," McMahon said postgame. "So, the league hits me for five grand, and I figure, I'll give Pete some pub. Maybe he needs it."

Labeled by many as the best commissioner in the history of sports, Rozelle saw the value of great public relations. Before he penned a postgame note to McMahon thanking him for making the commissioner "famous," he told reporters the headbands "broke me up. I'm just upset that I wasn't able to get a shoe model out in time." Rozelle handled the headband situation very well. When we opened McMahon's restaurant in 1986, Rozelle sent McMahon an autographed picture inscribed with, "Thanks for making me famous," and I think he was wearing a headband. We hung it in the restaurant in a prominent place for two years.

Even the cerebral Bears' owner, Michael McCaskey, got the joke.

"Why didn't he have the McCaskeys written out? Or Halas?" the Bears president said. "That would have been a nice touch. What will Jim think of now? With his fertile imagination, there's no telling what he could come up with in the next couple of weeks. 'This Space For Rent'?"

Rozelle could not have effectively argued the basis for McMahon's creativity and enjoyment of the byplay in a money-oriented circuit sometimes called the "No Fun League." The commissioner got additional publicity from David Letterman, who presented McMahon a "Late Night" headband on his then-wee hours NBC show on an off-night during the playoffs.

"I like to think I helped bring their personalities out," McMahon said. "When I first came here, I could say that maybe some of the guys were a little tight, a little afraid to let themselves go. But there's no reason why you can't be a little crazy, be yourself and still play good football."

From the frying pan to the fire! During the Rams game, Jim was speared in the left buttock. The afflicted cheek sported all the darker colors of the rainbow. The soreness did not abate the following week when the Bears, then lacking their own indoor practice facility, worked out 170 miles from their suburban-Chicago Lake Forest home base under a bubble at the University of Illinois.

McMahon had undergone acupuncture treatments at his alma mater, Brigham Young. Now he thought of it as a quick fix with the game less than one week away. Speedy wide receiver Willie Gault had invited Japanese celebrated acupuncturist Hiroshi Shiriashi from Tokyo to treat his ailments, so McMahon figured he could get relief in a similar manner. Payton and other Bears had used Shiriashi during the regular season. Shiriashi treated McMahon at Halas Hall in Lake Forest, relieving some of the pressure, just hours before the Bears' team flight departed for New Orleans. Although old school, Ditka and then General Manager Jerry Vainisi endorsed the treatment — acupuncture wasn't exactly unknown and untested in 1986.

But when McCaskey heard about Shiriashi, he hit the ceiling. Gault relayed McCaskey's comments to McMahon: "Let's get one thing straight. This isn't Jerry Vainisi's team. This isn't Mike Ditka's team. I'm running the Chicago Bears." Such a statement had unforeseen consequences in this anticipatory moment of Bears triumph.

When Shiriashi showed up at O'Hare Airport for the team flight, McCaskey barred him from getting on the team plane. But events would soon overtake the neophyte football man.

Naturally, soon after McMahon and the team landed in the Crescent City, an initial night on the town beckoned. But before merriment ensued, he was mobbed by the gathered national media to discuss his latest "sticking point" with the Bears. I was getting my rite of passage in ringmaster duties. Fortunately, I planned to stay the whole week. Every bit of my creativity, advice and persuasive power were needed to deal with the daily drama.

Bernie Lincicome, a sports columnist and lifetime purveyor of sarcasm with the *Chicago Tribune*, wrote, "it will be determined if (Jim McMahon) is a cocky eccentric or, if I have come to suspect, a thorough churl," his fancy way of calling him a wise guy which McMahon did not appreciate. On a second go-round with the *Tribune* on a weekly basis 32 years later,

Lincicome was still known to take similar shots at McMahon.

But still in New Orleans and with McMahon now one of the country's centers of attention, I orchestrated the alternative headline-making thread of Super Bowl week. When finally relieved of press conference duties, McMahon did what came naturally to so many New Orleans visitors. He went out drinking the first night, but he was a pied piper. Walking down the street, he reportedly had an entourage of hundreds following him. People screamed at him walking down the street. Women were flaunting their physical attributes and flashing at him. McMahon just might have made more women dedicated football fans than any other personality of the time.

Meanwhile, McCaskey could not stop the dam from breaking. While asking McMahon how he felt at the first Super Bowl practice that Tuesday preceding the game, McCaskey knew the Illinois Acupuncture Association had announced it was flying Shiriashi to New Orleans on its dime. Shiriashi treated McMahon in his hotel room that Wednesday while McMahon road roommate Kurt Becker, an acupuncture association official Bill Anderson and I looked on. The scene was almost surrealistic: Shiriashi sticking needles one by one in McMahon's butt while he lay quietly on the bed. The best line delivered was Becker's: "All the nice-looking women in the world, and I gotta watch this." I laughed in response. Shiriashi shushed us all for quiet so as to better needle McMahon, literally.

The human pincushion immediately improved, moving around much more freely at practice on Wednesday. To reveal what only a handful of us had witnessed, McMahon mooned a helicopter hovering over practice. "That's no big deal. I just let them know where it hurt," he said. His real motivation is he did not want the helicopter taping practice. On the same day, McMahon wore an "Acupuncture" headband at his press conference.

Shiriashi applied another treatment early Thursday after McMahon had blown the 11:00 p.m. curfew by 2½ hours. McCaskey though, subsequently bent, saying he would not forbid players from taking acupuncture. Meanwhile, Bears trainer Fred Caito, to whom McMahon's care was originally assigned by McCaskey, made no comment about the sharp turn of events.

McMahon got only the equivalent of a power nap before one controversy melded into another—and one far bigger. After fielding several irate calls in his hotel room (apparently, Bears players did not use aliases on the road), McMahon was puzzled about the motivation for the calls. Going to a team meeting and breakfast, he could not figure out why the Bears management triumvirate of McCaskey, Vainisi and Ditka were angry.

Exhibiting the laziest and most unprofessional of work habits, the late WDSU-TV sports anchor Buddy Diliberto aired allegations on Wednesday night that McMahon had called New Orleans women "sluts" and the men "idiots." I persuaded the Bears to practice damage control by calling a press conference at midday Thursday.

But McMahon was reluctant at first. We went up to his room. McMahon was extremely angry and did not want to do the press conference to absolutely refute Diliberto's unsourced reporting, which nowadays might be called "fake news." I worked for an hour and finally convinced him he had to nip this. I told Vainisi and Ditka that McMahon did not say what Diliberto had accused him of doing. I told McMahon to just tell the truth. He entered the room, which had only a few reporters at first. Word spread quickly and soon the room was jammed with media. McMahon was fabulous. At first, I considered a slander suit against Diliberto. Then I sent a letter desiring an apology. WDSU did just that after suspending Diliberto, who continued on in a long career talking sports on the air in New Orleans.

And as absolute proof McMahon had been falsely accused, the Bears quarterback sported still another headband, "I Love New Orleans," at the Friday practice.

Somehow, in spite of the daily drama and nocturnal forays, Jim guested on Bob Hope's pre-Super Bowl TV show, and led a delegation of his linemen to Hope's hotel suite, which they promptly trashed. More surreptitiously, we squeezed in a photo shoot for the cover of *Rolling Stone* magazine. The Bears did not know about the session. *Rolling Stone* rented a local house for four hours one evening. McMahon wore a *Rolling Stone* headband with his Bears No. 9 uniform. The cover ran March 13, 1986. McMahon was the first athlete to appear on the cover. Like it or not, the country music fan now was synonymous with a rebellious rock image, an appealing semi-bad boy.

"Jim has turned into a fascinating folk hero, but I do feel he can cross that line," Rozelle said before the game.

The biggest advantage of the McMahon-generated histrionics was the pressure taken off most of his teammates. Two days before the game, Ditka said the daily thread had removed the focus from Walter Payton, who was in position to collect his just due after 11 seasons of absolute selflessness and excellence. In the same breath, Ditka suggested he'd use Fridge Perry as a blocker in goal-line situations. The two high-profile Bears would supplant McMahon as the main distraction of the big game.

As the Bears counted down to the 4:00 p.m. Sunday kickoff, mine and I gathered for dinner Friday night with Jim and Nancy McMahon. We discussed the absolute craziness of the past five days. With the country's biggest TV audience set to convene Sunday night, the time was right to send a positive message to contrast with all the controversy, much of which could have been taken the wrong way by millions of fans. I asked McMahon which headband he'd wear for the game — by now everyone expected a distinctive new model for the mass viewership. Shelly suggested a headband promoting a charity.

We began talking about the Juvenile Diabetes Foundation, in honor of our then-15-year-old son, Herbie. Nearly a decade earlier, we were on vacation in the south of France when we got a call that Herbie, who had been urinating frequently, was admitted to Michael Reese Hospital in Chicago. He was diagnosed with what was commonly called "juvenile diabetes." We quickly flew home to take care of Herbie and to be educated about Type 1 diabetes and insulin injections. Along with six other couples whose children also had the disease, we started the diabetes foundation.

Herbie and Jim had gotten to know each other, tossing a football around in our backyard. The headband would promote JDF. McMahon was enthusiastically in favor of his latest headband-modeling assignment. So Shelly jumped from the table to call old friend Joan Beaubaire, also a founding member, and still on the board of JDF. Joan worked all night into Saturday morning to get the headband labeled with "JDF Cure" delivered in time for the game. The timing was just right.

So when McMahon came running on the field at the Superdome with the new headband, the sportscasters had no idea what JDF stood for. Shelly and I were in our seats waiting for the Bears to appear and to see if he was wearing the JDF headband. When we saw the headband, I yelled to Shelly, "Go!" We had press releases from the JDF office, for which Mary Tyler Moore, also a Type 1 diabetic, served as spokesperson. Shelly dashed for the press boxes on the other side of the stadium. Rather than a humorous or damage-control angle, the "JDF Cure" headband showed Jim cared about good causes while putting JDF on the map.

McMahon did not waste an opportunity for good causes with the whole world watching. In the second quarter, he changed to a headband labeled "POW MIA." Finally, he allowed himself some personal promotion in the third quarter as his playing time was ebbing due to the Bears' huge lead. The final headband read "PLUTO," his nickname for buddy and favorite receiver Dan Plater from his BYU years.

No Vikings-style quick-strike rallies were needed in this game. Nervousness for all Chicago sports fans, too many decades of failures and coming up just short, were put to rest by the second quarter. The Bears took apart the New England Patriots in a 46-10 thrashing. Ron Rapoport of the *Chicago*

Jim McMahon wearing Juvenile Diabetes Foundation headband

Sun-Times summed it up best with his Page One story beneath the headline, "Number 1!" large enough to befit world-shaking news. Rapoport began with a Carl Sandburg-type poem:

Pigskin victor of the world,
Helmet breaker, sacker of quarterbacks,
Toyer with opponents and the nation's headhunters:
City of the Swelled Chest.

And only two Rapoport sentences needed to be cranked to analyze one of the most resounding victories: "All the Bears had to do was lineup, look the New England Patriots in the eye and it was done. If it was as easy as all this, you could not help asking yourself, why had it taken so long?"

Indeed. I was a middle-age man of 45 with four kids assigning myself to the McMahon Watch in Super Bowl Week. When these same Bears won Chicago's last sports championship in 1963, I was 23, footloose, free and needing an adult anchor. There had been 103- and 106-loss seasons for both of Chicago's baseball teams with just two divisional titles to their credit. The Bulls had reached the conference finals just once. A seemingly fluke Montreal Canadiens goal half lost in the fog above the ice on a humid 80-degree day, killed the Blackhawks in Game 7 of the Stanley Cup Finals.

The "Super Bowl Shuffle" Bears backed up the team's vows and dance moves while partially removing the monkey off the back of a sports-crazed city. By 2016, every pro franchise in town had broken its own championship drought. But the Bears' title still resonates as the icebreaker, crafted by a team still rated as one of the most dominant in pro sports history for its singular championship season.

Richard Dent came away with the game's Most Valuable Player Award. But McMahon made a strong case by completing 12 of 20 passes for 265 yards while scoring two TDs on the ground himself. Passes of 60 and 43 yards to Gault were crucial in setting up scores.

The only black mark on the fun was not serving Payton with a TD opportunity. With the Bears leading 37-3 and 3:22 remaining in the third quarter, Perry was in the goal-line offense. But instead of merely blocking, as was Ditka's original plan, the order came in for McMahon to hand off to The Fridge. Of course the man-monster blasted into the end zone in the last piece of true entertainment in the blowout. But after the game, McMahon told me the biggest mistake in his career was not calling an audible on the play, and not giving the ball to the deserving Payton. He admired the greatest-ever Bear so much.

Payton walked off the field virtually alone while most of his teammates whooped it up. Ditka and Ryan earned the distinction of two coaches on the same team being carried away on their players' shoulders. Sweetness hid the obvious disappointment of being shut out in the scoring column.

"Yes, I was surprised," Payton said. "Yes, I was disappointed. I feel bad, but that's the way it goes. There's been other games where I didn't get into the end zone. I don't mind being a rabbit. When they key on me, it opens it up for other people."

McMahon's own feelings on the goal-line efforts to get Payton into the end zone were expressed in his 1986 autobiography with the *Chicago Tribune*'s Bob Verdi: "We could have done something for him, and I'm partly at fault there. I went for one touchdown from the two, midway into the second quarter. It was an option play. Either Wally would get it or me. He came around for the pitchout, but they smelled it coming, so I found the lane and I did what I was supposed to do.

"Where I screwed up was when we gave the ball to 'The Fridge' about four minutes later. He scored from the one to make it 44-3. Ditka got caught up a little too much in his innovations here. He'd made a star out of his big rookie defensive tackle; made him into a touchdown hero. Now, Ditka wanted him to become president of the United States, too. So, Ditka called for Perry to get the ball, and that's where I should have just given it to Wally and the hell with what Ditka wanted.

"The way things were going, I thought there'd be plenty more chances for Wally to score. I thought for sure he'd get a shot. I thought I could give him a shot."

Such memories enveloped Jim and Nancy McMahon, and me. We attended Walter's funeral together in 1999 after he died of liver disease at just 45. An element of life not being fair was present in the Payton timeline. But the respect he garnered from every direction cannot be matched in Bears annals, and maybe in all of all sports, for that matter.

Payton celebrated in his own subdued way with an unlit

cigar postgame while the entire Bears organization let loose. McCaskey and the Lombardi Trophy were seemingly joined at the hip amid the celebration. Eventually they were separated, never to reunite. The city of Chicago geared up for its first championship parade in modern times on a frigid Monday. McMahon, though, detoured to the sheltering palms of the Pro Bowl in Hawaii.

None of the Bears would get a chance to celebrate their hard-earned title at the White House, though. The Challenger space-shuttle disaster cast a pall on such celebrations. That's why at the very end of his career, as a little-used Green Bay Packer backup on a championship team in 1997, McMahon wore a Bears jersey under his shirt during the visit to Bill Clinton, in honor of his old teammates who were not able to bask in presidential glory 11 years earlier.

The entire football community celebrated the restoration of dominance to the old Monsters of the Midway. In my opinion, it was the greatest phenomenon on Rozelle's commissioner's watch. Bears TV ratings in Chicago alone dramatically boosted CBS' national numbers, the Bears' conference's primary carrier. Star anchor Bill Kurtis thanked the heavens for the financial bonanza that enveloped the Bears outlet, CBS Chicago (*nee* WBBM-TV). The station congratulated the team with a full-page newspaper ad: "You've been the gleam in our eye all season." They could have added the huge bulge in their pocketbook for record ratings, too.

In the frozen Chicago wasteland of Monday, January 27, 1986, more than a million Chicagoans braved frostbite, seeing their breaths constantly in the excitement of the Bears' parade. Even McCaskey, the former dignified academic, let his hair down—in primal fashion—like never before. "No one made fun of him when he 'woofed' at the downtown Chicago rally saluting the Bears," recalled longtime Chicago sportscaster Tom Shaer.

In harried catch-up mode back at my small suburban office, I began returning phone calls to a mass of companies that wanted to jump on the McMahon endorsement bandwagon. My friend and advertising executive, Rick Fizdale, said there was gold to be mined when the Bears won the Super Bowl. Just hold your fire until the Lombardi Trophy is in the Bears' hands, he said. I had negotiated with anti-war protestors, all aspects of the legal system and a Bears general manager, but now I'd get experience in the corporate marketing world.

Anyone associated with the Bears dealt with a different kind of animal — a tiger by the tail. When Bears management walked into the NFL meetings after Super Bowl XX, they were given a standing ovation, with profuse thanks from Rozelle. CBS-TV in particular, with an unprecedented national ratings boost from Bears' telecasts, could line up right behind the commissioner, bowing to its Chicago benefactors.

"We had attracted more women fans to the game," recalled then-GM Jerry Vainisi. The leading heartthrob was the headband model who doubled as a quarterback.

Blue skies enveloped the Bears Universe. Any storm clouds were saved for another season.

In the meantime, Part II of the McMahon phenomenon of travels and transactions that carried him from franchise to franchise and metropolis to metropolis was about to begin.

CHAPTER 8
THE SELLING OF JIM McMAHON

We had a glimpse for about a four-year window of just how popular a Chicago passer could be if he wins, is a team leader and has some colorful qualities.

Jim McMahon's endorsement portfolio was one of the NFL's top performers in the mid-1980s. I was fortunate to coordinate the off-the-field image of a man who many popularly viewed as "The Punky QB," but who in reality was a doting father of four just wanting to low-key it away from the limelight.

The McMahon phenomenon simply snowballed with every Bears victory and his on-field dramatics throughout the 1985 season. McMahon's quarterback productivity continued beyond that year's Super Bowl XX victory with a total of 22 regular-season winning starts in a row — 25 including the playoffs — through the middle of the 1987 season. Those feats followed setting 70 NCAA passing records at BYU. He was a brash quarterback with a direction all his own, playing off sometimes straight man/coach Mike Ditka, developing more appeal with each passing week.

McMahon did not want his near rock-star status, but he agreed to ride it for what it was worth as long as possible. He ranged the gamut from having his limousine mobbed by frantic fans at an autograph appearance to colorful national commercials to hobnobbing with the likes of Bruce Willis and Hugh Hefner. McMahon was not fated to have a long run as a Bear or even a starting quarterback, so his desire not to work after retirement — which would have been a challenge given debilitating injuries — was helped along when companies and fans alike wanted a piece of him from midway through the

1985 season on.

The thoroughly dominating Bears were so popular, extra work was available to all down to the last special-teams player. Which Bear *didn't* have a broadcast gig became the issue. As 1985's impact was digested, the Big Three in outside work were McMahon, Ditka and defensive lineman William "Refrigerator" Perry. Ditka, the most enduring symbol of the franchise after "Papa Bear" George Halas, has had the longest-lasting endorsement/broadcasting/restaurant image. Staying in the city at least part of each year helped "Iron Mike" stay front and center. He had expertly positioned himself as quintessentially Chicagoan — rough and tough — even though he grew up in Aliquippa, Pennsylvania, and attended the University of Pittsburgh.

Few, though, have shot up like a meteor as McMahon. All kinds of companies and individuals wanted McMahon in a fast and furious manner, and I had to hold off most of the bidders until McMahon was assured of his Super Bowl XX ring.

The real McMahon? He is an extremely loyal guy. He is shy, and not an extrovert. He is not a big conversationalist. He doesn't seek friends. In a crowded room, he'd stand on the edge. The press gave him the moniker the "Punky QB." But as he stated in his Foreword, McMahon attributed the nickname to a bad haircut in the summer of 1985. No rocker, McMahon is a country music fan.

As the commercial tide rolled over us, as his rep, I faced an interesting dichotomy. Wild-and-crazy sells, and big. The public wanted that side of McMahon. Who wouldn't want to rebel against authority as he did when he wore his Adidas headbands against the NFL's wishes, yet turned that into gold with NFL Commissioner Pete Rozelle when McMahon wore a headband bearing Rozelle's name? And who wouldn't want to get the best of a reluctant boss? As McMahon entertained the masses by engaging Ditka in sideline histrionics, "Da Coach" would eventually be caving in to let his quarterback generate championship momentum, according to some observers.

Almost everyone has their public and private sides, but if NFL players do it right—and some very publicly don't—they have an "off" switch for their game face. They actually can craft as close to a normal home life as possible under the circumstances. Jim and Nancy McMahon did just that, raising four really good kids in Ashley, Sean, Alexis and Zachary. The couple exposed them to real life in public schools, including Glenbrook North High School in Northbrook, Illinois, where Alexis served as her class president.

Anyone close to the McMahons knew of this side, including Ditka.

"He has a lot of qualities that are important to have, the way he treats his family and his kids and what's important to him," Ditka said of him.

When not sore from football, McMahon was delightfully earthy while circulating in the higher society than the working-class one in which he was raised. That certainly played into his slightly off-center commercial image.

For instance, when we took him to an upscale dinner party one night during the height of his popular "punky" image, we told him he had to behave accordingly. There were some very well-to-do people in attendance from Chicago's ritzy North Shore neighborhoods and suburbs.

Little Cornish Hens were being served, and when the one served to McMahon dropped off the serving dish and away from McMahon's plate, he had difficulty trying to scoop it up with his utensils. Finally, he picked it up with his hands, out of bounds for this North Shore crowd. I practically hit myself beside my head in amazement, but that was the real, unabashed McMahon.

Another time, McMahon joined us in the beautiful International Club of Chicago's famed Drake Hotel. Their specialty was stone crabs, which McMahon said he loved. We showed him the crab cutter and McMahon took the crab and proceeded to cut his hand. Rather than grab a napkin or other object, or leave the table, McMahon dipped the bloody hand in a goblet of water.

"His first instinct was to stick it in a glass of water," said his wife, Nancy McMahon. "His attitude was, 'I'll use what I have in front of me.' He just didn't get up and go to the restroom. Just contain it right here and not make a fuss. Jim's first thought is not proper etiquette. As a quarterback, he had to make split-second decisions. So he just stuck the hand in a glass and took care of it. It's not like he didn't have manners."

McMahon probably could have mimicked these comedic scenes in TV spots. He eventually performed other societal *faux pas* that can still be seen on social media. He had a slow start to his bountiful endorsement side. When it hit, though, the force was like a tidal wave.

The Bears were not winners in McMahon's first two seasons, 1982 and 1983, with his rookie campaign fractured by the NFL's first players' strike. He garnered the usual appearance and minor endorsement offers through the time I took over his representation in January 1984. The Bears officially began their revival that year by winning the NFC Central, but McMahon could not take full advantage of mounting public interest, having suffered a lacerated kidney on November 4 and then missing the rest of the season.

We entered a brave new world after game three in Minnesota in 1985. Coming out of Ditka's bullpen, a nicked-up McMahon, who didn't start, proceeded to startle a national TV audience with three TD strikes, the first two being scores in the comeback victory.

But even if a quarterback had a colorful personality, he was not going to garner a lot of outside income if he wasn't winning games. The triumph over the Vikings proved a lot to many. So my phone began ringing with endorsement and appearance pitches. The pace continued to pick up as the Bears' undefeated season moved into November.

My strategy was to defer most endorsements until after the season. Players' off-time is precious during the season. McMahon's only standing engagement was going out with his linemen for a bonding session at a bar every Thursday night, with a different Bear picking up the tab each time.

However, endorsement values would only increase with a Super Bowl victory, so I confidently told McMahon to just be himself and keep winning and that we'd make our money after we won the Super Bowl. Overall, football players typically have a harder time in landing endorsements. Because they wear helmets, not everybody knows their faces. So I just held McMahon back at first, although he controlled the authority to say yes or no to offers.

The one commercial McMahon did tape was after game 10 of that Super Bowl year. He joined Refrigerator Perry in a Coke commercial taped in a coffee shop in north suburban Wilmette. Agent Jim Steiner asked me to represent the Fridge on the commercial. The players spent five hours producing it, wearing full uniform and pads.

Then we did an autograph appearance at the Brickyard Mall on Chicago's northwest side. Perry had backed out and the promoter really wanted a star Bear. They doubled their offer from $10,000 to $20,000, turning McMahon's "no" to a "yes." Arriving in a limo, we found out how hot the '85 Bears had become. The crowd waiting our entourage rocked the car. McMahon's arrival was like that of a rock star. I had never seen anything like it.

"It was crazy," said Nancy McMahon. "To me, I'm very low key, nothing fazes me. Jim and I would look at each other and laugh. He didn't look at himself as Jim McMahon the football player. We just can't believe people are acting like this. He didn't think of himself as someone [people] would go crazy over."

Yet, so many thousands showed up at the Brickyard appearance that McMahon practically got writers' cramp signing.

"They advertised I'd be there for three hours," McMahon said. "I sat in the chair and signed for three hours. But I could have signed for a week, and not signed them all."

After McMahon had teamed with all-pro running back

Jim McMahon, Steve and Refrigerator Perry at filming of a Coke commercial, Wilmette, Illinois, 1986

Walter Payton to record a clip to be inserted into "The Super Bowl Shuffle" after the main taping, a flurry of endorsement work followed. A triumphant post-Super Bowl tour took us to New York, Washington, D.C., and Los Angeles. McMahon was not haughty at all about his victory tour. His first preference was surprisingly to hit as many big-name golf outings as possible.

The celebrations were still going on in icy Chicago when the Zuckers and the McMahons arrived in New York. Hosting us was Steve Rubell, owner of the Paramount nightclub, sister to Rubell's famed Studio 54 club. Entering the club through the back entrance, none other than Andy Warhol opened the door for us. Never one to miss out on such a fortuitous opportunity, I negotiated with Warhol to draw a portrait of McMahon, gratis. Unfortunately, Warhol died before he could embark on the project.

Rubell took us to the famed Peter Luger Steak House in Brooklyn. He excused himself to make a call and came back to announce his friend "Calvin," who lived near Central Park, would like to meet McMahon at his apartment. McMahon responded no—he was tired. Shelly, however, figured out to whom Rubell was referring. And so, sitting across from Jim, Shelly gave him a kick under the table. He reversed course to say OK. The visit to Calvin's penthouse was on—Calvin Klein, that is.

When we walked in, none other than gossip columnist Liz Smith was in attendance.

Klein told us he was coming out with a line of underwear. He showed us the storyboards, which included an image of his topless girlfriend Kelly modeling panties. The men giggled while Nancy McMahon and my wife Shelly helped themselves to souvenirs from the bathrooms—any item with Calvin's monogram on it. With McMahon's honor as pro quarterback of the year coming up at the Washington, D.C. Gridiron Dinner, a tuxedo was needed. I suggested, appropriate to our setting, that McMahon rent Calvin Klein formal wear.

Still, McMahon could not duck his new-found celebrity no matter how hard he tried. At lunch at New York's Columbus Café the next day, actor Sean Penn and comedian Billy Crystal were in the house. Nancy McMahon took notice of the pair. Interestingly, McMahon told his wife not to bother celebrities during their personal time just because they were out in public. But as McMahon got up to go to the bathroom, Crystal yelled, "Hey, McMahon!" Ironically, Jim McMahon was possibly the most famous guy in the room at that moment.

We then went on to the Gridiron Dinner where I got the two top quarterbacks in Bears history together. Also inducted as a Hall of Famer was Sid Luckman, who had been George Halas' championship Bears quarterback in the 1940s and a quarterback tutor thereafter. That began a bromance between Luckman and McMahon that lasted the rest of the latter Bears' career. McMahon also began friendships with dinner emcee and Super Bowl-winning coach John Madden and a former Redskins quarterback of renown, Sonny Jurgensen. I also planted the seed for a tuxedo deal with Calvin Klein for

Steve, Hugh Hefner and Jim McMahon at the Playboy Mansion, Los Angeles

McMahon by showing the designer's label on the tux to newspaper photographers. After the photos were published, I wrote Klein and soon we had a tuxedo deal.

Moving on to Los Angeles, we were invited to Hugh Hefner's Playboy Mansion for lunch and a personal tour of the property, which included a private zoo. During the tour, Hef's secretary slipped me a note from actor Bruce Willis, who wanted to meet McMahon. Since he was hit from all sides with such requests, I did not bring this to McMahon's immediate attention, as he had empowered me to say "no" to all offers. For a few hours, as I would learn, I had made a temporary mistake, but would have a chance to more than make up for it.

Hefner wound up giving McMahon a red Corvette for being judged Playboy's Super Bowl XX Most Valuable Player. All Hefner wanted to do was talk football with McMahon. In the tour of the mansion, each bedroom featured bottles of oil on the nightstands. Shelly and Nancy again busied themselves collecting more souvenirs.

Hours later at a dinner, Hefner's other guests included Motown impresario Berry Gordy and actors Tony Curtis and James Caan, who played the late Brian Piccolo in the famed *Brian's Song*, about a Bears running back's courage while fighting a deadly disease. This was long before he was Sonny Corleone in *The Godfather*.

Over in beautiful downtown Burbank, as we waited in the green room to go on Johnny Carson's *Tonight Show*, I got another note from Willis, again asking to meet McMahon. This time I shared this communique with McMahon, who was excited, a contrast from the majority of other offers we received. He revealed that Willis' TV series *Moonlighting* was one of his favorite shows. After the *Tonight Show* taping, we went to the *Moonlighting* set. I had called ahead to say we'd meet Willis. Upon arrival, Willis' co-star, Cybill Shepherd, and the rest of the cast and crew were wearing "McMahon" headbands.

Hungry after the early-evening Carson taping, I asked Willis for a dinner recommendation. He directed us to the Maryland Crabhouse, his favorite in Santa Monica, but he said he wouldn't be able to join us, claiming that *Moonlighting* was shooting until 3:00 a.m. Yet, after we arrived at the restaurant, who should walk in but Willis? He told us he wanted to talk with McMahon so much he shut down shooting. A great friendship among McMahon, Willis and me was born. The following year, the Zuckers and McMahons were invited to Willis' wedding to Demi Moore.

In any event, McMahon's passion for golf was widely known by now and he was invited to numerous PGA events. Due to scheduling, most were impossible to attend. However, soon after we returned to Chicago after our victory tour, we jetted back out to California, to Rancho Mirage where Shelly's parents had a snowbird residence at the Mission Hills club. McMahon played in the Dinah Shore-hosted event. He obviously loved the atmosphere and the repartee.

Jim McMahon, Steve and Bruce Willis

So the next year, after he had lost the second half of the season to shoulder surgery and the Bears had been knocked out of the playoffs early, he finally could RSVP positively to the annual invitation to the Bob Hope Classic in Rancho Mirage. I had assured the PGA officials McMahon would wear shoes, as he customarily played barefoot. On the 18th hole, I stood waiting with PGA officials for McMahon to finish. But he approached barefoot, playing in the Pro-Am event with golf legends Jack Nicklaus and Johnny Miller.

"I did what you told me to do," he said, "but my feet started bleeding at 16. Jack told me to take my shoes off." Eventually, we'd be invited to play Augusta, home of The Masters. I was not a golfer, and it showed. My veteran caddie told me on 16, "Mr. Zucker, I have been here 28 years, and you have taken me to parts of the course I've never seen before."

By the time we returned to Chicago, endorsement work was awaiting McMahon. I probably could have pushed the effort into TV gigs and movies, but McMahon did not want to endure the endless hours of preparation and repeated filming and taping that the takes required.

McMahon probably would have loved a guest gig on *Moonlighting*, due to the Willis connection. But Willis was not the show's producer, so a call never came. In the same breath, we did come close to McMahon working on *Miami Vice*, another of his favorites, playing a "heavy" in the top guest-star role. He would have worn his sunglasses. The deal-breaker was the producers needed McMahon for eight days of filming; he only had five. He also wanted Bears linemen Kurt Becker and Keith Van Horne to be on the show.

McMahon turned down guest-shot bids as a hero on *The Equalizer* and another on *The A-Team*. Some 10 to 12 movie productions also inquired, but the time commitment was too much or the format was not right.

Many years later, after his football career was over, CBS inquired about McMahon working as a football commentator on Sundays. Yet, McMahon did not want to show up on Fridays and Saturdays for the typical pre-game production meetings and player/coaches' interviews. If it was Sunday only, to just show up a few hours before game time, hobnob with some people on the field and then do the actual game, there might have been a deal.

Overall, the timing in early 1986 after the Super Bowl championship was perfect. Endorsers typically focus on the hottest, most compelling athletes on the nation's most popular team. McMahon, Perry and Ditka were magnets for offers. So many opportunities poured into the team headquarters at Halas Hall in suburban Lake Forest and the Bears referred many of these contacts to me, as I did commercial deals for players I otherwise did not represent.

Our Super Bowl week cover shoot for *Rolling Stone*'s March 13, 1986 issue was a massive free promotion for participating brands. Again wearing sunglasses and with a two-handed gesture, he was positioned as "Jim McMahon…Chicago's Rock & Roll Quarterback," playing to the image of what the public wanted. Inside, Becker and Van Horne were portrayed holding up Jim in another gag pose, while vintage photos from his career also were published.

No matter how modest their situation, everyone wanted a piece of McMahon. *Sports Illustrated* inquired about McMahon for a commercial, stating they were down to him or Joe Montana.

Callers asked about McMahon for appearances of all kinds — including bar mitzvahs. He passed those up, allowing favorite receiver Dennis McKinnon to become the "bar mitzvah king."

No other football player and very few other athletes were as magnetic as McMahon at the start of calendar 1986. Timing is crucial in landing these deals, as with any other aspect of sports, competitively or in contract negotiations. The path was wide open for McMahon to take advantage of the marketplace. Fifty calls per day asking about his availability streamed into my and the Bears' offices. The process was labor intensive and I had to reject the great majority of inquiries.

Interestingly, McMahon's and Michael Jordan's commercial paths did cross during this period. Arrangements were made for both athletes to get together for a photo shoot. Posing in their respective uniforms, McMahon held a basketball, using now league-banned stickum to make it appear as if he were palming it, while Jordan cradled a football. I placed the poster-sized photo on the wall behind my desk and made sure prospective clients saw it whenever they visited.

However, McMahon's rule was to endorse only products he used. We could exercise "no" at two key junctures: when an offer came in, and at the storyboard level. The latter is a production phase in which the commercial's producer sketches out on boards the different shots or poses by the endorser. If I were negotiating with a company and felt the spot put McMahon in a bad light or changed the perception of his personality, we would not proceed. We did not want to jeopardize his credibility.

But Jack Brickhouse, one of the most ubiquitous broadcasters in Chicago history, famously advised to never take the first "no" for an answer. And that's how I tried to handle rejections, even with big, market-dominant companies. Often though, the "no" was only for "now," leaving the door open for the future. And I learned in negotiating with teams that if they said "yes" the first time around in negotiations, I must have done something wrong by not asking for enough. No deal is worth it by reaching agreement too quickly when all possible financial and other benefits were still on the table.

One company emerged as first among equals in McMahon's mind as he got to work with sunglasses, makeup and sometimes rebellious-looking outfits. Taco Bell won his approval after a number of fast-food chains pitched us. He was a Taco Bell fan and happily munched on their offerings. My key was limiting the total amount of time Taco Bell could use him to one year.

"To this day I love Taco Bell," McMahon says. "I love tacos."

Clips of most of these spots still can be viewed on YouTube. Of course, McMahon had fun doing the Taco Bell commercial with a "Born to Be Wild" theme. He sat in an easy chair, devouring a taco. There'd be no complaints about multiple takes here.

But for one year, he loved hamburgers. Years after the Taco Bell deal ended, I signed him up for a Burger King Legends of College Football spot with Bo Jackson, Lou Holtz and Joe Paterno. Still, only one fast-food endorser could be credibly endorsed at a time.

Perhaps the wildest action in which McMahon engaged was for the "Gotcha" paintball gun spot for LJN Toys. Sitting poolside in a bathing suit, McMahon aimed the gun at a target carried by a dignified butler he called "Stetson." A whole bunch of other butlers are seen cowering off to the side. LJN toys rented a huge mansion in the hills above Los Angeles for the shoot.

A Honda commercial for its scooter—which McMahon used to zip around training camp—proved to be more work for its "outrageousness" theme and the quarterback's many faces.

"I didn't like doing the Honda commercial," Jim said. "There were 22 wardrobe changes. All those different outfits, the same thing over and over again."

The somewhat-reluctant McMahon, always wanting to go off to do his thing at home or on the golf course, perked up once the cameras began shooting and clicking. By no means was he an endorsement hog. The money was too good to pass up and he overcame his natural reluctance to promote himself.

"I really wasn't interested in doing half these commercials, but I was getting between $100,000 and $300,000 for a commercial," he noted.

But it all added up. On September 28, 1987, *Sports Marketing News*, a now-defunct publication, reported just five quarterbacks handled national endorsements other than footballs and shoes. McMahon was far ahead of the pack with an estimated $3 million in earnings, far outstripping his Bears salary. The Giants' Phil Simms was a distant second with $900,000, his team having won Super Bowl XXI. Years removed from his last Super Bowl title, the 49ers' Joe Montana was just behind Simms at $850,000. In smaller-market Miami and with just one Super Bowl appearance, but no title to his credit. The Dolphins' prolific and Hall of Fame-bound Dan Marino was fourth at $700,000.

"I think McMahon has moved to the next level," ProServ agency's Andy Brandt, who represented the Bengals' Boomer Esiason, said in the *Sports Marketing News* article. "He's not a football player anymore. He's a celebrity. He has reached rock-star proportions."

McMahon's celebrity status moved him from just a desired football endorser to the August 31, 1987 cover of *Businessweek* magazine, this time with a Taco Bell headband. Furthering the good timing of his commercial portfolio were more available TV channels on which commercials could run.

The 1980s were cable TV's first big decade. ESPN had signed on in September 1979, at first with anything that moved on a field. Half a decade later, the eventual "World Wide Leader" gradually added mainstream events going into McMahon's endorsement boom.

Regional sports networks also were starting up, taking some of the local team telecasts formerly limited to over-the-air TV. The RSN's, who now face declines due to cable cord-cutters a generation-plus later, enabled teams to start televising home games which formerly were blacked out on over-the-air channels. Supplemented by still-fledgling cable news networks, the scenario simply represented more exposures for the outwardly wild-and-crazy quarterback hawking his wares compared to the primarily three-channel, three-network days of the 1970s.

At the same time, the more McMahon was exposed, the more there was the chance of his "the truth hurts" verbal style throwing a potential monkey wrench into his commercial momentum. But we achieved the high ground of daytime guest-star credibility when Oprah Winfrey, skyrocketing to fame in 1986 with her Chicago-based show, booked McMahon for a live-on-tape production for airing the day after Thanksgiving in '86.

We were also in the process of locking down a deal for Kraft Food's Miracle Whip topping. Nancy McMahon used Miracle Whip on Jim's lunch sandwiches for practice, but he really did not like it. I told Oprah we just did the deal with Miracle Whip, so could she mention it on the show in some way? She was very accommodating, asking McMahon about doing the commercial. He replied, "I hate the stuff." During the next commercial break, I asked Oprah if she could take out that comment, otherwise we could lose the deal. She said "I'll take care of it." So she put Nancy McMahon on the next segment, and asked how does her husband really feel about Miracle Whip? Nancy saved the day by stating he loves it and that she puts it on his plate every day.

Other instances of McMahon's public stance could have deep-sixed some work, but his strong appeal post-Super Bowl XX overcame the negatives. He was not a media politician like some superstars and just garden-variety athletes. He did not play up to the press. He could be a little curt even with beat writers covering the Bears daily.

In spite of that chasm, I always told him to be himself: Don't be phony and always tell the truth. I don't think that was difficult—there is not a phony bone in McMahon's body. Still, he would not sit down and entertain reporters for long periods of time. As a result, I sometimes had to be the buffer, to be the man explaining McMahon to the media, adding to my similar role as a go-between for McMahon and Ditka.

The next step in cashing in on McMahon's image and fame was the most risky—a restaurant in his name. Restaurants in general have a high mortality rate, and an athlete's name on the front door never insulates it from the problems of making money. I would not have initiated the deal. Instead, I was approached by a restaurateur to open McMahon's eatery at the site of a closed restaurant at Armitage and Lincoln avenues in Chicago's upscale Lincoln Park neighborhood. I put a group together, cutting McMahon in for a good amount of the gross. But it cost $1.2 million to open. I asked Rich Melman, Chicago's leading restaurant innovator with his Lettuce Entertain You Enterprises, to take over and run the restaurant as a favor to me.

But McMahon's restaurant had a short life, closing in February of 1988. Melman told me the key to a successful restaurant is size and lease. We had a small restaurant and a lousy lease. We could seat a maximum of 110 people, but we needed 300 to make money. And we had people lined up to get in, adhering to a dress code—against McMahon's casual image. Melman came to me and said you'll make money in seven years or we can shut down now. Under the circumstances, the decision was simple.

Harry Caray's, starting at about the same time, was successful partly because the famed broadcaster and carouser was often there to rub shoulders, sign autographs, kiss the women and yell out a few of his signature "Holy Cows!" Managed by the adept Grant DePorter, Harry Caray's expanded to a small Chicago-area chain and has been popular for three decades. Meanwhile, Ditka gained credibility for his second restaurant in Chicago, near downtown, by appearing regularly. In contrast, McMahon only showed up occasionally at his own place. He'd sit in back and sneak out through the kitchen.

I learned a business lesson, putting in some money and losing it. The only advice I can give in a tough restaurant business is get a professional you can trust, and make sure you partner with the right people. The odds will still be against you.

While throwing all these balls in the air and hoping none missed on the way down like the Cornish hen had done with McMahon, I had to dampen down the truly wild-and-crazy side effects of McMahon's fame. He indeed brought more women to football, some of whom wanted a close encounter of the first kind. Shelly had to steel herself while helping sort her husband's torrent of mail. The receivables included extremely candid photos of women, far greater in number than exhibitionists who tried to stop McMahon on his after-hours rounds during Super Bowl week. When I brought McMahon's mail to his locker at Halas Hall, the picturesque mash notes were directed to the circular file.

Nor would McMahon be posed in commercial deals in any risqué manner. Always a devout Mormon, Nancy McMahon ensured her husband would not pose with models garbed suggestively when her husband did a *Town and Country* magazine "beauty issue" photo shoot with the artistic Victor Skrebneski at his LaSalle Street studio. The models were portrayed in separate photos and the closest to them McMahon got was his photo on a facing page.

During the shoot, Skrebneski asked if I had a jewelry deal. I said just hold on. I quickly drove to Trabert and Hoeffer jewelers on Oak Street along the famed Magnificent Mile shopping district. I asked if I could get a high-end watch for the shoot, the Ebel Beluga brand being my favorite model. I went back to the studio, affixed the watch to McMahon and then called Ebel Beluga corporate. I asked, how would you like your product featured in the *Town and Country* "beauty issue?" We cut a deal for products. They responded with a cache of free watches. In turn, companies could sometimes piggyback onto McMahon's deals. Revo sunglasses could not afford a commercial but I got them value-added exposure by putting a different pair of Revo glasses on McMahon during his many Honda wardrobe changes.

Amazingly, after all these decades, McMahon, now a grandfather, still gets inquiries about his services. I even heard of a new medical practice wanting Jim's endorsement, given the physical challenges of his post-football life. So I still wonder if I would have had to defer retirement had he been blessed with better health and would've had a longer run as a winning Bears quarterback.

When not detoured by domesticity, McMahon still could generate laughs and mild outrage when the mood hit him.

On August 24, 2000, our daughter Jenny was married in a black-tie ceremony at our Chicago north suburban home. McMahon showed up — *sans* teeth and adorned with his trademark sunglasses. I think he wanted to put on a show for my more "proper" mother-in-law. She took one look at him and asked about the whereabouts of his choppers. She pleaded: put your teeth back in now! McMahon dutifully complied, but only after the pair posed for toothless McMahon photos.

McMahon was in character for someone whose favorite movie was *One Flew Over the Cuckoo's Nest*. Jack Nicholson, the movie's star and another with a rebellious image, was one of his favorite actors.

And even going further into the 21st century, a curious public still inquired about McMahon, who generated headlines whenever he spoke up. At its peak, the "McMahon Show" was an unforgettable ride and a major reason why I am able to lay down tens of thousands of words in these pages.

CHAPTER 9
MONKEY WRENCHES IN THE
WOULD-BE DYNASTY

I s that all there is?

More than three decades later, Jim McMahon, I and any-one else with a connection to the mid-1980s Bears still get bom-barded with questions about why the Super Bowl XX champs, one of the greatest teams in NFL history and possibly the most colorful, did not repeat their championship at least once.

The titlists were the youngest team in the NFL, the stocking of talent completed with a bountiful 1983 draft. Even given the normal attrition in the NFL and the crapshoot of the playoffs, when any team on a given day could pull an upset via a hot quarterback or turnovers, the ferocious defense combined with skilled players on offense should have been enough to at least reach another Super Bowl, if not win it all again.

Rolls of the dice certainly played a factor. But the answers are not wrapped up in mysticism or curses, as was a huge misdirection to the masses for the Chicago Cubs through their finally broken, 108-year championship drought. Injuries, bad fortune and perhaps above all, wayward management contrib-uted to the unraveling of the 1985–86 momentum.

The only major change affecting the Bears going into train-ing camp in 1986 had been the departure of defensive coor-dinator Buddy Ryan to the Philadelphia Eagles for a well-de-served head-coaching job. Vince Tobin, brother of Bears scouting chief, Bill Tobin, replaced Ryan. But his defenders were so strong, any change in the much-praised "46" scheme would not have affected their output due to their athleticism and smarts. Three future NFL head coaches — Ron Rivera, Mike Singletary and Leslie Frazier — had evolved from that '85 unit. A fourth, Jeff Fisher, spent the season on injured reserve, eventually enjoying the longest head coaching career of any Ryan alumnus.

Frazier was the only '85 defensive starter not to return, his career having ended prematurely due to a knee injury suffered on a punt return in Super Bowl XX. What was rated the NFL's greatest-ever defense was otherwise bolstered by the return of lineman Al Harris and safety Todd Bell, both of whom held out the entire 1985 season.

Meanwhile, McMahon was a young-veteran quarterback leader armed with a championship pedigree, still blessed with Walter Payton, 31, as the primary recipient of handoffs, and impact receivers in Willie Gault and Dennis McKinnon. Another offensive weapon was added in No. 1 pick Neal Anderson out of Florida, being groomed as Payton's successor.

The '86 defense actually went on to allow 11 fewer points — again ranking No. 1 in the NFL — than their unforgettable predecessors from the previous season. The Bears began 6-0. But the offense was not as efficient, sputtering at times when McMahon suffered a sore shoulder. McMahon missed three consecutive November starts against the Los Angeles Rams, Tampa Bay Buccaneers and Atlanta Falcons. He finally returned for a November 23 grudge match at Soldier Field against the archrival Green Bay Packers.

The Bears won 12-10. But it was a matter of winning the battle while losing the war. The Bears were stripped of their quarterback and their championship mojo — thanks to an out-of-control Packers lineman named Charles Martin. McMahon's career and Chicago's fortunes were forever changed by a fit of madness for which a suspension to Martin could not compensate.

McMahon and the Bears were the final victims of an elongated hot war between Ditka and Packers coach Forrest Gregg, carried over from their playing days two decades prior, when

Vince Lombardi's Packers usually got the best of George Halas' Bears. But Ditka stuck it to Gregg by employing William "Refrigerator" Perry, to this day the world's largest defensive tackle-turned-running back, to score two rushing touchdowns and one receiving six-pointer against the Packers in 1985. Angered at their inability to beat the far-more talented Bears, the Pack tried to beat up Payton and fullback Matt Suhey in that Bears' triumph at Lambeau Field.

On this day though, at Soldier Field, Gregg prompted the wound-too-tight defensive end Martin to sport a "hit list" of Bears on his towel—Nos. 9, 29, 34, 63 and 83—for McMahon, special-teams player Dennis Gentry, Payton, center Jay Hilgenberg and Gault.

Gregg apparently picked the right man for the job. When his family and friends gathered for his funeral in 2005 after he died of kidney failure in Houston at just 46, his football style was recalled: "'Too Mean' just didn't want to run across the field without hitting someone that day. That's the way he was." Martin was renowned all the way back in high school in Canton, Georgia, for playing after the whistle blew. If he slammed the running back halfway to China as a play was being blown dead by officials, well, that was just Martin, the hyper-aggressive defensive stopper, according to reputation. Amazingly, after his death, a friend called him "gentle, childlike."

After the Packers' Mark Lee intercepted a pass in the second quarter, Martin kept coming long after the ball went downfield. Martin came up from McMahon's blind, left side, grabbed him by the chest and slammed his right shoulder and head onto the artificial turf. McMahon's shoulder was severely injured and he also could trace long-term spinal injuries to this play. Referee Jerry Markbreit quickly prevented an on-field brawl by immediately ejecting Martin, who accepted congratulations by the Packers' bench. CBS-TV analyst Johnny Morris expressed shock at the mini-celebration for the banished Martin.

But Markbreit never expected to enter into a tinderbox. A longtime north suburban Skokie resident, he always passed up hometown NFL assignments to avoid the attendant pressures from fans in the stadium and in his personal and business rounds. But in the rare Soldier Field duty, he took control quickly.

"It was at least 20 seconds after the interception," Markbreit said of the play to the *Chicago Tribune*'s David Haugh after Martin's death. "I don't think he had an awareness of how late it was, or that the play was over. McMahon was walking to the sideline, had relaxed, and he picked him up and smashed him to the ground."

Markbreit, who was later actually fired for refusing to train officials — termed Martin's ejection "the biggest call of my 43-year career." Martin's ejection was the first in NFL history for a violent act other than fighting.

Martin lollygagged on the field after Markbreit's thumb. Spotting him nearly 10 inches and 100 pounds, Markbreit grabbed Martin by the arm. "If you don't come with me now, I'll let the Bears kill you," he claimed he told the lineman.

"I was afraid of nobody," added Markbreit. "I felt so powerful (as a referee) out there."

Martin went on to earn a two-game suspension. Then-Bears general manager Jerry Vainisi recalled being so enraged he wanted the NFL to suspend Martin until McMahon's injury healed. Martin was fortunate the incident took place in a more tolerant era for such on-field incidents.

"The way the rules are now, he'd be banned for life," McMahon said, looking back.

Watching from the second row at the 35-yard-line, I believed Martin's slam down was an outright mugging. As a former prosecutor and defense attorney, one of my first thoughts was a lawsuit. Today, there's no question Martin would have had to defend a huge civil action, if not criminal penalties. I talked to who I perceived as the top civil attorney in the city at Kennelly and Associates. He thought we had a good case and was willing to take it on and so I brought the legal facts to McMahon. But he was from the old school and told me he did not want me to pursue legal relief. "I have to still play in this league," McMahon told me at the time. The macho code was not to put the hammer on fellow players, no matter how grievous their acts. He had a great instinct about the reaction of NFL players, and I trusted his instinct.

"I'm the one who said 'no,'" McMahon recalled 31 years later.

Martin was not blackballed in the least. He played in the final two Packers games in 1986, began the 1987 season with Green Bay and finished out his career through 1988 as a backup with the Houston Oilers and Atlanta Falcons.

Once Martin's fate moved out of our immediate concern though, I had to laser-focus on McMahon's health, a quarterback's arm being his bread and butter. He needed total shoulder reconstruction. I decided to bypass the Bears' medical staff to seek out the best orthopedic surgeon for shoulders in the country — Los Angeles-based Dr. Frank Jobe, father of baseball's famed "Tommy John Surgery" back in 1974. On something as serious as a player's career, I did not want him to see team physicians, as doctors paid by the team have a mandate to get the player back on the field, whether via painkilling shots or pills.

Media swarmed out to the West Coast to follow the medical soap opera. Jobe had mentor Dr. Robert Kerlan come in on the consult. Kerlan put crutches aside and manipulated McMahon's shoulder. Jobe ended up performing the total reconstruction with Dr. Clinton Fossier, the Bears team physician, in the operating room as an observer. He put McMahon's cast up high to get his range of motion back more quickly. Jobe set up McMahon with famed Chicago-area trainer Bob Gajda for his rehabilitation.

But even Jobe's surgical talents could not restore McMahon to his old form. He was never the same player. He couldn't throw the same ball as before. McMahon's post-surgical arm in returning to the Bears in 1987 would not have set 70 NCAA records. He was just an OK player. I can recall talking to NFL

Hall-of-Fame writer Dan Pompeii, who asked about McMahon being a backup going forward.

However, Ditka employed his own brainstorm—the diminutive Doug Flutie to replace McMahon on the roster for the remainder of the 1987 season. Despite the Boston College product's 1984 Heisman Trophy pedigree and one of the top Hail Mary passes of all time to beat the University of Miami that same year, Flutie did not hit it off with his new Bears teammates from the start. His arrival was the first real chasm threatening the momentum of the budding dynasty.

The Bears had acquired Flutie's NFL rights, at Ditka's behest, from the Rams in mid-October, after the 5-foot-9 Flutie had played the '85 season for Donald Trump's New Jersey Generals in the USFL's final season. Even with longtime backup Steve Fuller and second-year quarterback Mike Tomczak already on the roster, Flutie started one regular season-game, a too-close 16-13 victory over the Detroit Lions. But the players already were agitated after Ditka hosted Flutie at his home for Thanksgiving. Tight end Emery Moorehead would not soon forget the locker-room feelings two years later when Flutie, by then helming the New England Patriots, returned to play for the Bears.

"I think everybody wants to squash him and eliminate him," Moorehead told the *Chicago Tribune*. "We'd like to put him down early and get someone else in the game.

"There were some bad feelings between some people and him. I think we will have some bad feelings. He just got started off on the wrong foot. First thing, he gets to town and has Thanksgiving dinner at Coach Ditka's house. He was getting special treatment. Nobody else ever had Thanksgiving dinner with Ditka. Nobody else ever had dinner at his restaurant. It separated him from the other guys."

McMahon had his own take on Flutie. Prior to Flutie's return, he showed up at practice with real thick glasses wearing a mock New England uniform. He threw a couple of real off-kilter passes as if to channel the Bears-era Flutie.

In remembering his Bears arrival, Flutie said he knew he was an interloper creating bitterness in a McMahon-led organization.

"That's Jim's team," he said. "He's the No. 1 guy and the player that makes the team click. I don't worry about it."

But Flutie cemented his position as a divisive force when Ditka chose him to start the January 3, 1987, divisional-play-off game against the Washington Redskins at Soldier Field. Although the 14-2 Bears were favored, the Redskins shocked their hosts with a 27-13 victory in which Flutie was not competitive enough. He'd play in just one Bears game in the 1987 regular season before moving on to the Buffalo Bills, whom he guided to the playoffs, via the Canadian Football League and several championships there, and eventually to the Patriots, where he enjoyed a modicum of success

But only three days after the Redskins playoff victory, Bears president Michael McCaskey apparently fired General Manager Jerry Vainisi, a move that was kept under wraps except for a *Daily Southtown* newspaper report. The sacking was widely reported by January 16 with official announcements from the Bears that day.

Vainisi was a straight shooter across the negotiating table. He had done McMahon's contract in 1984 after some lengthy talks. And he was an advocate of McMahon as the franchise quarterback, despite the histrionics of 1985–86. However, while Vainisi carried out his general manager duties as proscribed by George S. Halas as Papa Bears' final front-office promotion in 1983, Halas presidential successor McCaskey began growing more imperial and less accessible as the franchise headed toward the Super Bowl. The breath-of-fresh air, next-generation Bears executive of 1984 apparently was consigned to history. Like other sports executives who came from the ranks of business or other professions, he began to see himself as a player-personnel and contract expert in relatively short order.

Vainisi initially believed he worked well with McCaskey. He never asked for an increase in player payroll behind his initially budgeted number. Vainisi designated wiggle room for each player's projected contract to provide for the give-and-take of contract talks. In 1984, the general manager adjusted the timing—but not the money—under which rookie Ron Rivera's contract bonus would be paid. McCaskey had wanted no changes in the Rivera contract. He was upset when he learned of the relatively-minor Rivera bonus shift.

"That was the first crack in the dike," Vainisi said. McCaskey wanted more of a day-to-day contract and personnel presence. He couldn't scout, he couldn't coach, so he wanted to be involved."

Over the next 2½ years, "ego, a small word with a large impact," prompted McCaskey to involve himself more in personnel decisions. He could not learn on his own, though. Vainisi said McCaskey enlisted longtime scouting chief Bill Tobin to teach him Football 101 and then some. "Bill agreed, because he could see how things were starting to go," Vainisi said.

Over time, as McCaskey exercised more direct control over contracts and player personnel, he eliminated signing bonuses for veterans and desired contracts emphasizing team incentives.

One motivation could have been to break up a potentially opposing power base in the Bears organization. "My relationship with Ditka became too close, and I was perceived as having lost my independence," Vainisi said. "I didn't, but I did what I felt Mike needed to operate. He wasn't the easiest guy to work with. We had a common purpose—it was unspoken. We just knew what the other one wanted."

Under McCaskey, the Bears were run by what the media termed a management triumvirate of Vainisi, Ditka and Tobin. "That was the wish of George Halas," Vainisi said of Papa Bear's final days running the Bears in 1983. McCaskey said on January 16, 1987, he would soon fill Vainisi's general manager position. But the general manager's job was officially never filled until 2001, when Jerry Angelo assumed the title. For 14 years, first Tobin, then Rod Graves and finally Mark Hatley would assume some general manager roles under the title of player personnel director. McCaskey, who studiously read books in the car to and from Bears games at Wrigley Field in the days of his youth, served as a kind of executive general manager. He reversed the organizational structure back to the pre-Jim Finks days of the early 1970s, one of the most inept periods in Bears history.

Emotionally handling the firing at the time, an upset Ditka termed Vainisi his "best friend." With one year to go in his contract, Ditka suggested he would not coach the Bears beyond 1987. The pair reportedly favored the signing of quarterback Doug Flutie — even while also backing McMahon — the previous fall. Remember, Ditka and Vainisi were business partners in Ditka's first restaurant as well as the City Lights nightclub.

But the dismissal had been percolating for a while. Vainisi continued to show up at Halas Hall for more than a week after getting the bad news from McCaskey to ensure the two remaining years on his contract would be honored.

NFL colleagues, fans, players and media did not endorse McCaskey's political action and Vainisi was respected throughout the NFL. Green Bay Packers President Bob Harlan and New York Giants General Manager George Young, both Super Bowl winners, said they regularly called Vainisi for advice on their own player contract negotiations. Vainisi's predecessor Finks, who in 1987 was the general manager of the New Orleans Saints, called the dismissal "mind-boggling," adding that in talks with Vainisi over the previous few days he picked up that Vainisi was "crushed, shocked."

A vice president of an NFL team told the *Chicago Tribune* the "ego thing in this league is incredible. It has to be unparalleled in American society. The only thing close to it might be politics. Everyone is on a monster ego trip, and Michael McCaskey might be the worst offender." That team VP, quoted anonymously, also speculated that NFL Commissioner Pete Rozelle placed McCaskey on the Long Range Planning Committee "to teach him you don't just snap your fingers and get an answer."

Longtime Chicago sportscaster Tom Shaer said McCaskey's increasingly aloof management style had led to "valid and unrelenting criticism. Things got worse with his firing of Vainisi when McCaskey had only three years' experience in the NFL. Brutal."

The increasingly ivory-tower stance of McCaskey ran counter to his professed open-door philosophy during his spring 1984 interview with sports writer George Castle in George Halas' Edgewater Beach Apartments residence. He talked about being advised by his grandfather to take a public-speaking course. "There should be mutual respect from both sides," he said of team management and media. "For those of us in pro sports, it's critical. The only way we can be in business is if the fans are interested, and the chief way to reach them is through the media."

Looking back more than three decades later, McMahon said he "didn't know what they were thinking" in dumping Vainisi. He recalled being put off by a kind of money quote from McCaskey.

"I just remember meeting Mike McCaskey once," said McMahon. "He said his idea is we don't have to win each year—just keep the stadium filled. I said to him we're not on the same page."

In contrast, McMahon had always gotten along with Michael McCaskey's father, team chairman Ed McCaskey. Every time the elder McCaskey went into the locker room, he left a cigar for McMahon. I was the recipient of the same brand of stogie from Halas' son-in-law. But there would be no such outlays of goodwill from his son.

"They lacked a [Hall-of-Famer,] Bill Polian-type football guy," McMahon said of the post-Vainisi management structure. He felt a president of football operations would have been ideal. "No question about it, they should have had a football guy in charge."

For me, I began to think this was the end of the championship Bears and McMahon's time at Soldier Field. Like Tobin allying with McCaskey, I could see the winds starting to turn.

One less McMahon backer was in the house after Vainisi's departure. At the time, I represented 10 Bears players and Cincinnati Bengals wide receiver Tim McGee, who led the NFL in kickoff return yards in his 1986 rookie season. I thought I'd better spread my wings. Early on, I switched the loyalties of Washington defensive lineman Reggie Rogers from then-suspected and later-convicted corrupt agent Norby Walters prior to the 1987 draft.

Initially I did not think the Bears would select a quarterback in 1987. Although still under contract as a possible backup, Flutie seemed a bust off his brief Bears performances and did not appear to be a threat to McMahon. But in the weeks leading up to the draft, McCaskey told me in all probability he would pick a quarterback. On Draft Day, I was in Detroit talking about Rogers' first contract with Lions owner William Clay Ford and General Manager Russ Thomas. I planned to stay overnight.

But then I got a call the Bears had picked quarterback Jim Harbaugh out of Michigan in the first round. Vainisi recalled the Bears' scouting staff had placed third-round grades on Harbaugh months before the '87 draft. I informed McMahon, who was in Las Vegas. He said to get him out of the Bears organization. I immediately got on a plane to Chicago and made a beeline to Halas Hall around 10:00 p.m. I went to McCaskey to ask him to trade McMahon.

In the hallway, Ditka saw me, and told me to come into his office. At first he asked why I was in the building. I informed him McMahon wanted to be traded. In his office, he said he too had quit the team after the Harbaugh pick.

After Ditka announced his intentions to leave, he went back in his office, sat for 20 minutes and asked himself, "What do I want in life?" The answer was clear: coaching the Chicago Bears, even though he had classified himself as a "Halas Bear" at the time of Vainisi's firing by McCaskey. So he "un-quit." Ditka continued to coach the Bears in a kind of cold peace until McCaskey called his number early in 1993.

Ditka did ask about McMahon's whereabouts. He called McMahon, telling him how much he liked him and how much he wanted him to stay. Da Coach then talked McMahon out of wanting to be traded. After hearing from Ditka, I told McMahon to go along with it and see what happens. That's when I realized Ditka loved him. But he couldn't say that publicly.

Now though, without Vainisi, Ditka was out-numbered in Halas Hall office politics. Exercising more authority, but still answering to a boss who had increased his own power, Tobin later would be proud of his Harbaugh selection.

"I took a lot of heat for taking Harbaugh in the first round," Tobin said years later. "But I know I was right as far as the person I got and the ability that I got."

Ditka's pitch to McMahon turned out to be a kind of short-term reprieve. McMahon came back for two more seasons, running his winning streak as a starter to 22 in a row in 1987, 25 including playoffs. Late in that streak, McMahon went 23 for 34 for 287 yards and three touchdowns with a 110.8 quarterback rating for engineering a 31-28 comeback win over the Kansas City Chiefs at Soldier Field. Ditka's tongue was loosened a bit by his typical postgame victory celebration. Later that night, on Ditka's regular appearance on WBBM-TV's *Bears Extra* program, McMahon booster Johnny Morris asked if his old Bears teammate-turned-coach would split play-calling with McMahon. Ditka swiped the air with his fist. "What we're going to do...I'll call some, he'll call some," he said. Pressing, Morris asked if the Bears were "late and behind" and if would it be more economical to let McMahon call the plays at the line of scrimmage? "It's easier that way," Ditka replied, with a telltale smile as the night grew long.

But whatever positives arose from that game soon disappeared. The Bears limped to the finish line in 1987. They embarrassed themselves on *Monday Night Football* on December 14 with a 41-0 loss at San Francisco, with an angry Ditka hitting a female fan in Candlestick Park at halftime after hurling a wad of chewing gum toward the stands. McMahon was sidelined with a strained right hamstring. Amazingly, longtime McMahon critic Bernie Lincicome of the *Tribune* wrote about what would cure the team's ailments: "The visible and unsurprising lesson is the Bears must have McMahon. He is more essential than (Joe) Montana to his team's success." But McMahon did not return in good health. For the second straight season, the Bears lost to the Redskins in a division playoff game at Soldier Field, this time by a 21-17 tally on January 10, 1988.

Now Super Bowl XX receded further into memory. The momentum of that "shufflin' crew" was officially gone. The players still endured somewhat sour after effects from the October 1987 walkout in which Ditka embraced the "Spare Bears" strikebreaker subs. Meanwhile, the Bears' informal team salary cap took effect. I now negotiated contracts with team financial man Ted Phillips, eventually destined to succeed McCaskey as team president. I got along very well with the amiable Phillips. But at various junctures of each negotiation, he had to interrupt to go to the back office to check on contractual clauses and team policy with McCaskey. Only one other executive with whom I ever dealt, the Redskins' Charley Casserly, was under such strictures.

One by one, the components of the '85 titlists were dismantled. Only 25, All-Pro linebacker Wilber Marshall became the first NFL free agent in 11 years to sign with another team in the spring of 1988. Marshall garnered a five-year, $6 million deal with the Redskins. Declining to match the offer, McCaskey and Co. corralled first-round picks in the next two drafts as compensation. If the Bears had matched Washington's offer, they would have dramatically skewed their carefully-constructed player payroll. Middle linebacker Mike Singletary's contract required him to be the Bears' highest-paid defensive player. At that point in time, a pair of $1 million linebackers would have severely cut into the dividends of a family-run business with more than a dozen heirs, while causing restiveness among other players.

Later, during 1988 training camp, the Bears were forced to

trade McMahon's best deep threat, Willie Gault. A holdout who wanted a trade to the West Coast, partially to help boost his budding movie interests, Gault, 27, soon departed for the Los Angeles Raiders, with whom he played out the rest of his NFL career.

My own true breakout from my Chicago-centric stage would have to wait for the turn of the calendar to 1989, when I staged a bread-and-circuses production for eventual Hall-of-Famer Deion Sanders' nationally-televised Prime Time Draft party at my home. But at heart, I was a Bears fan and my heart was starting to bleed. Eventually though, I'd root against the Bears. My clients at Halas Hall would play through the early 1990s. Never again, though, would the charter NFL franchise match the fun of 1985, even with another trip to the Super Bowl 21 years later.

Yet, I get the feeling the same things that have kept the Bears from even more Super Bowl wins are stuck in a time warp to this very day. Rick Morrissey of the *Chicago Sun-Times* summed up the dilemma facing the proud, but bowed, franchise in a November 19, 2017, column:

"Let's pretend that my dad was a brilliant scientist who founded a rocket company that became a billion-dollar corporation. And let's pretend that I, whose aptitude was more suited for, I don't know, 18th century French literature, took over the company upon his death.

"At some point, as the math and technology that went into the rockets continued to make no sense to me, my family or anyone we hired (which explains the rockets exploding over and over upon liftoff), I think I'd say to myself, 'You know, I might not be cut out for the aerospace engineering industry.'

"But here's the craziest part: People still keep buying our rockets! Year after year! The bigger the catastrophes, the more sales seem to increase! We're wealthy beyond almost anyone's wildest dreams!"

In real life, a pro football franchise dear to my heart since pre-school, also was wealthy, but not in a victory column that so many less-pedigreed franchises have long since mastered.

CHAPTER 10
IS THE NFL READY FOR PRIME TIME?

A ll my bread and circuses—the noise of my public persona, that is—up to the spring of 1989 were far from
my Chicago north suburban home. Jim McMahon's endorsements, appearances, photo shoots and rubbing shoulders with
celebrities who wanted a piece of the Chicago Bears quarterback had me on the road.

Little could I figure my lower-level living room would almost
be the show-biz capital of sports for NFL Draft Day, Sunday,
April 23, 1989, which was also my wife, Shelly's, birthday.

Minus any celebratory cake, the Zucker home was the NFL
coming-out party for Deion Sanders, the man who patented
Prime Time, both in nickname and performance. Two other
of my drafted clients and a big dash of a McMahon sideshow,
via a trade that never was consummated during the live event,
set the tone.

My wife Shelly and I like to keep well-groomed grounds,
front and back. After that Draft Day, landscapers had to do
some post-event cleaning up as reporters and cameramen
tromped all over the place while an ESPN remote truck
camped out on the driveway for a live broadcast conducted
by reporter Andrea Kremer. I had been an agent for nearly 4½
years, but now I developed a truly national profile with profuse
thanks to Sanders' showmanship and McMahon's mirth.

The road to my own prime time had begun the previous
month. Among his three-sports feats, Sanders had completed
his eligibility as an absolute shutdown cornerback at Florida
State. He also starred for the baseball team and ran track. His
multi-tasking in sports seemed out of the early 20th century.

On one astounding day, outfielder Sanders played the first game of a Seminoles doubleheader, then took a break to run a leg of a 4-by-100 relay for the track team and then dashed back to the baseball field to play another game.

Any agent would have given a chunk of his business to represent Sanders. He came out of school as a two-time consensus All-American cornerback in 1987–88. He had intercepted 14 passes, including three in bowl games. He returned one interception a record-breaking 100 yards. His final collegiate interception, with five seconds left, locked up the Seminoles' 13-7 victory over Auburn in the 1989 Sugar Bowl.

Opponents only got a break when the Seminoles had the ball. Sanders was also the country's best punt returner, leading the nation in average yards per return, finishing with 126 returns for 1,429 yards.

So then, how could he do so much over three sports, sometimes two simultaneously, all the way through his pro career? To Sanders, enjoying such variety was second nature, having done it from almost the first day he picked up a football or baseball. He had been drafted by the New York Yankees in the 30th round and signed a few weeks later, in 1988. One month after the televised soiree at my home, he made his big-league debut as a Bronx Bomber.

"I played multiple sports my whole life," Sanders said of his roots in Ft. Myers, Florida. "Doing that at another level was nothing new to me. It was just new to (the pro) level. It was new to the country. I had been playing two sports and three sports since I was five-, six-, seven-years old. The demands on the body were not strenuous whatsoever because this is what you do and this is who you are."

Sanders comprised his own legend long before he sniffed the NFL. He brashly acquired the nickname "Prime Time" early on and had the athletic stones to back it up. And how many athletes could comfortably be known by a flashy second nickname: "Neon Deion?"

It was hard to catch Sanders once he had the ball, but the

odds were a bit better off the field. I made my run at him at the NFL Combine in 1989. I lusted after a shutdown cornerback, a true game-changer for any defense. But I already represented Florida defensive back Louis Oliver, who had appeared on a magazine cover with Sanders.

In a hotel lobby, I saw Louis accompanied by "some guy." I wasn't sure of the latter's identity, but I walked up to Louis and asked, "Who's this?" I'd never forget "some guy's" name again. It turned out to be Sanders and I told him, "When you get serious about choosing an agent, please give me a call." Perhaps it was a little arrogant. But prominent agents — Leigh Steinberg, Marvin Demoff, Ralph Cindrich — were going after him, especially after Sanders ran a record-breaking 4.27 in the 40-yard dash. He would go out for an exercise run, showboating in sweats and his trademark jewelry.

After Sanders' amazing dash, he gave his phone number in Tallahassee to Gene Burroughs, my right-hand man. Getting ready for my presentation, I called lifelong friend Rick Fizdale, then chief creative officer of the Leo Burnett ad agency. We agreed we had to appeal to his ego. So Fizdale made up a poster reading, "Is the NFL Ready For Prime Time?"

Setting up a suite in a Tallahassee hotel, I put the poster in the other room. After I began pitching Sanders, I went into the second room, told him I had a gift for him and brought back the poster for display. Sanders loved the poster and the entire concept of putting him in a special category of a prime-time star. The presentation surely appealed to his pride. Sanders confirmed for me in 2017 that the poster clinched his commitment to hire me as his football agent.

He attributed much of what he had achieved to Connie Knight, his mother, so much so that he bought her a Mercedes and acquired a personalized license plate, "Ms. Time." So Knight joined Sanders' aunt and girlfriend on the trip to Chicago. I flew them all first class for the first time for any client's family. I put them all up in a boutique hotel. And then I took them to the famed Palm restaurant, where they all ordered seven-pound lobsters at $105 each. Remember, this is 1989. Later, in a tour of my offices and meetings with my 16 staffers, Sanders remarked, "I am impressed."

So I wound up getting Sanders' business from what I believed was a personalized style he picked up on immediately. Plus, he was well aware of my success in marketing McMahon nationally.

"First and foremost, he represented successful people already," Sanders said. "That led you to understand he knew what he was doing. Secondly, he had a knack for marketing. He was a wonderful marketing guy. I knew what I wanted to attain at the professional level. I thought he was a good fit."

For our draft strategy, Sanders said he did not want to sign with the Detroit Lions or Kansas City Chiefs, who selected ahead of his preferred Atlanta Falcons, who held the number five pick.

"I went to Atlanta on All-American visits," Sanders said. "I understood the ethnicity of the city, the dynamics of the city and I knew I would have much more acceptance there than in a Green Bay, a KC or Detroit."

Armed with that information, I called the Lions and Chiefs to wave them away, stating Sanders would play baseball rather than signing with them. Then I called the Falcons, who loved Sanders. But I cautioned that for committing to Sanders at number five, they'd have to pay him number three money.

In the meantime, the Zucker family had its first experience as unpaid ESPN production assistants. The cable network, which had built a huge audience of 10 million for the draft since first televising it in 1983, wanted to piggyback onto Sanders, the hottest player in the country. And the broadcast would give the talented Kremer, just hired as ESPN's first female reporter, live national exposure. A Chicagoan, Kremer had recently earned an Emmy Award nomination as an NFL Films producer.

"It's almost like a snowball going downhill — it just builds and gets bigger and bigger," John Wildhack, ESPN's NFL coordinating producer, said of the media crush around Sanders to the *Chicago Tribune*'s Steve Nidetz just before the draft.

But if Sanders had any doubts he was heading into new and exalted territory, they should have been erased the night before the draft at dinner at Stefani's restaurant in Chicago. I was fortunate to have clients thrilled to cross paths with Michael Jordan as they began working with me. Jordan was a clincher in so many ways away from the court. On this night, Jordan, perhaps the ultimate prime-time clutch performer, happened to be there and greeted Sanders at the eatery.

On Draft Day, ESPN staged two remotes from the Chicago north suburbs — my home and Bears headquarters a little further north in Lake Forest. Correspondent and brilliant wordsmith Pete Axthelm reported on the fate of the Bears' trio of first-round picks.

As to Sanders, he liked the semi-homey, living-room atmosphere, even with the TV lights and crush of visitors.

"I didn't care for a huge auditorium or a TV studio," he said of the usual draft backdrop. "I believe in relationships, and there were no relationships. The relationship Steve and I had warranted me to be at his home. I was comfortable there. I was relaxed there. It was a great atmosphere there. It showed me it was someone handling my business who was successful, and it meant a lot to me."

I had barely put my head down on my pillow the night before the big show when I got an after-midnight call from a West Coast source that the San Diego Chargers would trade for McMahon. On Draft Day, anything could happen. With 1987 number one pick Jim Harbaugh going into his third year and the Bears coming off three straight disappointing playoff eliminations, the Bears seemed primed to finally dispatch McMahon. But I could not confirm the trade by the time the telecast went on the air.

Meanwhile, cameras set up in our living room as a bejeweled Deion and Connie Knight posed for photos and waited for the number five pick. He was adorned with five gold necklaces

*Deion Sanders shows the poster created by Rick Fizdale on
NFL Draft Day in Zucker's home in Winnetka, 1989*

with charms. The biggest one was festooned with a diamond dollar sign. I knew we would change the way a player could be marketed. We had trademarked the term "PrimeTime." A buffet kept the media sated. In those days, the pen and mic crowd typically did not pay for food in press boxes and I wasn't going to start a new trend a decade too early.

"It was very good of Steve to invite the media to his house on NFL Draft days, where we'd not only get interviews with him and players but also be treated as guests of his family," said longtime Chicago sportscaster Tom Shaer. "That was Steve, knowing we had a job to do, but also being gracious and building relationships. Believe me, as a media person, I felt it went both ways.

"I vividly recall Draft Day 1989, standing with my NBC-5 videographer next to Jim McMahon on the Zucker family's front lawn when Jay Hilgenberg arrived and immediately asked McMahon if he'd been traded. 'Not yet,' replied McMahon. The trade occurred four months later."

Any forward progress in the McMahon trade the Bears wanted to make was likely halted due to the reports coming

Steve interviewed by ESPN reporter Andrea Kremer as Deion Sanders looks on, NFL Draft Day, 1989

on the live broadcast from my living room. On top of all the arrangements to set up the ESPN show, I had several plates spinning in the air.

McMahon had arrived alone in his blue-and-white Cleret convertible. He soon was joined by wife Nancy and their then-three children. ESPN tried to get McMahon to go on live to talk about a trade that hadn't been consummated. He declined until there was news to talk about. McMahon passed the time playing with his son Sean in the backyard. He also rocked one of his daughters in a hammock and ate lunch.

Meanwhile, my assistant, David Powers, had to retrieve both Sanders and his girlfriend down our side street. Apparently, the young woman had some sort of fit and ran out the front door, upset.

Meanwhile, I also had to give a pep-talk to Florida's Oliver, who was stationed in an upstairs bedroom. Oliver was somewhat removed from the inside-outside tumult, but nevertheless was stewing. The Gator safety was upset he was not taken in the top ten. Instead, he went at number 25 to the Miami Dolphins. Oliver was knocked lower in the draft due to rumors associating him with drugs. So I had to ad lib with an upstairs-downstairs style involving three separate personalities and a media contingent clamoring for information.

After the ESPN programming concluded with Sanders a Falcons' draftee and McMahon still a Bear, Sanders and I prepared for the business part of the Prime Time Show. Indeed, this was serious business.

Our original request was for six years, totaling $10.7 million. Sanders' goal was $1 million per season for five years with a $1 million signing bonus. The financial package was identical to Atlanta's contract with defensive tackle Aundray Bruce, the number one pick of the entire 1988 draft. The Falcons countered at $4.5 million for five years. I did not budge at first, but then threw in a voidable option on a four-year contract. If he made All-Pro two of the four years, the contract would be void and we'd start over again.

Sanders joined an oddly crowded initial contract negotiation held at Atlanta's Hartsfield International Airport on June 12, 1989. Falcons' owner Rankin Smith was joined by son Taylor Smith and head coach Marion Campbell. Georgia Governor Joe Frank Harris also dropped in, the first and last time an elected official took part in my negotiations. But the meeting, which lasted a bit more than an hour, left Sanders upset as he walked out believing the Falcons wanted him "to just return punts." We did not meet again with Falcons Chief Financial Officer Jim Hay until two and a half months later, in early September, right before the opening game. Hay told me the team would simply sit on the sidelines, with no endgame in sight. I was sweating it out. I'd talk to the Falcons on the phone, telling them you'll see how crazy he is. He'll fire me, but he won't play for you and he'll end up in baseball full-time.

"By today's standards, I would have held out. But I didn't have a contract," said Sanders.

Finally, late on September 6, 1989, the Falcons came up to meet our demands without any concessions on our part. Sanders would get the richest contract ever for a defensive back, a four-year, $4.4 million payday. Included was a $2 million cash bonus, biggest ever non-deferred bonus for an NFL draft pick. Sanders' contract in totality was better than number one pick Troy Aikman of the Cowboys and his six-year settlement. To my knowledge, the deal had the first voidable option in the history of the NFL. The contract would not have been done without the voidable part and now is the standard for top players.

By the standards of "present value," measuring the value of a contract adjusted to interest rates, the contract paid Sanders more than Tony Mandarich's, the number one pick and monster offensive lineman selected by the Green Bay Packers. And Sanders' contract provided for a full season of Falcons football, not a mid-season transition from baseball to football that was two-sport star Bo Jackson's arrangement with the Los Angeles Raiders.

Sanders had previously worn the number 2 in college. But the NFL dictates numbers according to player positions. A defensive back had to wear a number starting in the 20s. Sanders asked me what number he should choose. I suggested 21 — simply my lucky number, as I was born on August 21. He agreed.

The Falcons deal meant Sanders finished his second stint with the Yankees with a flourish late on September 5, 1989, in Seattle. Playing left field, he slugged his second career homer off the Mariners' Jerry Reed with a man on. He added two doubles and drove in four runs. He also started the September 6 game in left, learning just before the first pitch, via a call from me, that he was a new Falcon. After striking out in the sixth, Sanders left the game and departed, shaking hands with his teammates in the dugout before flying almost 2,200 miles overnight to Atlanta.

"I'm sorry to be leaving," Sanders said of his departure from the Yankees. "Mr. (George) Steinbrenner has been very good to me, and I plan to come back next year. This has been a good experience for me."

Arriving with little preparation and travel-logged, Sanders

showed the Falcons' avid interest was justified. He fumbled, but recovered, his first punt return, which fortunately was re-kicked due to a penalty. The second time he touched the ball, Sanders took a punt 68 yards for a touchdown, the first score in the game in the Falcons' 31-21 loss to the Los Angeles Rams on Sunday, September 10. He thus surely became the only professional athlete in history to hit a Major League home run and score an NFL touchdown in the same week. He'd finish the '89 season with five interceptions in 15 games.

Like McMahon though, Sanders was marketable. I assisted in coming out with a line of "Prime Time" clothing. And playing two sports did not hurt. No matter how glamorous, Sanders knew he had to produce to make the dollars off the field.

"You'd be a fool to think you could be marketed and not have the goods, and not a lot of work put into being marketed," Sanders said. "You have the marketing team on standby ready to capitalize on your exploits." And that's what (Zucker Sports Management) did.

"McMahon had the ball. He had to produce. Steve could do what he does best. The same went for me as well, taking advantage of the opportunity Jim McMahon did what he did on the field. The quarterback is the only player, along with the team itself, which has a record. Defensive back, receiver and other positions don't get measured with wins. Being a winner means you're dominant. Being a winner means you're successful. Being a winner means you're voted to all these (all-everything) teams because of your exploits. It's different when it comes to quarterback. I don't think anyone could tell a defensive back or any other positions to hold off (on endorsements) 'til you win it all. That's not wise."

Yet, all along, Sanders did not seek role-model status with his commercial work.

"I was thinking about securing my mother for the rest of her life," he said. "That was my whole marketing picture."

But to maintain the endorsers' desires for Sanders' services, he had to fine-tune his image a bit.

Sanders knew the fundamentals of both football and baseball. There could be a situation where you can come off too flashy and thus not represent yourself in the right way to the public.

However, on May 22, 1990, Sanders' Yankees played the Chicago White Sox at Yankee Stadium. In the first inning, Sanders drew a dollar sign in the dirt as he prepared to hit, attracting the unapproving eye of ultimate old-school Sox catcher Carlton Fisk, a soon-to-be Hall of Famer. Then, in the third inning, Sanders drew another dollar sign in the dirt before he took his cuts. With a runner on third and one out, he then popped to short. Sanders apparently did not run out the ball to Fisk's satisfaction. He allegedly yelled: "Run the fucking ball out" and called Sanders a "piece of shit."

Tensions were at a boil in Sanders' third at-bat in the fifth inning. Sanders and Fisk began jawing at each other when the former batted. "The days of slavery are over," Sanders told Fisk. The catcher responded that he did not care if Sanders was black or blue or red, but that he was playing the game wrong. "I didn't think Deion had much respect for the game or the players," Fisk said later. "He'd saunter up to the plate like he owned the stadium."

Plate umpire John Hirschbeck was joined by his crewmates, along with all Yankees and White Sox players, managers and coaches, who served as spectators to the Sanders-Fisk debate. The pair did not make contact, and Sox and Yankees players played the distraction for its humorous aspects.

"It looked like more than it was," Sanders said to reporters after the game. "We were just telling each other how much we loved each other."

Fortunately, I was at the game, in position to give Sanders a bit of counsel afterward. I told him he cannot battle with a surefire Hall-of-Famer like Fisk. I advised him before the next White Sox-Yankees game on May 28, 1990, at old Comiskey Park, to shake Fisk's hand. Sanders initiated just that as lead-off man to start the contest and the two extended greetings.

"It was totally unexpected, but it was nice," Fisk said.

Sanders went on to catch three Fisk fly balls in the game. On the last one, near the left-field wall, he was doused with beer by a rowdy fan.

"I don't believe that was right," Fisk said.

However, I did not serve as Sanders' baseball agent. Barry Axelrod had that role. Had I repped Sanders for baseball, I likely would have made out just as well as in football from his deals. Hitting just .158 with three homers and eight steals in limited action, Sanders was released by the Yankees late in the 1990 season. Yankees General Manager Gene Michael said the media attention in New York for a part-time player and his commitment to the Falcons retarded his baseball development.

"In a different town, he might be better," Michael added. Earlier, Steinbrenner had offered him almost $2 million for the last two months of the 1990 season and all of 1991, but rescinded the offer just before he went on suspension from his active ownership role. Sanders soon caught on with the up-and-coming Atlanta Braves. He thus had the rare convenience of playing for both of his teams in the same city, fulfilling his full-time duties with the Falcons.

But Braves old-school Manager Bobby Cox did not permit bad apples in his clubhouse. If Sanders' character and dedication were a question, he would not have been signed. He played all three outfield positions in Atlanta, hitting .304 and leading the National League with 14 triples in 1992.

The '92 season thus was extremely busy for Sanders. He'd go on to lead the NFL in kickoff return yards (1,067), yards per return (26.7) and return touchdowns (two). He tried to add to his multi-sport legend on October 11, 1992. He first played in the Falcons game in Miami at 1:00 p.m. He then flew to Pittsburgh with the goal of playing in the National League Championship Series game that night against the Pirates. He would have earned the once-in-a-lifetime status as the first athlete to play in two professional leagues in the same day. But with no pre-game batting practice and obviously concerned about Sanders' late arrival time, Cox did not put him in the game.

Sanders made up for his absence that night with a typical Sanders center-stage performance in the Braves' World Series loss against the Toronto Blue Jays. He went 8-for-15 (.533), including two doubles.

He went on to play with the San Francisco Giants and Cincinnati Reds, who reactivated Sanders twice after he skipped baseball the entire 1996 and 1998–99 seasons to concentrate on the NFL. In spite of the fractured seasons, he still hit .263 lifetime with 186 stolen bases.

Sanders' status as an NFL Hall of Famer came in 2011 with high induction. He had succeeded to a good degree in demonstrating that with remarkable talent, sometimes you can excel without a lot of practice. His baseball tenure did not slow down his production once he transitioned to football.

He finished his 17-year football career in 2005 with nine interception returns for TDs, while returning six punts and three kickoffs for scores. He led the NFL in interception return yardage with 303 on three runbacks in his only season with the San Francisco 49ers in 1994. More importantly, for his standards, he started at cornerback on back-to-back Super Bowl winners for the 49ers and then the Dallas Cowboys in 1995.

Sanders had helped put me on the map nationally in 1989, expanding from my Bears-centric base of clients. I'd go on to represent two NFL first rounders in 1990 and three first rounders in 1992.

Now Sanders coaches high school football while serving as an analyst for CBS and the NFL Network. He's surely smart enough to coach in the NFL, but why would he want to deal with the embedded politics? I told Sanders in 2017 I was proud of all he accomplished on and off the field, and he responded that he owed it all to me. I appreciated such kudos, but without Sanders' talent and savvy, we surely would not have gotten very far.

Given his style and his dedication to the game, Sanders is probably right where he should be. I'm happy I had a modest part in getting Prime Time to that point.

CHAPTER 11
LET'S MAKE A DEAL!

You'd think professional sports' owners, general managers and bean counters are either saints or sinners.

I believe they fall in-between. They're not either/or. They all want to win — but they have varying philosophies related to their pocketbooks on how to do it. Sometimes they have pressures from debt or team investors that govern their behavior. Some are far better at running an organization than others.

I try to meet them in what I call the middle ground in which some of them operate. I'll state again, 'til I'm blue in the face, I much prefer my clients settle into a stable, long-term situation in a first-year contract with a fair front-end bonus, or a multi-year deal for a veteran. If I was the anti-Scott Boras, known for his hardcore negotiating tactics in not taking clients to free agency, then so be it. Changing comfortable surroundings for the unknown can be risky in sports. The competitive situation and coaching and managing philosophies can be dramatically different. The proverbial grass is rarely greener on the other side — unless athletes need to divorce themselves from absolutely irreconcilable differences in financials or personalities in their present teams.

I also hoped never to be intimidated by anyone with whom I was negotiating. I adapted myself and my style to that of my negotiating "opponent." Remember, almost all owners are self-made.

This is where I learned about people, having been a prosecutor and then a criminal defense attorney. I'd like to believe it made me a good judge of people. I would know what areas to aim at in people with whom I was dealing. I was trying for commonality of interests. But you couldn't make negotiating mistakes.

If you had a great owner, invariably he had a great GM and a great coach. It filtered down. The majority were good human beings. You didn't become a self-made man by hurting people, with some very standout exceptions. Treat the janitor and everyone else the same. If owners were well-grounded, they didn't flaunt their wealth.

I did find, however, variances in the style of negotiating among the different sports, as I was one of the few agents who handled three major sports. In my predominant representation, football men were tougher. They could be firmly that way with no real free agency back then. At the same time, baseball general managers almost always were baseball men who came through the ranks. They were easier to deal with and had navigated through long-established free agency by the time I was an agent. Contrasted to the pre-expansion days, you've now got Harvard and Yale-educated baseball execs, many of whom did not grow up in the game. They're a different breed.

But no matter their specific sport, personal background or size of pocketbook, I believe in always leave 'em laughing. You always want them to like you. I was selling myself. I tried to become very friendly with them, if possible.

So I'll take you through my negotiating tracks and give you an insight into the sports executives with whom I've dealt. I don't believe there's a honcho in any league with whom I couldn't have at least a civil conversation. No one will pound his shoe like former Russian Communist leader Nikita Khrushchev. But there have been some examples of the lively art of conversation with a touch of cloak-and-dagger intrigue in sports-contract negotiations.

The team I rated most difficult with which to negotiate, the Cincinnati Bengals, was a multi-generational, family-run operation started by patriarch Paul Brown. This 1968 AFL expansion team did not have an owner with an outside business as a source of the majority of his or her income. Brown's son, Mike Brown, traditionally kept careful watch on the exchequer. Team cash flow and revenue were his family's bread and butter. It's his money and he protected it. He reportedly did not like agents. Mike Brown's reputation preceded him by the time I had my first negotiation with him.

Brown was a tough guy, a lot like Bill Tobin, the crusty scout who became unofficial general manager of the Bears. People told me when negotiating with the Bengals to look out, that it the toughest team with which to negotiate in the league. I had to re-tool my style to become friendly with Mike Brown. I was going to find common ground to make Brown "my friend."

We'd talk sports. We'd talk about his dad, also the patriarch of the original Cleveland Browns. I'd chat about all the old Browns Hall of Famers. I used my knowledge of the powerhouse 1948–50 Browns of the old All-American Football Conference, before the franchise was absorbed by the NFL. Mike had been at his father's knee, so he was a football man. There was lots of small talk. I'm not just another agent and I knew Brown's team and family histories. I did whatever I had to do to relate to him and to get to know him.

I had no transition period from doing almost exclusively Bears contracts to dealing with financial tough guys like Brown. My first major non-Bears client was Tim McGee, the Bengals number one pick in 1986.

The McGee process was two-fold. First, I had to sweet-talk University of Tennessee product McGee away from Michael Jordan-agent David Falk, who had gotten him courtside seats at a Bulls game at old Chicago Stadium. Tim waved to me in my ninth-row seat from his on the floor. I ran down to meet him at halftime and pitched him again. No decision. Weeks later, on Draft Day, I was not going to try McGee again.

But my wife Shelly said, "What do you have to lose? Give him a call." So I finally decided to contact McGee that day. McGee had claimed several days previously to me that I was his choice for representation, but in reality he had never said that. So I arranged to meet him, flying to the Cleveland airport to do so. He was a Cleveland resident. I waited for his flight to deplane. All the passengers came off except McGee. I was about to leave, feeling defeated, and suddenly McGee came off and signed with me, just like that. I missed my plane back to Chicago, but the stakeout was worth it.

My goal with that contract was to get McGee a market-rate deal. So when I negotiate, I always do so off the team's need, on what the player could do for the team.

Once I got into Mike Brown's office, I showed him the "comparables," in other words, what the contracts for the numbers 20 and 22 picks got. It was easy, friendly, not contentious. If Brown thought I was just some agent bargaining strictly from a monetary standpoint, the approach would not have worked. Representing Jim McMahon had given me credibility. McGee got his market rate and after a break-in period as a kick returner, he had a productive Bengals career as a wide receiver.

The toughest challenge with Brown was the big-money contract due receiver Carl Pickens. He had 99 receptions and an NFL-pacing 17 touchdowns in 1995. He followed that up with 100 receptions in 1996. I represented Pickens in mid-career with a boost from Michael Jordan, who said some good words about me when he met Pickens. After his 82-reception season in 1998, I wanted to break the bank, the ultimate challenge with Brown. Pickens announced he'd never play football again unless he got his money. The Cincinnati Reds, playing hometown helpers, provided leverage, saying they'd keep Pickens in town and make him a center fielder. I reminded Pickens of the risks, pointing to the Al Harris/Todd Bell season holdouts with the Bears in 1985. Holding out was not my style, but I believed we'd win—somehow.

I finally convinced Brown the Bengals could not compete without Pickens. Initially, Brown offered between $3 and $4 million. But when you're negotiating in the monopolistic NFL with more restrictive free agency than baseball or basketball, you're negotiating with yourself sometimes. We had to create something, a market. Pickens' threat to retire factored in.

Remember, the winner in negotiations is whoever is willing to walk away from the table.

Brown brought in daughter Katie Blackburn and her husband Paul Blackburn, who by then were assuming more day-to-day responsibilities as team officials. As a negotiating tactic, I depicted Pickens as a tough guy—that he wouldn't do the contract they were offering. Brown finally agreed to $8 million, including a signing bonus for the first year of a five-year, $23.25 million contract. I remember walking out of the talks. The waiting media were amazed. They were shocked to see me coming out with the deal. I was trying to hold back a smile. We couldn't believe the size of the contract we landed, almost $24 million without going to training camp.

"It was bizarre. This was the strangest I remember," I told the media of the entire process.

I did a number of contracts with Brown. He never thought we ripped him off. In his mind, I believe he didn't think he lost in the Pickens deal. How come? Because you never make the team negotiators feel you beat them and that everything is positioned as a fair deal.

Pickens only lasted one more year in Cincinnati. Brown had suggested after the deal was completed that he hoped the receiver would spend his "golden years" with the Bengals. But he released Pickens in the 2000 off-season after he re-signed assistant coach and offensive coordinator, Bruce Coslet, in spite of a 21-36 career record. Pickens ripped the Coslet re-upping: "We're trying to win…and they bring (Coslet) back."

So Pickens signed as a free agent with the Tennessee Titans. Brown thereafter instituted a "loyalty contract clause," nicknamed the "Carl Pickens Clause," to deny various bonuses in contracts going forward if Bengals players disparaged the organization. Releasing Pickens with four years to go on a handsome contract meant Brown just might have cleared a good amount of salary-cap space as well.

At least with Brown, I dickered with the bottom-line man in the organization, the guardian of the vault. With the

Washington Redskins I dealt with General Manager Charley Casserly, who did the bidding of billionaire Jack Kent Cooke. I was cautioned that nobody beats Cooke on contracts; he simply said "no" and won, and won and won again.

In 1995, I had tried to land University of Colorado wide receiver Michael Westbrook, the Redskins' top pick at number four in the draft, but I initially lost out to agent Joel Segal. During negotiations with Casserly, Westbrook wasn't getting anywhere near the money Segal promised. So he fired Segal and hired me, all before the NFL instituted its now-famous rookie salary cap in the 2011 Collective Bargaining Agreement, and I began negotiating with Casserly. The system was similar to the Chicago Bears, where the negotiator had to keep checking with the man behind the curtain. At one point I walked out, believing I couldn't get it done. But I had a hunch to sit tight nearby — literally. I checked out of the Hyatt Hotel in suburban Virginia, but then quietly got a small room in another hotel across the street from Redskins headquarters.

I waited for three days for Charley to call me at my Chicago north suburban office, figuring my absence would make Casserly's and Cooke's hearts grow fonder. Casserly finally punched in my number, leaving the message that they would do the deal — and how soon could I get there? Sooner than they thought — the "flight went smoothly." I loved the subterfuge about my whereabouts. I got Westbrook $18.5 million, which was three times more than the same pick, defensive end Willie McGinnis, got from the New England Patriots in 1994.

The Dallas Cowboys presented a different kind of challenge though in ownership personalities. You'd have thought the urban kid in me and a small-town Arkansas guy like Cowboys owner Jerry Jones wouldn't necessarily mesh. But we did, and with son Stephen Jones, too, who was in day-to-day charge of personnel. Stephen turned out be the best NFL executive with whom I ever negotiated.

I knew Jerry, a strong maverick owner, was my kind of guy. He knew to do the right thing. Some thought he was grandstanding. He started out taking a lot of heat for replacing Tom Landry as coach. But Jerry Jones was tough. Whenever he told you something you could take it to the bank. He built one of the best stadiums in the NFL. The Jones Boys were my favorites. They were always willing to pay above-market rate because winning was primary. They exceeded the salary cap for four years before the salary negotiations and their roster composition caught up to them.

Our relationship helped greatly though when Jerry Jones zeroed in on a man to play for him who I had also wanted to represent.

Cornerback Kevin Smith, linebacker Quentin Coryatt's roommate at Texas A&M, both needed representation. I flew to Houston to sign Smith and Coryatt. After initially meeting them, I arranged to sign both at Coryatt's parents' home. But Smith was not there. Coryatt signed with me, and I asked him about Smith's whereabouts.

Coryatt said his roommate had gone back to school. I gave up and returned to the airport. I returned my rent-a-car. Two minutes before I was due to board my flight, I called Shelly. As with McGee, she is an advocate of, "It ain't over 'til it's over." She urged me to drive to College Station. I got another rent-a-car and did just that. In the meantime, Coryatt had returned to school. I called Smith at his college apartment. Coryatt picked up the phone to say Smith had left. For a moment, I felt I was chasing a ghost. But then Coryatt picked me up from the depths to inform me Smith had left an envelope—our signed contract. So the wildest of wild goose chases ended well.

And Smith had it even better in the 1992 draft. Jones coveted him as the 13th pick. But a trade offer enticed Jones with extra picks to move down in the draft to number 17, which he did, but still remained locked into our commitment to sign Smith with the Cowboys, and to give us number 13 money. Jones went on TV to deny he had given his commitment to take Smith at 17. I agreed for public consumption that we did not have a previous deal.

But I felt I could always make a better market for my clients and eventually Smith became one of the highest-paid players in the league. Jerry Jones got us a huge signing bonus with each new deal as Smith played on his rookie contracts. Smith did not forget either—he got me Super Bowl tickets every year.

I brought even more show-biz to Jones' football empire in 2000 when I pursued defensive back Dwayne Goodrich of the University of Tennessee, the Cowboys' top pick. The Chicago-area native wanted me as his agent, but his entourage also liked hip-hopster Jay Z and his Roc-a-Fella Records organization. I decided to team up with them and give Roc-a-Fella half the fee. The same arrangement worked with several future draftees in splitting the fee. I saw the attention Roc-A-Fella drew. They could get a meeting with anybody. I was the business guy. Everybody got along.

Come draft time in 1992, Coryatt was thankful he was where he was supposed to be during our collegiate courtship. The Indianapolis Colts had the first and second picks. Owner Bob Irsay, whose Skokie, Illinois, business office with the outside sign "Colts" on the second floor, was a few miles south of my home. I had an 11-hour negotiation on the phone with Irsay and top financial man Mike Chernoff, in which the owner got more agitated as the hours mounted, but was positively boisterous at the end. Having always enjoyed a good relationship with Irsay, we stayed on point. He sent his private jet for me and Coryatt to make the 31-minute flight to Indianapolis. That meant Irsay was serious. We agreed they would commit to take Coryatt number one.

But defensive tackle Steve Emtman was seen as a consensus number one throughout the NFL and The Colts went with the madding crowd. Chernoff called back to ask what would it take for Coryatt to go number two so they could pick Emtman. My reply: $1 million more will do it. We agreed, and Emtman and Coryatt had almost identical contracts. "It's like giving me $1 million to step in front of the line," Coryatt cracked.

Emtman had an injury-shortened six-year career, a 90-yard

interception return for a TD—of all things for a lineman—his signature feat. He was the Tony Mandarich of the Colts though a total bust from the top of the draft. Nobody was a wasted pick at the level of Mandarich, but Emtman came close in my opinion. Appreciative of the extra million bucks, Coryatt always thought I did the right thing. The Colts never used Coryatt quite right. He got an offer as a restricted free agent four years later for a lot of money from the Jacksonville Jaguars, but Indy matched it. He finished with a final season as a Dallas Cowboy.

Irsay always took a bushel full of knocks for moving the Colts from Baltimore to Indianapolis, sneaking out under cover of darkness. Years before, people thought he was crazy for trading franchises—the Rams for the Colts—with Carroll Rosenbloom. But the Los Angeles market left a lot to be desired as its decades without an NFL team proved at the time. Irsay left some extremely devoted fans behind in Baltimore, but gained new ones in Indiana's capital city while the Ravens (*nee*, Browns) became a good replacement team years later. He was a self-made man in the heating and air-conditioning business. I liked him. When not talking football, we chatted about buying Walgreens stock, of which Irsay was very bullish. He made a fortune on Walgreens; me, less so.

The Irsay family certainly was able to attract and pay Super Bowl-caliber talent to Indy, a cold-weather city. Jimmy Irsay had taken over for his father, having the franchise simply handed to him. Initially, Jimmy Irsay was more interested in weightlifting. He became a players' owner. He paid way over market rate to get quarterback Peyton Manning. Give him credit though, Jimmy Irsay did know football.

But two franchises with different kinds of underlying cash resources and market size shared a common goal—winning—in the years I dealt with them.

The San Francisco 49ers front office, under owner Eddie DeBartolo, Jr., was of one mind. DeBartolo, Jr. would say he was making the money available. He was surrounded by knowledgeable people in a trio of good football men in Carmen Policy, John McVay and Head Coach Bill Walsh. The system paid off with five Super Bowl championships. I had an especially good rapport with McVay. "How are things, John?" I'd ask. "Dodging and weaving," was his response. DeBartolo and Policy both grew up in blue-collar Youngstown, Ohio, but you'd never know DeBartolo was a billionaire. He was a regular street guy. I was honored to be invited to the 50th anniversary celebration of the 49ers franchise. In more recent years, the team's fortunes declined with DeBartolo nephew, Jed York, taking control.

But while one man sat on a mountain of personal cash in running a championship team, another franchise literally was community-owned, consistently winning in the NFL's smallest market. The Green Bay Packers spread their stock among scores of avid fans. The Pack is the NFL's only community-owned team, as they sold near unlimited amounts of "stock," all for the same price, to raise funds, "stocks" that got owners no special privileges, like ticket assurances. The franchise had to be adept in its front office without tapping into personal fortunes. General Manager Ron Wolf was a terrific football man. Top financial officer Mike Reinfeldt did many of the contracts, and I got to know him well. They paid market rate for the right people in spite of the tiny market and lack of backup financial support. I even got Jim McMahon and Steve McMichael paid well at the end of their careers in Green Bay. Other clients who landed with the Pack were LeRoy Butler, Edgar Bennett, Ni'al Diggs and Anthony Morgan.

I got up close and personal via a lot of dealings with the legendary Al Davis, patriarch of the Oakland-Los Angeles-Oakland-Las Vegas Raiders. Davis talked to me, but he was a tough guy who was self-made. I hounded Davis when McMahon wanted to be a Raider, to keep in that rebel spirit. I tried, but failed to engineer a trade with Davis while McMahon was still Bears property. Whenever I saw Davis at owners meetings, I told him McMahon had wanted to play for him, but he responded that he couldn't do it.

A longtime Raiders rival dating back to AFL days was Lamar Hunt's Kansas City Chiefs. Carl Peterson ran the team on behalf of Hunt. He was one of the best football guys in the league, a good-looking, sharp guy.

However, I just missed dealing with Jim Finks when he was Bears general manager. But I had plenty of discourse with Finks when he was named to run the New Orleans Saints two years after he left Chicago. I could see why Finks was admired in Chicago. Our personalities meshed right away. He was never contentious, a very straightforward guy. Finks was a football man, a regular guy. I could always tell him about his Steelers tailback days in the early 1950s. I keep wondering how the Bears could let both Finks and assistant coach George Allen get away.

Finks no doubt had many dealings with Detroit Lions owner, William Clay Ford, and General Manager, Russ Thomas. I had my inaugural dealings with the duo when I maneuvered Reggie Rogers—whom assistant Kathe Clements and I had taken away from the shady (more on him later) Norby Walters—to the number seven pick in the 1987 draft. I stashed Rogers in Chicago until the last minute. Rogers had a tough off-the-field reputation and I had to convince Thomas and Ford about him. Thomas was tough. I got along with Ford. He was relatively quiet. He would sit in the corner and say I'm not going to pay him the money. I kept my tongue, remembering I certainly did not agree with grandfather Henry Ford's anti-Semitic politics. It became a matter of softening up Thomas. I got Rogers a fair contract.

Battling the Lions in the Central Division annually were the Minnesota Vikings. I was fortunate to have a good rapport with longtime General Manager, Jeff Diamond. In his post-Bears days, McMahon saw service throughout the old NFC Central. I went to Palm Springs to convince Diamond that McMahon was a winner and could improve his team. The contract they granted McMahon could have gotten him $3 million after he topped out with the Bears at $800,000. It was a meeting of the minds.

Still though, one of the best old-school front office personnel packages was that of the New York Giants — Ernie Accorsi, George Young and Super Bowl-winning Head Coach Bill Parcells. Players loved Parcells. After his Bears days, I helped Dave Duerson land with the Giants. I'd call Accorsi every now and then on who to go after for the draft.

Old-school also worked with the old Cleveland Browns and Art Modell. A longtime friend gave me an introduction to Modell. He was accessible and a terrific guy, although old Browns fans will disagree due to the franchise move to Baltimore. I had talked to the Browns and they rejected on Friday my proposals to sign running back Leroy Hoard. On Saturday, I went to a party given by a friend. Modell was in attendance. I chatted him up with my friend. On Monday morning, I got a call from the Browns okaying the deal.

Meanwhile, I was fortunate to have made trips to France in my travels over the decades. I was able to talk about that country with Philadelphia Eagles owner Norman Braman, who had a house in the south of France. That kind of commonality worked out well, along with relationships with General Manager, Harry Gamble, and Coach Jeff Fisher, a former Bear, in landing a good deal for cornerback Eric Allen.

Last but never least in the NFL is Bob Kraft, owner of the New England Patriots. With their quintet of titles, Kraft and DeBartolo have got to go down as the most successful owners in history in my opinion with their quintet of titles. Kraft was terrific, putting winning first. He is sharp. Having threatened to pull the Patriots out to Connecticut, he got the stadium back in the Boston suburb of Foxboro. Kraft also made perhaps the greatest coaching hire in history in Bill Belichick. He did not hire Belichick for one-liners in press conferences. Belichick's very dry, but a great football man.

In the summer game that was my original passion with rooting interest in the St. Louis Cardinals, I'd have to rate John

Hart in his Cleveland Indians days as the best baseball executive with whom I've dealt. He ranks with Theo Epstein and Hall-of-Famer John Schuerholz for overall prowess. Hart was ably assisted by Dan O'Dowd, who became a general manager in his own right with the Colorado Rockies. I did some good deals for Kenny Lofton, perhaps the fastest man in baseball, with Hart. He was well ahead of the rest of baseball for locking up his young stars for long-term contracts before they could become arbitration- and free-agent-eligible. He would pay over-market rate, but he knew talent. Like the earlier Pittsburgh Pirates' Lumber Company, loaded with sluggers, Hart developed so many good hitters he couldn't keep them all. He got the previously moribund Indians to a pair of World Series, but never got the credit because Cleveland never won it all.

In dealing with Schuerholz, you could see why Cooperstown welcomed him. His Atlanta Braves had 14 consecutive National League East division titles. Schuerholz was level-headed and down to earth. There was little haggling. If he told you something, it was true.

Much closer to my home though was White Sox chairman Jerry Reinsdorf. The man reputed to be baseball's best handler of money—being both a CPA and an attorney—Reinsdorf is known as an expert negotiator. Fortunately, there was no carry-over in enmity after I represented 1982 Sox player Ron LeFlore on a drug possession charge, two years before I became an agent. I represented outfielder Daryl Boston as his agent, now a Sox coach. I got Boston paid well over market. Reinsdorf sent aide Jack Gould to negotiate. You knew Gould had internal toughness. He was an Army Air Corps bombardier in World War II. Reinsdorf has a great philosophy of at least breaking even, and not losing money. He puts revenue back into the team.

Reinsdorf certainly got to know fellow cigar-smoker and basketball Hall-of-Famer Red Auerbach when the former bought the Chicago Bulls in 1985. Longtime Boston Celtics boss Auerbach was backing away from day-to-day activity when I worked

Dee Brown with Steve

on 1990 number one pick Dee Brown's contract. Brown was one of the first-rounders in all three sports I represented in '90. Most of my dealings for Dee were with General Manager Jan Volk. But I got to hobnob somewhat with Auerbach to finish up the Brown contract. I had two Cuban cigars and I peeled off one to him. We had a grand time talking about his friend Sid Luckman and Auerbach's playing days at Oshkosh, Wisconsin, in the semi-barnstorming days of early pro basketball prior to the NBA's formation. With all the Celtics' titles, Auerbach knew talent — an understatement, surely.

Auerbach certainly rates as one of sports' all-time coaches and executives. And although fans love rankings, I'm not going to rate owners one through four, but I will rank in my era DeBartolo and Jones as the best owners in football. Art and Dan Rooney were one step below. Also up there is Lamar Hunt.

The best baseball owners were George Steinbrenner, who restored the Yankees to their dynastic glory; Mike Ilitch, who left no penny unspent in trying to build a Tigers winner; Ted Turner, underrated in his management shift from free agency to player development with the Braves; and Jerry Colangelo, who earned plaudits because he got a franchise for Arizona in the mid-1990s despite not having any money.

Bud Selig loved baseball and brought the game back to Milwaukee in 1970 following a five-year absence after the Braves fled to Atlanta. He rates a mention for getting the admired Miller Park built under tough political circumstances. I knew Selig needed an improved ballpark in my visits to homey-but-creaky County Stadium. In the 1982 World Series at that ballpark, I caught a foul ball off the bat of the Brewers' Don Money. A few years later, my son Herbie Zucker met Money in Arizona and got the ball signed. Managing a Brewers affiliate, Money told his players the ball was a home run.

As commissioner, Selig's only bad move was giving World Series home-field advantage to the All-Star Game winner, although the Cubs surely thanked him in 2016. With the Indians getting the home-field nod, the Cubs were able to use knee surgery-rehabbing Kyle Schwarber—who could not play the field—as the Designated Hitter in the Progressive Field games. And the rest is history.

There certainly are side benefits to negotiating. I went to Dodgertown in Florida to deal with Los Angeles owner Peter O'Malley on pitcher Rick Gorecki's contract. While in Vero Beach, I had lunch with Sandy Koufax, the Hall-of-Fame southpaw and probably the most respected former superstar in all of sports. I must have given several thoughts to how many zeroes a Koufax agent would have to count after the first contractual number if he played in the free-agent era. In a later visit to Vero Beach, Herbie Zucker snared Koufax's autograph, one of my treasured sports possessions.

In real life, the salary and bonus numbers were still impressive. So was the daily stimulation of dealing with men who would eventually agree to them in contracts.

Basketball Hall-of-Famer Red Auerbach and Steve celebrating with a cigar after doing the Dee Brown contract, 1990

CHAPTER 12

O.J. AND HALLE—A STARTLING SUCCESS AND BIG ONES WHO GOT AWAY

As the hackneyed phrase goes, "You win some, you lose some."

Indeed. Good fortune plays a big role in sports and entertainment. Yet, conscious decisions by athletes, executives and, yes, agents, are a deciding factor in whether a game or representation is successful.

That's why I have to accept the several images that flash in my mind that are down in my personal record books.

There were the show-stopping sights of the slow-speed Ford Bronco chase and O.J. Simpson in an orange jail jumpsuit. Next was a resulting image that went off in my head based on a simple pre-*Trial of the Century* transaction that succeeded beyond anyone's wildest dreams.

In contrast, there was a stunning image of a tearful Halle Berry accepting the 2002 best actress Oscar for *Monsters' Ball*, reminding me that I had fumbled away a chance to represent Miss Berry when she came to me more than a decade earlier.

And I could only shake my head when I witnessed Joe Girardi managing the Yankees in their last World Series championship in 2009, knowing I was the former All-America Baseball Academic Team player's first choice as an impact agent.

These memories are a big reason I am hesitant to roast top sports executives on their long-term records, unless they are willfully incompetent or refuse to admit they know what they don't know. Everyone managing a business for the public's entertainment will have his hits and misses. If the perfect executive exists, I am not aware of him or her, nor have I negotiated with or for him or her.

In hindsight, if I had made the correct decision on everyone with whom I had contact, I might have been labeled the best agent ever. But no one can be that perceptive or that exact in his judgment.

Still, my path was eye-opening when it took me through Simpson, Berry, Girardi and a dash of Muhammad Ali, Reggie White and Emmitt Smith. And to do what I did, I needed help from unlikely sources. Michael Jordan, for instance, often put in a good word for me with athletes he felt I would represent well, based on my history.

In Simpson's case, he signed a contract with Zucker Sports Management in 1994 to autograph 2,003 football cards to match his 1973 NFL rushing record. We learned that was the only pending signing deal he had. Then all hell broke loose a week later, on June 13, 1994, when ex-wife Nicole Brown Simpson and Ron Goldman were found murdered at her Brentwood, California, house. Four days later, O.J. had his truth-is-stranger-than fiction ride in the white Bronco, driven by buddy and former teammate Al Cowlings.

We had an existing deal with Simpson. And yes, a man is innocent until proven guilty — I knew that all too well as both a prosecutor and a criminal defense attorney. The card-signing contract was completed before Simpson was charged with murder. So how would I make money on it? I figured a way — I called the Los Angeles County administrator because I knew signing the cards in jail would be allowed. I got the approval and Simpson signed the cards. We thought we'd make some money, but under the high-profile circumstances, we actually made a fortune. The cards spiked in value while Simpson was in custody and during his trial. I still have the No. 1 card that he signed.

Do I have any feelings of guilt about the card deal? When I did the deal, Simpson was not notorious. Yes, he may have been guilty based on the actual evidence, but I believe the prosecutors made a mistake trying the case in downtown Los Angeles rather than out in a branch court in Santa Monica. As an experienced criminal defense attorney, I had a lot of respect for Johnnie Cochran and his strategy in the case. In such a trial, you must hire a great attorney like Cochran. The amount of justice you get is often tied to the amount of money you pay for your defense. Maybe Simpson would have been found "guilty" without Cochran.

And I had personal experience with Cochran. Representing a safety at Northwestern University who collapsed in summer practice, Cochran hired me as an expert witness to establish the player's value. I worked with him on another case of a Carolina Panthers player who was assaulted by a teammate at practice. I established the value of the player's lost income. Soon afterward, in 2005, Cochran died. Had he lived, who knows? I might have worked more cases with him.

Meanwhile, I still wonder about the lost value of not repre-senting Berry in her superstar career on the silver screen and TV. When word of letting her walk out of my office without a signed representation contract leaks to friends and colleagues today, I justifiably get severe razzing. I am the easy target of the peanut gallery.

A Cleveland native, Berry had moved to Chicago in the late 1980s to start a modeling career. She also studied at Second City, famed for launching so many comedians, actors and comedy writers to stardom.

In those years, my name was in the newspapers frequently thanks to my representation of Jim McMahon, a platoon of Bears players and Hall-of-Famer Deion Sanders. Berry was dating a dentist in the northern suburbs. One day, the couple walked in cold to my office in Northbrook. I had never heard of her but Berry told me she wanted to become an actress, and have me represent her. I explained what I did—I was a hired gun who got people paid. But Hollywood agents operate in a radically different system. They put whole movie deals together, from licensed merchandise to distribution down the line in video, online, on-demand and eventually over-the-air release rights.

By then though, I was friends with actor Bruce Willis and had met his agent, Arnie Rifkin. If I had acted more smartly then, I would have called Rifkin. Or I could have tried Sherry Lansing, CEO of Paramount Pictures, who knew my wife Shelly from their youth summer camp days. Lansing was nice enough to meet me back in 1981 when I tried to market "Spider Dan" Goodwin, the famed climber of the John Hancock Building and other skyscrapers.

But Berry did give me her picture. She was the most beautiful women I had ever seen. When Shelly saw the photo, she said, "Oh, my goodness," so I was kind of punching myself in the head as I watched Berry become the first woman of color to win the best-actress Oscar.

Another future star who was in and out of my grasp was Girardi. I was impressed the way he conducted himself as a young Chicago Cubs catcher starting in 1989. I told Nancy Mitchell, Zucker Sports Management's marketing director, that I'd really like to land Girardi. So Mitchell brought Girardi into my office. But the phone rang—the call part of an important, ongoing negotiation. Girardi sat there while I kept talking, but I did not get off the phone. Eventually he walked into the office of an associate who would go out on his own as an agent, taking Girardi with him.

Nancy always said Joe wanted to be with me, but taking that call—negotiating—was the most important thing in my life. In hindsight, I should have called Girardi back. After a respected career as a catcher, broadcaster and coach, Girardi was National League manager of the year with a sub-.500 Miami Marlins team in 2006. The Cubs considered Girardi the following year, but hired Lou Piniella instead. In 2008, Girardi began a 10-year run as Yankees skipper, winning it all in his second season in the Bronx. He would have been perfect with me, but I did not pull the trigger.

In the same breath, I'm happy Dr. Frank Jobe never

"fumbled" his scalpel as I did with his prospective representation. Jobe, of course, saved countless pitchers' careers with his creation of the groundbreaking Tommy John, tendon-transplant surgery, first performed in 1974. I brought McMahon to Jobe for shoulder reconstruction surgery late in 1986 after McMahon was slammed to the ground by the Green Bay Packers' Charles Martin. I believe McMahon never had the same zip on his passes post-surgery, but he still played another decade.

So in 1990, when I had open-heart surgery at Northwestern Memorial Hospital, Jobe was in town and came to see me. The nurses and doctors on the floor were wowed by Jobe's presence. He told me he wanted me to represent him, that he should have an agent to market his medical expertise and high profile. Unfortunately, I turned down Jobe, saying I did not have the time to properly work with him. Looking back on that, as the popular expression goes, "my bad."

Fortunately, along with legal associate Eldon Ham, I was able to corner Muhammad Ali and a smidgeon of his international fame in 1990.

We got a call from an attorney near St. Joseph, Michigan. He said he was doing some work for Ali, who lived nearby in the summer in the same home in which Al Capone once resided. The attorney wanted to know if we could do anything with Ali. The concept sounded incredible.

So Ham and I met Ali and his attorney at Gene and Georgetti's restaurant in Chicago for a two-hour lunch. The champ, still appearing in shape at 225 pounds, walked in wearing a full-length brownish-red leather trench coat. His speech was slow by then, but his trademark wit was still quick.

When my heart surgery came up, Ali wanted to know — with a twinkle in his eye — if I was still able to have sex post-surgery. He teased Ham for being a little young at 38. We had a great time and it was an iconic couple of hours. We were able to get some endorsement work for Ali, including a deal for NFL licensed clothing. We also did a partnership agreement and some legal work with Jabir Herbert Muhammad, one of the founders of Top Rank Boxing, with whom Ali was close. As a fringe benefit, the champ gave me a pair of personalized autographed boxing gloves.

Our relationship did not last all that long. Ali's overall popularity had declined after Larry Holmes soundly beat him and basically ended his boxing career a decade earlier. We may have worked with him a few years too early, but Ali's second coming came when, shaking from Parkinson's, he had the honor to light the Olympic torch at the 1996 Summer Games in Atlanta.

By 1990, Michael Jordan had a higher international profile than Ali, almost other-worldly as high-flying dunk master, "His Airness." But he had already registered a key assist for me.

In 1986, I had no idea football wide receiver Terance Mathis was a "Jordannaire" when I squired him after he led the country in receptions at the University New Mexico. I flew Mathis in from Albuquerque and took him to a Bulls game at my Chicago Stadium midcourt seats, nine rows up. As he sat with me, he saw Jordan and proclaimed, "Michael, Michael, I'm here." I turned to him and confirmed he liked Mike. So at the end of the game, I took him to the locker room. I asked Jordan if he would do me a favor and say hello to Mathis, a collegiate record-breaker. He stepped out of the then-tiny home locker room and happily shook Mathis' hand.

The next day, Mathis was at my office, where I pitched him on the beneficial representation I could provide for him. "Stop, stop, you know Michael Jordan. I'm signing with you," he shot back. With a similar good word from Jordan in a brief meeting, the megastar later would help me retain wide receiver Carl Pickens of the Cincinnati Bengals.

Jordan could have been an edge to land Hall-of-Fame defensive end Reggie White, the NFL's "Minister of Defense" and one of the most respected players of our time. First though, White was literally too close to home for me.

White's agent could not continue representing the budding

Steve with Michael Jordan

superstar for conflict-of-interest reasons, so he literally handed off White me. As I recruited White, he stayed at my house. He was coming out of the bathroom at 2:00 a.m., the same time my son Herbie was going into the same bathroom, with no idea White was sleeping over. He saw this 300-pound giant coming out of the bathroom — quite a shock to the system. He jumped back, but White said, "Don't worry, I'm a client of your dad's."

I thought I had gotten White. But a pair of agents offered to charge Reggie just one-half of a percent commission, which I could not do. It would not be fair to my other clients, who I charged the then-standard three percent.

You cannot be upset with anything the dignified, model-citizen White did, except perhaps his remarks to the Wisconsin state legislature condemning homosexuality and mischaracterizing Hispanics. He otherwise trail-blazed Green Bay as an attractive destination for African-American players in a manner the smallest NFL market could never have accomplished prior to White's 1993 arrival.

I also was nosed out for another Hall of Famer—all-time leading rusher (18,355 yards) Emmitt Smith. I tried to land Smith for the 1990 draft, in which he ended up being picked 17th by the Cowboys. I flew into Gainesville, Florida to compete among four agents meeting with Smith. Three already knew Smith; I was the only newcomer.

Some 30 people were in a meeting room with a huge desk. I felt my presentation was really good and I felt Smith was spellbound. Mary Smith, his mother, grabbed me and asked if we could we meet later. We really hit it off.

Later, only two agents were invited to the family home in Pensacola. I began negotiating a contract with his sister, Peaches. My assistant, Gene Burrough, said though he didn't think we had Smith.

"You see the Rolex on his wrist?" Burrough pointed out. He already was committed to another agent for two years. Emmitt Smith, Jr., his father, said I had the best presentation, but was just tardy enough in locking down their loyalty. The elder Smith and his family said they wished we had met earlier.

A third Hall-of-Famer also was a near-miss. Jerome Bettis was down to a pair of agent candidates in 1993. Like White, Bettis visited my home and I in turn visited him at his dorm room at Notre Dame. I also had lunch with his family in Detroit, but was nosed out by a Colorado-based agent. I had communicated with Bettis for five months, we had developed a very close relationship and we are friends to this day. Although he never became a client, I have always rooted for him.

But sometimes patience — meaning years into one's career — was a virtue in snaring a Hall-of-Fame client; my second after Deion Sanders. I thought I had defensive tackle Cortez Kennedy out of Miami in 1990. At my office, his step-father said the tank was filled and all we had to do is step on the gas. He said the family liked me, but I just needed to lower my fee to 2½ percent. The competition had been between me and Bob Fraley, late golfer Payne Stewart's agent.

Kennedy lived in a small town not far from Memphis. I flew to Memphis and waited for my office to finalize arrangements to drive to meet with Kennedy. But Farley sent Stewart's jet and picked up Kennedy to fly him to his Orlando office. Sadly, Fraley and Stewart were killed in 1999 in the crash of a private jet on which they were flying to a golf tourney. Meanwhile, I eventually did get Kennedy later in his stellar Seattle Seahawks career.

Meanwhile though, representing TV and radio personalities did not make up for missing out on Berry's Hollywood ascent. But they did pay some bills as the 1990s proceeded. A typical agent's cut for a broadcast contract was 10 percent. Plus free lunches and dinners were fringes as station general managers usually had hefty expense accounts.

One such delicious negotiation benefited the late Tim Wei-gel, middleman in a three-generation broadcast family in Chicago. A longtime newscaster and sportscaster at WLS-TV [now ABC Chicago], Weigel began falling out of favor with WLS boss man Joe Ahern due to what were considered by the boss to be wild man, prospectively unethical on-air antics. Doing one more contract for Weigel with Ahern, I put in a clause that if he was fired, WLS would pay the difference between what he would have continued to get at that station and any new outlet at which he landed.

When Weigel was given the hook at WLS, I went to General Manager Bill Applegate at rival CBS-owned WBBM-TV [now

CBS Chicago]. He said he'd love Weigel, but could not afford his going-rate as a station with smaller viewership. So I offered Applegate his services at just $100,000, and would get WLS to pay the rest. Applegate agreed. I called Ahern with the news. He was stunned, although it's hard to believe after that deal that we're still friends.

It's people themselves who generate money. So do good ideas — under the proper circumstances. But let an idea go and you can give yourself a lot of aggravation.

In the early 1990s, Zucker Sports Management came up with a concept with American Greeting Card Co. to have NFL-type greeting cards with messages like "Having a Bear of a birthday." The logos of all the teams and similar messages would be used in the cards. Other sports would also be included in this pace-setting concept.

We hired artists to sketch renderings. American Greeting Cards said they had an interest, but eventually said they'd pass on the idea. We got a provisional license from the NFL noting we owned the property if we got a distributor. Talks with other companies did not land a deal. But then we found a greeting-card machine with NFL-licensed products supplied by American Greetings Cards in a big-box store. The cards had a similarity to the mockups we commissioned.

We filed suit in U.S. District Court in Chicago, then agreed to go to arbitration, also in Chicago, to move the proceedings along more quickly. Our argument was that we developed this trade innovation. American Greeting Cards countered there was nothing unique in the idea. We won the arbitration and were awarded a large, six-figure settlement. That should send another message to people in negotiations — do not steal other people's ideas.

In the end, the life of an agent centers on people, laws and fairness. You'll win, you'll lose, but you've got to keep moving forward or else you'll quickly go into reverse.

CHAPTER 13
RICHMOND WEBB
FOR THE HALL OF FAME

There's no other simple way to declare it: I strongly believe and can make a good case that Miami Dolphin left tackle Richmond Webb should be in the Pro Football Hall of Fame.

Offensive linemen like Webb get the least amount of publicity in the NFL. Casual fans probably can't name their favorite team's entire line. They only seem to stand out when their quarterback is sacked. Yet, that's their extreme value: they permit the most successful passers just enough time to survey the field and aim for their targets.

Dan Marino's own Hall-of-Fame career stemmed from his deadly quick release. But even Marino, a right-hander, would have been hampered if he had to worry about his blind, or left side. That's the hole the gentlemanly giant Webb plugged up in Marino's prime, keeping the likes of Hall-of-Famer Bruce Smith off the quarterback. I am proud to have represented Webb, and he should join Marino and Smith in Canton.

Webb and I have an important endorser for that advocacy.

"We have three pretty good ones in the Hall—Jim Langer, Dwight Stephenson, and Larry Little," said Canton enshrinee Don Shula, the head coach and one of the all-time developers of great linemen, first with the Baltimore Colts, then with his much longer run with the Dolphins. "If you take Richmond's body of work over the course of his career and acknowledge the things he accomplished, you certainly can think they are as good or better than the ones that are already in there and he deserves that recognition."

Shula did more than just back Webb for the Hall of Fame. He played an active, but uncredited role in helping me get this number one draft pick signed as Dolphins training camp began in 1990. When an agent has a legendary coach backing his efforts, you just can't lose. He gained a key cog to his offense, and the NFL added one of its most high-character personalities.

"He just gave me that feeling of confidence that Dan was going to be protected on his blind side and that he could devote all his time and decision-making scanning the entire field," Shula said. "Dan didn't have to worry what was going on behind him, and it allowed him to concentrate on looking at his receivers.

"The thing about Richmond was that he was just what you were looking for at left tackle — the size, the strength, the agility, the quickness and the footwork. He had it all, and you could see that even as a rookie."

The measuring stick was Webb's work against Bruce Smith. In 14 games between the archrival Dolphins and Smith's Buffalo Bills, Webb gave up just three sacks to Smith. The two Hall-of-Fame coaches involved in these duels doffed their hats to Webb.

"Anyone who can hold Bruce Smith to just three sacks over a 14-game span sure does sound like a good one to me," said Bills coach Marv Levy. "It helps me understand even a little bit better how great a quarterback he helped Dan Marino to be."

Said Shula, "The fact that he changed the way he blocked Bruce made a big difference. Sometimes he went aggressively and sometimes he would sit back. He never did the same thing where Bruce could think, 'This is what he's going to do and I can beat it.' When you combine that with Richmond's talent, it made it much harder for Bruce."

In addition to keeping Smith off Marino most of the time, Richmond was honored by his peers from the get-go by being selected to the Pro Bowl seven straight years, starting in his rookie season in 1990. Even Hall-of-Famer Anthony Munoz of the Cincinnati Bengals, generally rated the greatest left

Steve with Richmond Webb, Pro Bowl, Hawaii

tackle in history, did not make the Pro Bowl as a rookie. Webb also was named first-team All-Pro twice, in 1992 and 1994.

Most of Hall-of-Fame linemen were first-rounders. They kept their opponents out of the backfield no matter what great talent staffed the defensive lines. The left tackle must hang back a bit to protect the quarterback's blind side. He's almost always the largest guy on the line. He needs quick feet to hold his ground and match the defender's moves going forward.

My time with Webb started in his college days at Texas

A&M. He was such a great blocker—defensive linemen couldn't go through him and could not go around him. I felt he was the best left tackle in the country.

Typical of Webb's insights, he can specifically define the best qualities of a left tackle.

"You've got to be smart," he said. "You need to have good feet. You have to be able to adjust as outside rushers are smaller guys and you got to be able to counteract if they give you a different move. You have to be athletic with long arms. But you also have to be mentally tough because sometimes you are going to get beat.

"You've got to be a student of the game. Once you get to that level, mental preparation is huge. You study the guy you play against. Does he line up wide or in multiple positions? Make as many mental notes as you can. Otherwise it's a guessing game. You got to treat it like homework, watch an extra hour of film each day."

But the most important side of Dallas-native Webb was his off-the-field personality and upbringing. He was just a gentle giant. As great as he was, he didn't have a mean bone in his body. He was very intelligent, a very well-grounded person. You knew you didn't have to worry about Webb off the field.

His parents are Richmond, Sr. and Bobbie Webb, both preachers. Their pulpit was the House of Prayer in Dallas. I loved the way they talked. Richmond, Sr. spoke like a country preacher. He would tell me great stories and had a nice sense of humor. The family prayed for my son, Herbie, to deal successfully with his Type 1 Diabetes. I still write a check every year to the House of Prayer.

"The discipline I had in life, all of it, came from being raised in church from as young as I can remember," said Richmond, Jr. He now lives in Houston with wife Chandra and family while owning the Environmental Machines and Services Company, handling pollution-control equipment.

"It's faith in God, treating people the way you wanted to be treated," Webb said. "Don't burn bridges. The same people you'll meet on the way up, you'll meet on the way back down. Put value in relationships and honor your word. Your name will carry you longer than any money."

Contract talks with Dolphins personnel director Charley Winner carried over to the first day of training camp at St. Thomas University in Miami Gardens, Florida. Early on the day of the opening practice, we were still far apart. We had to get a lot done in a short time. Shula called me and said he would do his part to get the deal done. I never had a coach call and state he'd be in my corner. Winner did not know of Shula's contact with me. That gave me a big edge, knowing Shula wanted him on the field.

Webb did not know of the backchannel Shula contact. Learning of his coach's support decades later, he was grateful.

"I had tremendous respect for Coach Shula," he said. "(Guard) Keith Sims was the number two pick. We both started on the left side. Two veterans were still out of camp, trying to renegotiate their contracts, so they wanted to get the two young guys prepped. That's why it was such a push. Miami was known for being hard negotiators. But it was almost unheard of for the coach to support (the agent).

"As a player, you always see a great coach like Shula on the sidelines. You see him on *Monday Night Football*. You pinch yourself that it's real. A coach is going to push you harder than you push yourself in training camp.

"You got a Hall-of-Fame quarter back, the coaches want to get these guys in. More important, if you miss the majority of training camp, every day you're installing the offense and you're missing out. All you have to do is learn the plays. That can be frustrating for a player. Steve understood the need to get me signed."

I certainly did, and knowing Shula was pulling on his end, I was not going to let Winner out of the room in which we were negotiating until we had the deal. I felt I was a good negotiator. Always make the other guy know he had a good deal, and always make him look good in his town.

Winner told reporters that day he was not going anywhere on the St. Thomas campus until a deal had been struck.

"Steve Zucker's persistence in getting the player signed helped," he said. "He came down here and wouldn't let me out of my room until this morning when we concluded."

With Webb's uniform waiting for him in the locker room, Winner and I finally agreed on a five-year, $3.77 million contract. His $1.35 million signing bonus plus $330,000 in base salary enabled Webb to earn more in his first year than Marino's $1.5 million.

Webb's average annual salary of $754,000 was 14.1 percent more than the Dolphins paid Sammie Smith, their number one draft pick of 1989, also picked at number nine. Smith's total deal was $2.59 million for 4 years.

Shula was not the only Miamian extending the big welcome mat for Webb. The ink on the contract was hardly dry before Webb practiced in the afternoon session. Some 300 fans cheered every time he was inserted into a scrimmage.

Webb went on to be Marino's left tackle for the remainder of the latter's career, through 1999. Marino would typically rank as the least-tackled quarterback in the NFL. Meanwhile, Webb would go on to start all but one of the 184 NFL games in which he played over 12 seasons. He finished up with 1½ seasons with the Cincinnati Bengals. I believe he was the best left tackle in the era.

"I do remember early on in camp, Marino walked up to me and Keith (Sims), and asked 'What's the most important thing we got to remember?'" Webb recalled. "We say the play, the snap count. But Dan said it's most important to protect him. I always had a great relationship with Dan, and the Marks brothers, (wide receivers) (Mark) Duper and (Mark) Clayton. You don't have to re-invent the wheel.

"I knew who I was blocking for. I always had it in the back of my mind, my motivation was I don't want to be the guy who gets this guy hurt. That's what kept me going. He always told us, in the two-minute offense, we've got to go down and score.

He was a fierce competitor. If you have this guy in the game, you always have a chance to come back in the game.

"We knew Dan wasn't going to run, he was not a mobile quarterback. We knew he had that quick release. You can go back in coverage, but if you blitz him, he got rid of the ball so fast. We saw stunts and blitzes that were unorthodox. If you gamble (on defense), he'd make you pay."

Webb arrived with the Dolphins in the first season of the Bills' four consecutive Super Bowl trips. Buffalo had to get through Miami in the AFC East. And Bruce Smith, perhaps the all-time greatest defensive end, had to get through Webb to slow Marino. Smith was strong with a great "swim" move, where the defensive lineman employs an arm maneuver like a freestyle swimming stroke to get past the blocker. Webb worked with Sims to counter him.

"When I first got there, Dolphins-Bills was already a rivalry," Webb said. "Bruce Smith was a guy you knew you had to play non-stop. He's giving 1,000 percent on every play. You get ready for 60 minutes of hell. At that time it was him and Reggie White as the two best linemen. It was always a challenge to just slow him down. With Bruce, he would line up wide over left tackle, then jump down over center or guard and rush the passer.

"He'd rush from anywhere on the field. He'd use his spin move and speed rush, use his hands well. He was doing anything possible. He'd line up, as Dan does a cadence, and jump over center. The center was looking back at Marino, so we had to do a good job of communicating. We were all good communicators. Darryl Talley, the outside linebacker, would help Bruce by sliding down over Sims. We just communicated and reacted to what was happening. They had some good stunts (defensive linemen switching pass-rushing routes), too. You had to really bear down."

Webb and I both lost a good advocate when Shula retired from his 33 years as an NFL head coach at age 65 in 1995. After a two-year break from his Super Bowl run in Dallas,

Jimmy Johnson took over. He wanted to change the system. Every coach is different. Winner had retired. I now dealt with General Manager Eddie Jones, but Johnson called the personnel shots.

The Dolphins put the franchise tag on Webb two years in a row under Johnson. One year, they were about to take the tag off to stop me from trying for a multi-year deal. I got wind of the Dolphins' plans and accepted the franchise tag at a salary at the average of the top six linemen. Johnson said that was the first time he was beaten by an agent.

Johnson and Marino departed Miami at the same time as Webb. He was allowed to walk as a free agent. Although Webb still started at his accustomed position in Cincinnati in 2000, it wasn't the same organization and quarterback.

His body of work still speaks for itself. Richmond is Hall of Fame-worthy as the man blocking the door to his quarterback through brains and brawn. But his character is the standout thing about this role model. We last did a contract nearly 20 years ago, but relationships are forever.

"He did a good job for me, and more importantly, we remain friends," Webb said.

Whether you're an agent, coach or even a media member, there's hardly any more you can ask from a player.

CHAPTER 14
LOFTON NIXES FORTUNE WITH
TRUE BLUE BREW CREW

I like Kenny Lofton, my most prominent baseball client during my prime years as an agent.

When I think back to some unlikely negotiations with the then-interim commissioner of baseball who could have made the five-time American League stolen-base king a very wealthy man, I now realize what Kenny was thinking. He did not want to play in the National League. He wanted to go back to the American League and steal bases as before. All you need to do is to compare 1995 as an Atlanta Brave with his Cleveland years at it pertains to stolen bases.

Several things did not compute when I was summoned to talk in the cramped Milwaukee County Stadium office of Brewers-owner-turned-interim commissioner Bud Selig, during the off-season of 1997–98. Now it all makes sense.

Lofton, the pride of East Chicago, Indiana, some 45 miles south of my home, had departed the Cleveland Indians, for whom he had swiped all those bases, in a spring training trade in 1997. Cleveland General Manager John Hart was not sure he could retain Lofton after his outstanding '97 free-agent season. So in a trade with John Schuerholz and the Atlanta Braves, Hart landed two good outfielders for Lofton — slugger David Justice and center fielder Marquis Grissom, who also plays a role in this story.

Lofton did not choose to stay with the Braves despite their status as a perennial National League East titlist and World Series contender. He did not want to play in the National

League. So I called Hart, suggesting he could have both Lofton *and* Justice in his lineup. Hart initially offered about $5.5 million for three years with a $1.5 million buyout for Lofton. Schuerholz countered with a $5 million annual, multi-year offer. My goal? Make Lofton the highest-paid non-power hitter in history.

At the same time, I connected with Selig and the Milwaukee Brewers with the help of Chicago attorney Mel Pearl, a fraternity brother of Selig's in the 1950s at the University of Wisconsin. Unlike Lofton's Indians, who lost to the Braves in the 1995 World Series and were nosed out again, this time by the Marlins without him in the 1997 Fall Classic, the financially-strapped Brewers had not had a winning season since 1992. They would not have another one until 2007, after the arrivals of slugging first baseman Prince Fielder and power-hitting outfielder Ryan Braun.

So along with Lofton and my son Herbie, I met with Selig and Brewers General Manager Sal Bando. Selig still officially ran the Brewers as principal owner, doubling up on his interim commissioner's job. When named permanent commissioner later in 1998, he had to formally disassociate himself from the Brewers, installing daughter Wendy Selig-Prieb as team president.

Selig went after Lofton in the wake of finishing the politically arduous task of getting the Miller Park project for his Brewers approved by the state of Wisconsin. Almost obsessively, Selig would drive around the construction site daily, with the projected stadium scheduled to open in 2000.

The owner/commissioner said the Brewers would make a lot of money in Miller Park, so he astoundingly offered free-agent Lofton $41.5 million, guaranteed over five years. You'd never have expected that kind of offer from Selig, who had endured declining attendance and revenue in old County Stadium since 1992.

But Lofton said no.

Given the alternative contract offers, I told Lofton to look at what he was leaving on the table. But one year in the National League with the Braves was enough for him. He had his worst year running the bases to date after his dominance as an American League base thief. In Atlanta, Lofton had a career-low 27 steals while getting caught a hefty 20 times. Meanwhile, he communicated with fellow free agent Grissom, a friend, who also was entertaining a $5 million Brewers offer. Grissom, who I considered one of the game's class men at the time, said he would not undercut Lofton by taking the deal, which in essence was a backup for Selig in case Lofton said no. Lofton told Grissom to take the Brewers deal while he would go back to Cleveland.

Weeks passed. I did not say yes to Selig and eventually did a three-year, $24 million-guaranteed deal ($7.5 million per year plus a $1.5 million buyout going into a fourth team-option year at $8.5 million non-guaranteed in the option year). As I was agreeing to terms with Hart in Cleveland, oddly enough the Brewers were holding on my other line. I told Milwaukee that Kenny was signing with the Indians and that was it.

The main reason that Kenny turned down the larger contract was two-fold. Kenny wanted it that way, and I never forgot that the client is the boss not the agent.

Lofton played another four seasons in Cleveland, making good coin. But he still left $16 million on the table, probably the most of any of my clients in the negotiation process. As an agent, I was sick about it. Baseball salaries, though, had risen so high compared to football that players got paid well with guaranteed deals no matter where they landed. Lofton's football counterparts could never walk away from such a rich deal, if it would have been offered in the first place.

Cleveland, like Milwaukee, was hardly the garden spot of the big leagues. But Hart had built up such a powerful offensive machine that he couldn't keep all his home-grown hitters. Players like Richie Sexson, Sean Casey and Brian Giles would all have to go elsewhere eventually to firmly establish themselves, in Milwaukee, Cincinnati and Pittsburgh, respectively. Manny

Ramirez even spent the first part of his career in Cleveland before he went to a lofty albeit controversial level in Boston, with his signature dreadlocks and sometimes odd behavior.

But Lofton wanted to be on a familiar winner, even at the cost to his pocketbook. After three years, Cleveland picked up the team option for $8.5 mil in 2001 for the popular veteran, canceling out the $1.5 million buyout. That took some of the sting out of the difference between the 1998 Milwaukee and Cleveland contracts. When the Indians let him go for the last time late in 2001, he became a pennant-contention insurance policy, but at a much lower salary, a veteran to plug a hole in the outfield for a contender at mid-season. That's how he came to his childhood-favorite Chicago Cubs in July 2003, his leadoff talents helping spark the Cubs to within five outs of a World Series appearance.

As a final twist in the story, Miller Park construction was delayed. The retractable-roof ballpark, praised by most fans, did not open until 2001, so Selig's timetable on Lofton's projected payments would have been off. Attendance did rise, but the real payoff did not come until 2007–08 when the team finally got to 3 million in attendance.

Repping a baseball star like Lofton was the exception in my practice. I was busy pursuing NFL first-round draft choices and did not have the time for chases of similarly qualified baseball prospects. MLB had big-name agents who specialized in deal-making in the free-agent era. Yet, I had dabbled enough in baseball to see what kind of leverage I had compared to the more-restrictive NFL.

To me, Lofton's base paths' stardom made him logical for a Nike shoe deal, so I went with Lofton to Nike headquarters in Beaverton, Oregon, to seal the deal. As a side benefit, we were allowed to shop in the Nike store. We each filled a shopping cart and only found out at the checkout line the goods were being comp'd. Had we known beforehand, we might have careened through the aisles, loading up the cart like on the old TV hit, *Supermarket Sweep*.

We also commissioned a poster put together by John Costacos, the famed artist who had put together all the vintage 1985 Chicago Bears posters, and we called it "90 Feet," or the distance between bases. The image depicted Lofton leading off first, ready to steal.

I had landed Lofton as a client as a side benefit of going to the University of Arizona to recruit Darrell Lewis, who had won the Thorpe Award as the best cornerback in the country. At the time, Lofton was best known as a skilled sixth man on Lute Olsen's great Wildcats basketball teams. As good a centerfielder and base-running threat as he was, Lofton only played baseball on a lark, something to do in the off-season. I wasn't originally going after him. But a coach from East Chicago asked me to say hello to him on my trip. Later, the coach paid for Lofton to come back home. He visited me in my office, and as a favor to his old coach, I signed him.

Lofton joined pitcher LaTroy Hawkins as longtime quality big-leaguers coming out of the inner city in Northwest Indiana. The city of Gary honored him by naming the street in front of his grandmother's house Kenny Lofton Lane. Although blind, his grandmother was key in raising Lofton. In my opinion, he should merit consideration for the Hall of Fame for his all-around talents. I believe many voters view him as a cut below Hall-of-Famers Rickey Henderson and Tim Raines as an impact leadoff man with game-changing speed. Plus, Lofton not being a media darling probably cost him some writers' votes.

Lofton's progression into pro ball and to the majors showed how sketchy the representation of a baseball prospect could be compared to other sports. Out of 15 young players you'd represent, maybe two would make it. In contrast, an NFL first-rounder is locked into a good contract. An NBA first-rounder almost always makes it.

For instance, I represented outfielder Jeff Jackson, a consensus sensational prospect out of Chicago's Simeon High School as the fourth pick in the 1990 MLB draft. Jackson did not make it out of Double-A ball in the Philadelphia Phillies system. Meanwhile, Lofton was a mere 17th-round pick of the Houston Astros in 1988. He was a late bloomer. The Astros traded him to Cleveland in late 1991, a team about to blossom under Hart.

As a rookie in 1992, Lofton hit .285. He was one of three players who hit .285 and added 20 points each of the next two years, rising to .349 in the strike-shortened 1994 season. Before his second year, Hart offered a five-year deal. I bit my lip. That was a risk, but Hart was confident both locking up his prime young players and motivating them would work. He was brilliant in the strategy of avoiding arbitration, a bigger elevator of salaries than free agency itself. In four of Lofton's first five full seasons, he stole at least 60 bases. But when you rely on your speed, your career generally goes on the downside earlier, another reason why I really wanted him to take that Brewers deal. Lofton wound up taking much lower-value contracts as more of a role player in the 2000s.

However, early on, I represented several of my hometown Cubs and White Sox. Chico Walker, a Cubs role player, was my first baseball client. He called me asking for representation. Then I signed Sox center fielder Daryl Boston, now a Sox coach. Sox reliever Donn Pall came into the fold. And in 1991, I landed my first manager—the Cubs' Jim Lefebvre. Tagged with the nickname "Frenchy," he and I got along well. He was intense, just like Mike Ditka. But Lefebvre only lasted two seasons on the North Side, caught up in the political swirl of the unfortunately typical Cub front office then directed by General Manager Larry Himes.

But as my overall prominence as an agent grew and I began representing baseball players to augment my football clientele, I ended up having interesting conversations with Scott Boras, probably MLB's best agent over the past 25 years. Boras would call me for advice on a football player who'd come into his fold. And if I got a baseball player, I'd in turn call him for advice.

If I was a good baseball player, though, I'd go to Boras. He's not impossible to work with at all, despite his reputation. The Cubs always signed his clients—sort of like the old relationship system that I practiced. Boras client and Hall-of-Fame pitcher Greg Maddux returned to the Cubs in 2004 after a different, previous Cubs management screwed up his contract negotiations 12 years prior, in my opinion, and watched him walk away as a free agent to perennially NL championship-contending Atlanta.

But I had another baseball deal in the works besides the Lofton-Brewers talks that never really got publicity. Amid the 1994–95 strike in which Selig canceled the World Series, lifelong friend Rick Fizdale, then CEO of the Leo Burnett ad agency, combined with me to come up with the idea of a kind of a barnstorming tour of strike-sidelined, big-league stars. We would play in stadiums that weren't already tied up with leases with big-league teams. Lofton recruited some of his contemporaries while Fizdale initially tapped Reebok, a Burnett client, for sponsorship. I contacted MLB Players Association chief Don Fehr, who was supportive.

The idea became moot though when then-Federal Appeals Court Judge Sonia Sotomayor, now a Supreme Court justice, issued an injunction in the spring of 1995, essentially ending the strike.

But even more recently, I was asked if I would represent all Cuban players moving into pro baseball. I would have come out of retirement to be the agent handling the arrangement in which the Cubans would have come to the United States through the front door and would not have had to sneak out on rickety boats, go through third-party countries and fall prey to disreputable agents and money-grubbers, what with diplomatic relations having been re-established. However, the deal went awry when President Barack Obama and Baseball Commissioner Rob Manfred visited Havana in 2016. They made other arrangements with the baseball powers-that-be in Cuba and we were cut out of a prospective free-agent tidal wave. You can't fight City Hall, and you certainly cannot fight the White House.

I'm still pretty sure an uninterrupted, smooth progression of Cuban players to pro organizations will take a few more years to fully develop. But the national administration in 2017–18 was not conducive to further improvements in Cuban-American relations. I believe the eventual adding of a more free flow of Cubans to the baseball talent pool will be one of the ways baseball can reclaim some semblance of its old national pastime role in coming years.

A re-direction of talent away from a concussion-afflicted NFL will be another way the flow of top-athletic prospects could increase in baseball. But the lords of the sport must put a clamp on bloated game times for today's attention-deficit, video-game-driven younger generation of fans.

In selling baseball, the owners cannot have the catcher trudging out to the mound on numerous occasions, further adding to game times. Pitchers and batters must be ready to go when they face each other. The lords must cut at least a half-an-hour off game times to make them more attractive, in my opinion.

But let's face it—athletes will go where the money is. If baseball owners are still making the megabucks, the players will cut themselves in for their usual share. They've got by far the strongest sports union in history, if not one of the strongest unions overall in the world now. We'll see if the TV rights bubble bursts in upcoming years. That would probably be the only dampening factor on salaries.

That, and the rare ballplayer who takes much less to return to his favored team.

CHAPTER 15
RICHARD DENT VS. THE NFL

Sometimes a monolithic organization like the NFL needs to go back to school to get things right in the way it does business and treats people.

I was pleased to be a facilitator of such an educational process during an eventful week soon after the start of the 1988 NFL season. In one of the most sensational Cook County, Illinois, court cases of that year, a jam-packed courtroom witnessed one of the most popular sports outfits in the country quickly call timeout in a trial to negotiate with me and subsequently grant immediate relief to a former Super Bowl Most Valuable Player—likely ensuring his Hall of Fame induction—and begin the process of changing a flawed drug policy that likely impacted scores of players each season.

And in the process, an old adversary from 20 years in the past came back to side with me on the issue. We combined to put forth the concept of "fundamental fairness," in which a private organization cannot simply run roughshod over its people without procedures that provide the equivalent of due process in the courts.

To set the scene, the basis of one of the best actions I ever took as an attorney and agent came in regard to an NFL drug policy first enacted in 1986, in an era in which cocaine emerged to join marijuana as the drugs the league's investigators and administrators endeavored regularly to eliminate from the game.

Drug tests typically were administered at the start of training camp. If a player tested positive for any trace of drugs, he was put on a "reasonable cause" list to be retested at a random

Richard Dent at McMahon's restaurant, 1988

future date. A positive retest would result in an automatic four-game suspension. A player's refusal to take the retest would count as a positive result. However, the players were not automatically granted a hearing on the retest nor were they formally notified in writing of the result.

And so, my most deep-rooted defense-attorney's talents were put to the test, so to speak, when Bears Super Bowl-winning quarterback Jim McMahon, my most prominent client in 1988, apparently recommended me to teammate and two-time Pro Bowl defensive end Richard Dent, who was MVP of the Bears' Super Bowl XX victory. By then I did represent a platoon of Bears players, but Dent was not one of them.

Dent had been put on the league's "reasonable cause" testing list off of a positive result for "very, very low traces" of marijuana during a routine team drug test in August, 1987. Twice in 1988, in May and in August, new tests on Dent turned up nothing. But he was told he'd still be on the list for random testing for two years after the original positive test.

Dent was ordered to take another test on August 23. He refused and was subsequently suspended for the Bears' second game of the season on September 11, 1988, at Indianapolis.

And so Dent asked me to represent him. I quickly huddled with a great legal mind, attorney Eldon Ham, who I knew through my father-in-law, Herb Young, a prominent commodities broker in an industry in which Ham also worked at the time.

We did our own two-minute drill to research and file a lawsuit that would seek a lifting of the suspension because we knew anything else involving the NFL drug policy would likely be a court battle. But we knew almost immediately our side was apparently several steps ahead of the NFL in the interpretation of "fundamental fairness," more commonly known as "due process" in the private sector. But our dual minds in the legal red zone paid off. We were like an English courtroom team: Ham was like the solicitor, doing the legal preparation beforehand; I was like the barrister, arguing the case in court.

"There were established standards in the commodities industry providing for notice and hearings in disciplinary matters," recalled Ham, who would soon join my growing Zucker Sports Management firm as in-house counsel. "I knew where the bones were buried. I read the NFL drug policy and bylaws. When they enacted the policy, a suspension could happen without a hearing in a second test.

"But NFL bylaws require some kind of hearing in a disciplinary matter. In private-sector due process, you have to follow your own bylaws. My feeling was that the contradiction in the drug policy was an oversight—its makers did not think to compare it to the league's bylaws. A suspension was invalid without a hearing."

The normal procedure would be to file a suit in federal court, as the NFL is a national organization operating across state lines. But I knew I'd have a kind of home-court advantage if I instead filed in the Cook County Circuit Court in Illinois. As a former prosecutor and criminal defense attorney in that system, I had a good understanding of how it worked. Plus, Dent was a Chicago hero. I was always looking for every edge

I could find.

We filed the suit on Wednesday, September 7. The hearing was assigned for 10:00 a.m. Friday, September 9, in the courtroom of Judge Sophia Hall, a Northwestern University-educated straight shooter. We summarized that after the subsequent tests and passage of time, there was no reason to suspect Dent was now using drugs. The suit said that without a hearing in accordance with fundamental fairness standards, Dent could not present his own evidence, could not cross-examine witnesses or question the methods of testing. We added, "There appears to be substantial confusion about what (NFL drug) policies are and how they are enforced." We claimed the policy had no discernible definition of "reasonable cause."

The magnitude of the case quickly captured the media's and court watchers' imaginations. No one had ever sued the NFL about its drug policy. While scores of players had recently drawn suspensions, none had the profile of Super Bowl-MVP Dent. By the time of the hearing, some 150 observers had jammed into the 100 seat-capacity courtroom. Fifty more mingled outside with a phalanx of TV cameras.

Almost immediately, lead NFL attorney Michael Coffield was playing defense. Soon after the hearing started, Coffield asked Judge Hall and me if we could all adjourn to a nearby conference room. Once there, Coffield quickly cut to the chase. "What do you want?" he asked. I was startled at what appeared to be a quick attempt to construct a settlement, having expected a legal brawl to this point with the NFL. We wanted the suspension lifted immediately, a hearing with NFL Commissioner Pete Rozelle and major changes in the drug policy.

But Coffield called another time out. He dashed for a phone, likely to call Rozelle. When he returned, he informed us the suspension was temporarily lifted until an appeal meeting with Rozelle. Dent subsequently was able to join the Bears' traveling party for Indy the next day. Without that blot on his record for the moment, he would certainly have an easy road to the

Pro Football Hall of Fame with his fabulous career defensive statistics and that Super Bowl-MVP performance.

So I flew to New York to meet with Rozelle on Wednesday, September 14. I told the commissioner, who always had a keen sense of public relations, that the drug policy was unfair. Players had a right to a hearing and had to be notified in a formal manner. Dent did recall Bears trainer Fred Caito verbally informing him of the test.

And so, everything went relatively smoothly again. I already had a long-distance relationship with Rozelle after he craftily handled the McMahon headband affair in the 1986 playoffs, involving what the league considered illicit wording on McMahon's headgear.

But even in our first face-to-face meeting, I recalled Rozelle's early career, as sports information director at the University of San Francisco in the era of its undefeated football team's refusal to play in a bowl game without its black players in an unprecedented anti-racial stance in 1951. Know and be friendly with your opposite number.

In any event, Rozelle said he'd have his final decision to me in the morning, and in an express-delivery arriving that next morning, Rozelle permanently lifted Dent's suspension while agreeing to change the drug policy.

The NFL in essence admitting it had a flawed system on drugs suddenly made me the media expert on the issue. I was subsequently invited to make the newscast and talk-show rounds, including with Larry King on CNN and Ted Koppel on ABC's *Nightline*.

These national exposures prompted a phone call to my home from well-known '60s radical Abbie Hoffman, a co-defendant of my one-time 1968 Democratic Convention "Chicago 7" adversary and equally famed "Chicago 7" defendant, Jerry Rubin. Despite that, Hoffman expressed an affinity for my side in this fight.

But the final disposition of a new drug policy would have to be locked down via collective bargaining between the NFL and its Players Association. The union was unhappy. I had come out of left field to prompt drug-policy changes after they had sat on their hands while their members were exposed to summary rulings. They asked, "Why did you do this?" I responded, "Because you didn't." It shouldn't have been me, but it was. Neither the league nor I and my team were against drug testing. But it had to be done correctly without fundamental fairness rights being trampled upon, which the NFLPA had allowed for years. By comparison, they were a shadow of the Major League Baseball Players Association and its strength as sports' strongest union, nursed along by the legendary Marvin Miller.

In prompting the NFL to rework the policy, to which Rozelle and the union agreed, we asked that "split samples" of urine be collected, the better to prevent contamination by accident or willful action. Players would urinate into two different bottles. Sample A would be maintained by the league. Sample B would be in the possession of the player and his representative, and be available for independent, third-party analysis. The players also would have their right to a notice and a hearing. It was a simple three-word process: sample; hearing; notice. Finally, I asked that the NFL in-house drug test administrator be dismissed. In addition to the program being run shoddily in my opinion, too many leaks of results had been taking place, which from my point of view only could have come from the inside.

Fundamental fairness soon became ingrained in drug testing. I can recall handling more than 15 additional hearings in the post-Dent years. We got relief in all of them—either a suspension reduced or thrown out altogether. Interestingly, several players were sent to me in backchannel fashion at the behest of their own teams, who surely could not challenge their own league and didn't want some of their best players suspended.

Dent was satisfied personally and for the future testing of his fellow players.

"I'm glad everything is over, said and done," he said at the time. "I can get back to what I do best. Life is full of chances;

nothing is promised to you. Sometimes you have to do more to get certain things done. It was a challenge I took, and I was willing to suffer whatever the consequences were.

"I think it's over unless I decide to turn into a drug addict or something. But that's not the case. I feel good to get this thing resolved and get the cloud off my head. Now things are much clearer, and I can go about my business."

The late Bears safety Dave Duerson, one of my most memorable clients, said Dent was not willing to get rolled over in the manner identified with the Bears of the era.

"We're a bunch of guys who stand up for what we believe in," Duerson said at the time. "Richard felt his rights were impinged upon. The league knew going in that Richard was going to win because the policy was so bogus. They knew it was a battle they would lose, so they reached a settlement out of court.

"Most of the time," he continued, "when you find players doing drugs, it's already too late. More has to be done from the preventive end and not the rehabilitative."

Dent went on to a pair of additional Pro Bowl teams and a career that finally wrapped up after 15 seasons in 1997. He was inducted into the Hall of Fame in 2011. Not bad for an eighth-round Bears pick in 1983.

Renowned NFL reporter Will McDonough, wired into the lords of the game, told longtime Chicago sportscaster Tom Shaer that the refusal-to-take-tests tactic would not work in the future under tough-minded Rozelle successor Paul Tagliabue. But I'm nevertheless confident we would have prevailed in another drug-policy challenge because we had the law on our side.

Of course, there are always two sides to every story. Players still tried to game the system. I heard one player tried to transfer his wife's urine via a tube that ran down his arm and eventually was attached to his penis. He was OK until they said he was pregnant. One other reported case had players having a third party withdraw their urine via a catheter and having it replaced it with clean urine. To me, that sounds downright dangerous, far worse than taking a chance with conventional testing.

Our case was only one leg of a widespread pro football association with drugs. Recreational and performance-enhancing drugs had been on the watch list for decades. But all kinds of painkillers, with their horrific side effects—see the opioid crisis—are embedded in the game.

McMahon, for one, saw addiction and other severely negative physical and mental effects as a result of too many pills and injections, which in many cases had become the players' best friends.

"Adrenaline, muscle relaxers and painkillers," McMahon told *Chicago Sun-Times* columnist Rick Telander in 2015 about his regular consumption of painkilling cocktails just to get onto the field. "A bunch of pills. That's why I almost fell down on the first play. My legs were like spaghetti," he said in reference to a 1985 game against Minnesota. McMahon had flat-out admitted he was addicted, requiring medical marijuana to get unhooked.

"I was eating 100 Percs a month," he told Telander. "Percocets. A hundred a month. How'd I get off them? I started smoking medical marijuana. I got my card when I moved to Arizona. I haven't had a painkiller in 15 years," he noted.

Two years later, in a conversation for this book at my home, McMahon recalled the pressure to play while practically disabled, or what he called "robbing Peter to pay Paul."

"They kept shooting my shoulder (with pain killers)," he said. "I had no labrum at all. They claimed I was faking."

He decried "Big Pharma's" heavy-handed influence over the country, including the NFL, and conservative government elements' continued attempts to "demonize" marijuana, including its medicinal purposes.

I now perfectly understand how many players dovetail into addiction. In the old days, they'd have access in the locker room to a bowl of pills in which to dig in. But on Mondays, many players could hardly walk. Nancy McMahon had to help her husband get out of bed. Yet he'd be fine, officially, to play

Sundays. Team doctors would mask underlying ailments with pain killers and injections, then push the meat-on-the-hoof back onto the field. They were in a gray area with their Hippocratic Oath, but too many doctors loved the prestige of being associated with an NFL team. That's why, early on, I opted with few exceptions to send my clients to independent physicians.

In baseball, the old axiom is, an injury should not cost you your job. But there was no football counterpart and I suspect some 80 percent of the players were interchangeable. They were on the field, hobbled but dressed for two reasons: fear of losing their jobs; and the sheer desire of their teams wanting them to play. In the ultimate macho league, if they did not play hurt, they got a stigma slapped on them.

Beyond the injury factor though, I believe every sports league is in essence hypocritical on drugs. Alcohol is the most addictive drug of them all, but no pro organization or broadcast network could televise sports without beer sponsors. Days after the Dent case was settled, the *Chicago Tribune*'s Don Pierson, one of the most respected football writers, put it into perspective.

Pierson quoted from the NFL drug policy itself, stating alcohol was the most abused drug in the league. Always had been, and always will be, given DUI arrests and alcohol's likely role in domestic-violence and other assault cases. Pierson also drew from policy language banning NFL employees from beer and tobacco ads to prevent "a detrimental effect on the great number of young fans who follow our game."

But beer and football then and now go together like love and marriage. And despite drug-policy changes for the better, double standards, as described herein, still permeate the game at the point of entry of all that sponsorship money.

"No drug policy will be entirely fair until it fingers owners, coaches, officials and other people besides players in the industry," Pierson concluded.

I heartily concurred then — and still do now. I am just happy I helped move the chains down the field from where the NFL was backed up in its own half of the field, benefitting no one.

CHAPTER 16

CONCUSSIONS ARE NOTHING
TO MESS WITH

Unveiled in a January 25, 2018, news conference in Chicago was a new legislative initiative called the Dave Duerson Act, a law that would ban tackle football in the state of Illinois for players under 12.

The issue of chronic traumatic encephalopathy, more commonly known as CTE, had to come to this.

This proposed law movement was spreading like wildfire throughout football as NFL Commissioner Roger Goodell prepared for another Super Bowl. The issue of the game's core head-to-head contact literally scrambling brains promised to change the game as we know it in coming decades.

As I came to understand the disastrous effects of repeated blows to the head and their role in CTE, I came to lose my lifelong zest for football, a game I had loved since I sat on my father's lap at a Chicago Bears game in 1944. Knowing how the legal system works, I now firmly believed parents and attorneys would undercut the game in a manner more powerful than any class-action lawsuit against Goodell and the all-powerful NFL.

And now a lawmaker had formally joined the quest to cut down on head blows at players' contact points. The merits of the proposed Dave Duerson Act were immediately debated by the medical and legal community, but State Representative Carol Sente (D-Vernon Hills) was spot-on in introducing the legislation. It was something I believed in very strongly, and having Duerson's name attached to the bill was touching. I was happy and I knew he'd be happy.

Like anyone else connected to football through my fan-based, emotional interest and agent-based livelihood, I had put head blows on the back burner all those decades, paying more attention to the ravages of violent contact on knees, hips and shoulders.

But then the concept of CTE, the end result of repeated concussions eating away at a man's physical and mental health in his middle-age years, struck me in the gut. One of my most memorable clients, Duerson committed suicide by shooting himself in the heart at his Florida home on February 17, 2011. CTE, impossible to diagnose while alive, had hammered at Dave's personality and changed him from the positive, thoughtful achiever he had been since even before he was the starting strong safety on the Super Bowl XX champion Chicago Bears. But in a heroic last act before his compulsion to end his suffering kicked in, Duerson mandated his brain be donated to the ongoing study of CTE, which can only be formally diagnosed post-mortem.

In the years leading up to Duerson's death, we had some inkling an insidious condition was slowly killing a number of veterans, but hardly the knowledge and willpower we possessed at the end of the 2010 decade. Duerson had been a finance major at Notre Dame and had run a food-processing business in Kenosha, Wisconsin that had McDonald's as a major client. He was the only player I represented who I seriously considered taking into my Zucker Sports Management business. However, Duerson could not be pulled away from his activism with the NFL Players Association.

In his 40s, we saw that Duerson's life was steadily eroding. The four-time Pro Bowler had been voted NFL Man of the Year in 1987 for his philanthropic work. But 15 years later, he began displaying irrational behavior and I don't think people at first knew where it was coming from. He lost his business, he lost his marriage, he lost his seat on the University of Notre Dame board, his alma mater. And I'll admit I did not put all

Dave Duerson

the signs together.

But by 2012, it all began to add up. Multiple-time All-Pro linebacker Junior Seau also committed suicide with a shot to the chest more than a year after Duerson's death. Both were diagnosed post-mortem with CTE. I look back at Duerson's troubles and wish I could have done something—but what? I had talked with Duerson three weeks before his death and little seemed out of the ordinary.

Tregg Duerson, Dave's oldest son, attended the press conference to show his support for the bill. Nobody was advocating stamping out football entirely. But research to date had shown that the earlier a youth began playing tackle football, the more he stood a chance of developing CTE symptoms decades later from the additional head blows.

"To be clear, I'm not advocating for people not to play any form of football, but to play flag, or touch, and use that time to develop properly," Tregg Duerson told *Chicago Tribune* columnist John Kass. "There are a lot of things children can do to learn the game without hitting."

A prominent teammate of Duerson's father had summed up their press-conference points six months earlier in a wide-ranging interview in my living room.

"They should eliminate Pee Wee football," said Jim McMahon that teammate at that time. McMahon is the client with whom I'm most identified. "Don't have contact until they're juniors in high school. The body is not mature enough to wear a helmet. Meanwhile, they can learn the fundamentals of the game."

To drive home Duerson's points, former Bear and longtime sportscaster Mike Adamle appeared at the press conference as an example of an affliction-in-development. Nearing 70, the youthful-looking, always-effervescent Adamle remains an activist for CTE awareness and research. He is suffering from steadily-worsening dementia he believes is a symptom of the disease — but of course cannot be proven due to the post-mortem-only diagnostic possibility. Adamle has had bouts of forgetfulness. At times he wandered about downtown Chicago, near the NBC-Chicago offices where he worked, not aware of how to get home.

And so the die may have been cast to radically transform football from its gladiator-game status. Parents are bailing from youth-football participation — even with laws that would put off the start of tackle football until near teen-age years, even with more knowledge of CTE's affects, even with increased safety measures at all levels of the game and even with equipment manufacturer Riddell attempting to develop much safer helmets. Participation has fallen 20 percent in the last decade. Entire youth programs in the Chicago suburbs have shut down. In Highland Park, Illinois, where Tregg Duerson grew up, the park district ended its youth program when just 11 kids signed up. The program once attracted as many as 150. Several high schools around the country have dropped varsity football altogether.

"My son-in-law (Thomas Rogers) is principal of Geneva (Illinois) High School," said former Bears general manager Jerry Vainisi. "They had many fewer kids try out for football this year. I've seen schools consolidating their programs to field teams," in other words, combining varsity and junior varsity teams into one unit instead of two.

However, suggesting the proposed law was not the right vehicle to legislate against youth tackle football, the *Chicago Tribune* ran an editorial saying that parents and youth program operators should make the calls.

They are doing just that. And when attorneys get involved, it becomes a double-whammy against the origins of the NFL's bountiful meat market. Youth programs, park districts, elementary and high schools almost always do not have the resources to defend against injury lawsuits in the manner of the mega-rich NFL. But the highest-level of competition will be hurt nonetheless. A cut in participation at the entry level eventually will cascade, impacting college programs and perhaps, eventually, the NFL.

Commissioner Goodell probably couldn't help but cringe when Hall-of-Fame linebacker Nick Buoniconti, CTE-like impaired now in his late 70s, said in a TV interview that he cannot read a book or newspaper anymore. "I can't believe any parent would let their kid play tackle football," he said.

And none other than Mike Ditka, the modern-day symbol of rough, tough, take-no-prisoners football, remarked he would not allow his grandchildren to play tackle football. "Iron Mike," as he was known, played with a full facemask, which was only instituted in the 1960s when he was in his Bears prime.

But pundits are not stopping with youth or even high-school football being dropped. *Chicago Tribune* columnist Stephen

Chapman, known for libertarian views, suggested in a November 17, 2017, column that his alma mater, Harvard, should drop football as an example to others in the Ivy League and other conferences.

"Universities that are academic leaders have no business pretending there is no problem or waiting for others to act," Chapman wrote at the time. "Their stature also gives them outsized influence. If Yale's President Peter Salovey and Harvard's former president Drew Gilpin Faust were to move to abandon the sport for reasons of health and safety, administrators at other colleges would be confronted with the question in a way they could not avoid."

I believe the word is spreading about danger and there's nothing the Lords of the NFL can do about it.

"Football will not be a middle-class sport anymore," said former Lions and Bears General Manager Vainisi. "I think you're going to see fewer and fewer middle-class kids playing. You'll see where football becomes a sport as a way out of the ghetto, as a way out of (an) underprivileged area, at whatever (physical) cost. They're willing to pay that price to improve their lot in life.

"Why do any athletes box today? I wouldn't get in the ring in a million years," he went on in comparison.

"I already see a deterioration of the type of player in there. You won't have the talent pool previously out there. With CBA rules and so little hitting in practice, my perception is the game will not be as good as it used to be," he concluded.

I believe forces are in motion. Parents will act on CTE, but the NFL had to have been nervous at the very least with the release of the 2015 Will Smith *Concussion* movie. Smith played Dr. Bennet Omalu, a Pittsburgh forensic pathologist who discovered the link between concussions and brain damage, sparked by the death of Hall-of-Fame Steelers' center Mike Webster at age 50 in 2002, after a decade of physical and mental deterioration in his life.

Rumors swirled that the NFL tried to have producers tone

down the movie's premise to avoid antagonizing the athletic hierarchy. *The New York Times* reported a Sony Pictures attorney taking "most of the bite" out of the movie due to "legal reasons with the NFL."

Despite all the publicity, the movie going public apparently wanted lighter fare when *Concussion* opened in Christmas Week 2015.

Box Office reported the $35 million movie made just $11 million at 2,841 theaters ($3,872 per theater average) in its opening weekend.

"It was out for just a week," mused McMahon. "The movie was well-done. Will Smith was nominated for an Oscar. I want to meet the doctor he played."

But the old sports saying applied here — the "horse is out of the barn." And I believe the NFL still has no sway over the work of top CTE researcher Ann McKee of Boston University. Studying the brains of 202 deceased football players, McKee found markers of CTE in the brains of 99 percent of NFL veterans and in 91 percent of those who played through college.

Now then, First Amendment rights may overpower any attempts at NFL censorship of the overwhelming testimony of former players like Buoniconti, Adamle and others. On top of that, a 35-year, all-time broadcast pundit like Bob Costas sent a quote ringing in the ears of every pro and college commissioner: "The reality is that this game destroys people's brains."

Meanwhile, Dr. McKee has been getting even more brain-tissue samples for further study. Dana Buffone, widow of popular Bears linebacker-turned-radio host Doug Buffone, exhumed his body two years after his 2015 death, unofficially tied to a heart attack at 70. Buffone's brain was sent for CTE study, a long and laborious process.

Dana Buffone wondered about her husband's connection to CTE after he died, officially of a heart attack. She consulted with attorneys about a possible legal action if such a diagnosis was confirmed.

"He became reclusive," Dana Buffone told Rick Telander of

the *Chicago Sun-Times*. "As time went on, he definitely wasn't as social. If people came over to the house, he stayed downstairs. There were times when he would drive around all night long. Sleeping was always an issue."

"He would get lost (driving). And he drove so slowly, it would drive me insane. I'd say, 'You have to just put your foot on the gas!'"

Meanwhile, in a September 21, 2017 Facebook post, former All-Pro linebacker Thomas "Hollywood" Henderson said he was suffering memory loss in his 60s.

"Took a seven hour cognitive test. My short-term memory is suffering. This is not a test to pass or fail. It's for seeing how your brain works with words, symbols, math, visual, physical and memory. My short-term memory sucks.

"It actually surprised me how my brain can't remember something I was read or showed. Interesting science. As hard as I played and hit, I'm sure I have brain damage. It's embarrassing to not remember parts of the testing. Linebackers like me probably have CTE. Comes with the way we played the game we loved."

The sum total of "name" NFL players suffering from CTE is registering in the public's mindset, said Richmond Webb, another former client who fortunately has a great head on his shoulders.

"Problem is when you keep hearing former players pass away, you hear about autopsies and CTE," he said. "These were not just average guys. If it continues to come out that players keep dying early, I could see the issues (for the NFL) later down the road."

Rumors even swirled years ago that McMahon's suffering from dementia was connected with CTE onset. McMahon himself even had those fears. He is alive and well and with all his wits—but he paid a monstrous physical price taking the beatings of a quarterback and being dumped on his head and shoulders in 1986 on a personal foul penalty following a play's completion against the Green Bay Packers.

"We knew we'd be beat up, with our shoulders and knees," McMahon said in a pensive moment at my home in an interview in the summer of 2017. "You know you're going to have injuries and have after effects when you retire.

"I played concussed. I went back out there many times. In those days (on the sidelines after a head blow), all you do is follow a finger, and if you can do that, you're back in the game. It's long-term damage. The guy [who] works with me in New York (Dr. Raymond Damadian) sees 100 guys with their necks out of whack."

Damadian had a somewhat unconventional but specialty medical treatment that gave McMahon some lasting relief after years of pounding pain from four damaged vertebrae and spinal fluid backing up into his skull. Initially, we thought blood flow into his brain was being impeded. "At least I know what's wrong with me," McMahon said. "Before I was treated, if I had a gun, I wouldn't be here. When *SI* came out in 2012 (speculating about his physical condition), these doctors called me to say we think they can help you. They found out what was happening in my brain. After the treatment, it was instant relief."

McMahon put it an even earthier way in an interview with the *Sun-Times'* Telander:

"As soon as the guy adjusted me, it was like a toilet flushed."

I don't believe we had any way to head off this tidal wave of problems simply from the way football always was played. The game was violent from the very beginning, before players even wore the primitive leather helmets. Moves to outlaw football around the start of the 20th century did not go very far, as college football gained popularity. Hall-of-Fame end Bill Hewitt played without a helmet in the 1930s with the Bears and Philadelphia Eagles.

My father, Herb Zucker, wore a leather helmet playing linebacker and center in the Big Ten in the 1930s. He had terrible arthritis affecting most of his body as a result of playing. He had to wear a back brace. To be sure, he got his "bell rung," as concussions were labeled, in the tough-guy days of football.

These aftereffects kept him out of the Army in World War II.

Herb Zucker taught me how to long-snap, but did not encourage me to play football. He was unsuccessful. Our city-wide organized youth league was the Junior Bears, but I did not make the weight range at 90 to 110 pounds. So instead I played sandlot tackle football—without a helmet—as quarterback and safety at Green Briar Park with the neighborhood kids. I do not feel I ever was concussed, but I broke my nose a number of times.

Football was always touted as the ultimate team game, teaching you teamwork and sportsmanship. You must rely on the man next to you. Although also team games, I believe success in baseball and basketball rely more on individual skills. But football has the hard hitting that fans craved in a faster-paced society in the 1960s, when the NFL exploded in popularity under Commissioner Rozelle. A 1962 *Time* magazine story centered on Green Bay Packers coach Vince Lombardi's success as the centerpiece for the NFL's growing appeal, mentioned that the hits just kept on coming as a big audience lure.

While today's players are much bigger and faster—making full-speed collisions that much more potentially catastrophic—more questionable or even outright dirty play was allowed as I watched the game first sprout into mass appeal. Like the style of former Bear Ed Sprinkles, touted as "The Meanest Man in Pro Football" and was lofted to hero status among many fans, we cheered for even more of that style. Almost anything was allowed. You could even blindside hit, although now it's a penalty for unnecessary roughness.

You'd look at a guy's belt buckle and lead with your head—and tackle with your head. But then if a player put his head in the wrong position, it was head versus head. It caused shivers up and down the arm, all the way to the neck, but only now is drawing major penalties, although seen in almost every game.

Post-leather helmets were made out of plastic. The players had little to protect their faces with mostly just one protective face bar. Wearing a face mask was just not a macho thing to do.

But the players got progressively bigger and faster. No matter what year or era, we never realized the repercussions of what we were watching. Now I have trouble watching a game after witnessing it for a lifetime and dealing with star players from the inside-out. When I see one hit, I now know the repercussions. They accumulate.

Obviously, football is not going to be outlawed at the college level or above anytime soon. And while youth participation will likely continue to decrease, the long-term squeeze on NFL talent and mandatory changes in the game into a somewhat kinder, gentler form may take 15 years — down from the 20 years I had originally forecast. In the meantime, those who teach the game at the entry level are charged with making it as safe and fundamentally sound as possible.

Two of my top former clients have perspective into that process. Hall-of-Fame defensive back and premier kick returner Deion Sanders has long taught football at the youth and high-school levels since he retired from the NFL. And Webb, who I believe should be in Canton off his 1990's blocking talents with the Miami Dolphins, has long had an involvement in his native Texas, seemingly the capital of youth and high-school football.

"I coach five- to 12-year-old kids playing football, and I've coached high-school football. I love it," said Sanders. "We have proper teaching, proper techniques. It has a lot to do with who's coaching, who's teaching and the type of equipment you're wearing as well. I don't think pushing back the age (would help). Twenty-one is the drinking age — you still get (underage) drunk drivers all the time. You push back the age all you want, it's still going to be what it is.

"Your head is going to come into play anyway. If you lead with your shoulder, your head is going to hit something. You just need better coaching and teaching at the younger level."

Webb, meanwhile, cut his teeth as a tackle in the Dallas area and now runs a business in Houston. He does not have a son playing high-school football, so he is not conflicted.

"Youth football should be the developmental stage," he said. "You teach kids the proper way of not using your head as a weapon. Growing up, guys used the head as a spear, and were not thinking long-term. I started playing in middle school, seventh grade. Now they start earlier. You have to be concerned about CTE. I do think the more you delay starting tackle football, the more you lessen the risk.

"You were trained in early days to use your head first. At the time, I don't think the coaches who taught me how to play the game had the information that if you continue to do this, it would cause concussions. That was the norm, that was how it was taught. You can tackle without the head. They're doing it in college. It's all in the technique. In college, there's a huge penalty for targeting. It's big because you can lose your key player (to game disqualification penalty)."

Webb lives in a geographic area that can serve as the proverbial canary in the coal mine if youth participation drops. And if it does, I believe the ripple effect will emanate into the collegiate ranks.

Texas institutions have invested big money in high-school facilities.

"The city of Allen, north of Dallas, built a $60 million sports complex for high-school football," Webb said. "The city of Katy also built a big facility.

"It would be justified to be concerned. Texas, Florida and California put out a ton of athletes. Most people don't have the war chest. There could be a ton of lawsuits. If it happens in Texas, it will start happening in other states. Everybody is not the NFL or the University of Texas with a ton of money for athletic programs. It could be a grim situation if lawsuits start winning. It would be a domino effect.

"If participating is down and it gets to the college level, you'll have a substandard product. At Division I, football supports almost all the other schools' athletic programs. If football is affected, it could hurt the entire athletic program. You could be looking at sports demoted to the intramural level. It could be catastrophic."

Even with the advocacy of no-contact youth football — or no youth football at all — along with concussion protocols, stricter rules on hitting and Riddell's all-out effort to produce a much safer high-tech helmet, I believe the game of football will be changed irrevocably in the coming decades. We may not recognize the game in 15 years.

The tide cannot be reversed due to the advance of science. The bottom line is players cannot keep suffering, perhaps dying as a result of long-accepted head trauma. However the game is repaired, if it can be repaired at all, is up to people at a higher pay grade than mine.

Knowing what I know now, I can never look at football in the same way as I have since the T-formation was a relatively new fad and I sat on dad Herb Zucker's lap at my first Bears game in 1944, learning to love the rough, tough stuff before me on the field.

CHAPTER 17
UNDERSTANDING JDF
ONE PERSON AT A TIME

Type 1 diabetes, once called "Juvenile Diabetes," is an often misunderstood disease. It is not the same as Type 2 diabetes, which develops in a considerable chunk of the general population as they age.

Cubs' Hall-of-Fame third baseman Ron Santo even hid his Type 1 diagnosis from his front office and teammates, and only late in his career did he reveal his affliction.

My family and associates have been active in raising money for research under the Juvenile Diabetes Federation's Chicago chapter for more than 40 years — and we have first-hand experience to spur us.

Our son, Herbie, was diagnosed with it at age five in 1977. He has had a challenging health history as a result — but never more so than when a Wilmette, Illinois, police officer, who did not recognize the urgency of treating a diabetic seizure, detained my wife Shelly to give her a speeding ticket in the spring of 1986.

While I was out of town, Shelly was asleep around 3:00 a.m. when she heard a loud thump in Herbie's bedroom. He was on the floor, hardly breathing. His color was blue. He apparently had a seizure. Shelly thought she could get him to the hospital faster than waiting for an ambulance. With Herbie slumped over on the front seat, Shelly — still in her nightgown — raced at 55 mph on local Green Bay Road, the route to nearby Evanston Hospital, about four miles away.

About 1½ miles from the hospital, a Wilmette officer

stopped Shelly. Although he could see Herbie sliding in and out of consciousness in the front seat, and Shelly in her robe, he still asked to see Shelly's license and inquired about who owned the car. Shelly answered it was my vehicle. All the while, Herbie was in extreme distress. We believe the time elapsed was between 10 and 15 minutes when the ambulance arrived. In that period, Herbie could have already been in the emergency room getting initial treatment.

Shelly told the officer he could have escorted her to the hospital, and then written all the tickets he wanted. No matter—strict procedure had to be followed—be it "life or death" or not. The Wilmette Chief of Police later said his department did not provide escorts for vehicles transporting seriously ill individuals. Instead, the police officer made Shelly wait for the ambulance while writing the speeding ticket. Shelly's perception was that he was not primarily concerned with the medical emergency at hand and that he was more focused on giving out a moving violation while handing off to the paramedics when seconds counted.

In the hospital, Herbie's blood sugar was a life-threatening 560. He was diagnosed with diabetic ketoacidosis, a serious complication of diabetes when the body produces high levels of blood acids called ketones. Without enough insulin, the body begins to break down fat as fuel. Immediate emergency care is urgent as the condition can cause fatal complications for a diabetic. I would urge police departments to provide better training to put emergencies first and sort out the justice later.

Perhaps there's been some progress. In recent years, many public-safety vehicles and public facilities have been equipped with defibrillators at the ready. And maybe more police officers now would not lose precious seconds waiting for the paramedics to arrive if a diabetic youth is suffering terribly in a car stopped for speeding.

Herbie's condition committed us to become activists to raise money for Type 1 diabetes. And it was the main motivation for Jim McMahon, who became friends with Herbie. At our behest,

McMahon wore a "JDF Cure" headband in Super Bowl XX, which really raised awareness to a national TV audience.

Shelly and I, along with six other couples affected by Type 1 diabetes, started the Chicago chapter of JDF long before I entered the public domain as a sports agent. We developed the largest charity event in Chicago, with up to 4,000 in attendance at the top Hilton and then Sheraton hotels in downtown Chicago. We raffled off a Rolls Royce from a local dealer. The several million we raised was spent well on research and awareness. Eventually, a local business executive afflicted with the disease took over the charity efforts.

Type 1 provokes greater ravages on the body, earlier than Type 2. Herbie had a heart attack at 30 and required a pancreas transplant. In turn, the pancreas issues forced a kidney transplant.

Santo, meanwhile, in his 60s, needed both legs amputated. But he played with the disease in an era when diabetics could not accurately monitor their blood sugar as well as they can in modern times. Santo required clubhouse chief Yosh Kawano to bring him a can of Coke and a candy bar in the middle of games. When he was first diagnosed in 1959, doctors tried to regulate his condition through diet.

Santo joined Jim "Catfish" Hunter of the Oakland A's, also a diabetes 1 sufferer, as Hall-of-Famers. Hunter was diagnosed late in a career that featured five World Series rings and 224 victories, including a 1968 perfect game with the Athletics.

Now, Type 1 diabetics who play sports in the 21st century can regulate their conditions much better in the middle of games, thanks to medical advances not available to the likes of Santo.

That's why I greatly admired two other Chicago athletes. Quarterback Jay Cutler of the Bears played through controversies in Chicago, but he was able to monitor his blood sugar on the sidelines. He missed time due to major injuries, not diabetes. Meanwhile, Sam Fuld was a speedy center fielder who challenged walls to make catches for the Chicago Cubs,

Tampa Bay Rays and Oakland Athletics. Type 1 did not slow down Fuld at all.

But one entertaining way of raising awareness for JDF involved Lou Holtz, the former Notre Dame football coach and one of the most charismatic sports personalities in modern times. In 1992, Holtz was our Man of the Year at the fundraiser. Holtz's son, Kevin, had been diagnosed with Type 1 diabetes.

Trying to contact Holtz in the first place though showed Shelly that his secretary was as good a blocker as his Irish offensive line. She could not get through despite three attempts. But Shelly is a bit resourceful. She knew a prominent Notre Dame alum who was a neighbor of Shelly's father, Herb Young. The alum slipped Holtz's home number to Shelly. Like a great running back spotting a sliver of daylight, that was all she needed.

Holtz agreed to headline the dinner. Accompanying him were the Notre Dame Marching Band and cheerleaders. And Holtz, a captivating speaker, mentioned to the assembled that Shelly had the guts to call him at home and bypass his secretary. If Shelly could've play football, she'd have been the kind of player Holtz would want on his team.

• • •

Diabetes, however, did not affect Jim Mullen in the least. The courageous Chicago police officer had a huge physical—life-and-death, in fact—challenge. He and I connected in a different way though.

On October 16, 1996, Mullen and other officers answered a call about a man shooting at passing Red Line "el" or elevated trains in Chicago's Rogers Park neighborhood.

Mullen and Co. could not gain entry into the suspect's apartment. But as the officers began to leave the scene, the suspect burst out of his door and fired two shots from a .357 Magnum. One entered Mullen's cheek, severely damaging his spine. He nearly died. Doctors saved Mullen, but he was left a quadriplegic.

Mullen, though, was so strong of will that the catastrophic injuries only slowed him. Confined to a wheelchair and needing to breath with a tube, Mullen did not retire from public life. He still served in the Chicago Police Department and eventually began his own applesauce business.

I met Mullen when he and I were among the recipients of the Father of the Year award by the Chicagoland Fatherhood Council. The late comedian/director, Chicagoan Harold Ramis, most famous for *Ghostbusters*, had been another recipient. Even though Mullen had a good municipal medical plan, all too often someone in his condition never has enough money for the lifelong care required.

But I had an ace in the hole. Since our 1960s days starting out in the city corporation counsel's office, I had kept in touch with Chicago Mayor Richard M. Daley. Seeing Mullen's long-term needs, I went to Daley to request the heroic cop be promoted to the "exempt" personnel level. That was the "white shirt" level, the color of the uniforms worn by lieutenants and up. Mullen was granted that promotion by Daley, enabling Mullen to get a significant boost in salary and commensurate pension benefits.

I was also especially sensitive to a public figure paralyzed for life. Dick Elrod, my friend and mentor in the corporation counsel's office, had been immobilized during the Days of Rage demonstrations in 1969. Elrod went on to serve four terms as Cook County sheriff. I told Mullen about Elrod's example. Mullen went on to teach computer skills to the disabled.

Despite criticism, Daley did a tremendous amount of good for Chicago in a 22-year mayoral tenure that even exceeded in longevity that of Richard J. Daley, his famed father. In one-on-one situations like Mullen's, he proved to be significantly generous and kind.

• • •

Later in my career I would dovetail with Rich Daley in a football-themed process that never saw the light of day in publicity in the mid-2000s.

Daley approached me at a party one night. He grew up in the South Side Bridgeport neighborhood a few blocks from old Comiskey Park, then home of the White Sox. But he reportedly rooted for the Chicago Cardinals, his football team of favor before they moved to St. Louis in 1960. Daley thought Chicago could use another pro football team to break the Bears' monopoly—and the fact the Halas/McCaskey family would never sell.

But due to the provisions of the NFL's TV contract, any new team in a two-team market had to be an American Football Conference franchise, given the Bears' entrenched National Football Conference standing. So I inquired about acquiring and relocating the Buffalo Bills.

I said I would handle the TV contract issues with the NFL with my connections and the acquisition of the team. There surely would be no shortage of buyers with the city's sports-minded executives locked out of a piece of the Bears, with the exception of high-profile and prestigious businessmen Pat Ryan and Andy McKenna Sr. having bought 20 percent of the team a while back. Meanwhile, Daley would take care of all other issues, including a stadium, since another Chicago team could not play at natural-turf Soldier Field.

I reached Marv Levy, who at 80 was in his second tenure with the Bills as general manager. Levy, a Chicago native, and I had an old connection from summer camp way back in 1950, I as a camper and Levy as a counselor. The big question was if longtime Bills owner Ralph Wilson, with whom Levy was close, was open to selling. Levy cautioned, "I don't think the old man will sell in his lifetime," but he'd check. Wilson responded negatively, that he did not want the Bills to leave Buffalo. Eventually, after his death, the Bills were sold, but stayed in Buffalo.

The idea of a second team in Chicago was always intriguing to me. George Halas ran the Cardinals out of Chicago to enable the Bears to televise road games without a second franchise in the city's home games forcing a total blackout of the market, per NFL broadcast rules at the time. Neither Halas nor his heirs would take on significant ownership partners. I was confident that between Daley and me that we could have rounded up both moneyed and football-knowledgeable investors. The thirst for a piece of a Chicago NFL franchise is never quenched, in my opinion, even with the growing issue of CTE clouding pro football's future.

••

The investigation into moving the Bills was the second time I had linked to another city's NFL franchise. In the late 1980s, as my prominence as an agent grew, I was told at an NFL owners meeting that the Sullivan family, which owned the team, would consider selling the New England Patriots, a team the family founded. The Patriots at the time endured severe financial problems, at one point in 1988 requiring the NFL to advance the franchise $4 million just to make payroll.

The Sullivans asked for $200 million. I thought I could have put a group together in two seconds. I would have taken a piece of the team and become general manager. But I just let it go, since I was too busy pursuing first-round draft choices. It was one of my bigger regrets. The Sullivans soon sold to shaving-magnate Victor Kiam, who yielded to New England business magnate James Orthwein as owner. Foxboro Stadium, the Patriots home, lapsed into bankruptcy.

Paper magnate Robert Kraft owned some adjacent land and had an eye on the adjoining stadium. The rest is history as he would soon own both. The Patriots are now worth $2.7 billion and the crafty Kraft leveraged a threatened move to Connecticut to get a new stadium, hire Bill Belichick, after some misconnections from the Cleveland Browns where he was coach, and got a bargain in the sixth round, drafting Tom Brady. You think Kraft is not one of the NFL's greatest-ever owners?

I probably couldn't have matched Kraft's prowess as an owner. Still, it would have been interesting to see how I would have operated on the other side instead of representing Richard Dent in the landmark NFL drug-policy case in 1988.

• • •

Since I never became an owner or facilitator of a franchise move, I had to settle for status as an agent. I never had any regrets. Thus I was thrilled to become the first agent ever inducted into the Chicagoland Sports Hall of Fame in 2011.

Former Bears general manager Jerry Vainisi, the first sports executive with whom I negotiated as an agent in 1984, was inducted just before I was. Vainisi grew up only a few blocks from me on Chicago's far north side, and played youth sports, like me, at Green Briar Park. Ed Kelly, who coached both Vainisi and me at Green Briar, ran my candidacy up the flagpole.

It means a lot being the only agent inducted into my local Hall of Fame. Vainisi and I were the only sports contract negotiators who got in. I'm sure there will be room for more.

EPILOGUE

I would like to thank a number of people who helped me through the years.

First and foremost was my dad, Herb Zucker, who believed in me before anyone else. I was my father's son. My mother, Millie Zucker, was another true believer who taught me compassion and to care about people.

All of the good fortune and memories from my professional life pale in comparison to having been blessed with my life partner Shelly, my wife of 48 years. Also in the lineup are my sons Neal and Marko, both extremely successful businessmen; my son Herbie, brave and resilient; my daughters Jenny Healy and Tory Boyer, and my son-in-law Randy Boyer, all of whom are in a law practice together. Also, Denis John Healy, a great father and businessman and friend in need. To our six grandchildren, D.J, Ally, Cassidy, Sammy, Danny and Lizzie, of whom I am so proud and love very much, this book is for them.

As with my parents, lifelong friend Rick Fizdale has always been there for me from the beginning in our tenement building at Rosemont and Western avenues in Chicago. He would go on to become a prominent writer and author, deftly describing life in Chicago.

Ed Kelly was my mentor and friend. I first met Kelly when I was 8. He taught me to play ball at Chicago's Green Briar Park. Throughout my late teens and early 20s, I followed him from park to park, playing 16-inch softball, a version of the game unique in its origins to Chicago. Kelly later went on to be superintendent for the Chicago Park District. Kelly has always been there for me.

The cast of characters in public life who also boosted me

over the decades is impressive. There's Eddie Price, a Republican Ward committeeman, and Judge Irving Eiserman, who, helped me steer through some difficult times when I was a student at the University of Illinois. Pro basketball entrepreneur and former Chicago Zephyers' owner Dave Trager, Harold Schwartz, an attorney of labor-law fame; and legendary DePaul Blue Demons basketball coach Ray Meyer—all somehow helped get me into DePaul Law School.

A few years later, Illinois State Senator Robert Cherry got me my prosecutor's job. Once in the corporation counsel's office in Chicago's City Hall, Cook County Sheriff Dick Elrod taught me how to be a lawyer and a man. Jim McMahon, my first sports client, for no apparent reason off the bat, trusted me with managing his career. I must also mention former tennis pro Linda Harvey Wild, my only client in that sport, who somehow put me into position to be elected CEO of the Women's Professional Tennis Association. Wild also helped my daughter Tory gain access to the unique player's area at Wimbledon when Tory was studying in London.

But back on my first day of law school, the class was taught in a room donated by one of the men instrumental in getting me into the school. It was one of the great pleasures of my life to donate in return a room at DePaul, some 30 years later, in honor of my mom and dad.

However, I can't say enough in this mini-essay about mentor Elrod. His picture was in every courtroom in Cook County as its sheriff. The picture gave me a huge edge as a criminal defense attorney because I had been known by the judges and assistant state's attorneys as his right-hand man.

Famous clients skyscraper-climber "Spider Dan" Goodwin, pro football's Richard Dent, pro baseball's Ron LeFlore and edgy publisher Larry Flynt, to name a few, helped in making my name well-known in the legal field. Around the same time, my friend Terry Cohen helped me start in private practice when he made me the "Rush Street Lawyer" of the fast and famous crowd that frequented that well-known Chicago entertainment district.

I was likewise fortunate to run Zucker Sports Management, my own company of great achievement, staffed by fantastic people. In the beginning there was just myself, associate Kathe Clements and secretary, Jamie Zimberoff, in a small Skokie, Illinois office. A few years later, I added Gene Burrough as my main college recruiter and we moved on to a suite of offices in Northbrook, Illinois.

Eldon Ham, a fine attorney, joined us as we were near our peak and capably ran the office while managing legal matters. Zucker Sports Management intern Lamont Smith went on to sign the top QB in the country, Syracuse University's Donovan McNabb, a famed Chicago-area native and prep athlete. Later, Ian Greengross ran everything at Zucker Sports Management Group and went on to be a terrific agent. I can never forget loyal Zucker marketing directors Bonnie Rucks and later Nancy Mitchell, who would go on to win a Thousand Points of Light award from President George H.W. Bush for her work at our firm.

I owe a debt of gratitude to many members of the press who helped my career along the way: the late can't-miss columnist and broadcaster Irv Kupcinet; Wally Phillips, the longtime king of Chicago radio talent; ace Chicago sportswriters Dan Pompei and Don Pierson; famed newscaster Ted Koppel; interviewer supreme Larry King; ESPN football reporting insiders Chris Mortenson and John Clayton; Chicago sports-reporting staples Chet Coppock, Mike North, and Tom Shaer; ESPN and later NBC's Andrea Kremer; former Bear-turned-sportscaster Johnny Morris; and famed national-profile sports reporters Len Pasquarelli and George Michael.

The whole timeline was amazing since my sports life began when I was 4, sitting on my dad's lap at a Chicago Bears game. My father and I went to Bears home games at their then-home Wrigley Field until I went away to the University of Illinois. We saw the Bears win the NFL championship in arctic wind-chill on December 29, 1963, at Wrigley. We also saw Gale

Sayers run for six touchdowns.

"The Friendly Confines" as Wrigley Field was known at Clark and Addison streets was our year-round destination. Herb Zucker took me to more than 100 Cubs games, including ethnicity barrier-breaking Jackie Robinson's Chicago debut in 1947. We always sat in the first row. We loved the Cubbies. Those were long, hard years for the team. However, for me, I was so happy just sitting next to my dad.

He never got to live to see the Cubs win the World Series. He died in 1966, when he was 54. My dad died playing gin, listening to the Cubs game on his tiny transistor radio pressed to his ear.

In 2016, when the Cubs *finally* won the World Series after 108 years, I was a season ticket holder, along with Rick Fizdale. We saw all the games. After they won, I went to the cemetery where my dad is buried. I brought with me a Cub World Series hat, Cubs T-shirt and his transistor radio, still tuned to AM 720, the 1966 Cubs radio flagship, WGN. They lost 103 games that season and finished dead last, in 10th place. But at last the world turned. I "told" my father what the Cubs had finally accomplished. I will always remember that moment because I was able to share everything with my dad, who first taught me to love sports.

Playing Games is Serious Business, for those of us who love sports. I hope you have enjoyed reading this memoir as much as I have enjoyed living it. Reach for the stars, live your dreams.

I have.

Acknowledgements

I have had the privilege to represent and defend many notable clients in court, work with many professional sports teams, and negotiate some of the top sports contracts at the time on behalf of my clients. I thank them all for entrusting me with some of the most significant dealings of their careers and for challenging me to be the best attorney and sports agent possible.

I thank the many partners, associates, and mentors I've had over the years. Ed Kelly (former superintendent of the Chicago Park District) and Rick Fizdale (former chairman and chief executive of the Leo Burnett Company) are both old friends who graciously participated in and supported me throughout the writing of this book. And a sincere thanks to my former law partner, Eldon Ham, whose partnership and brilliant legal work paved the path for many through the legal precedents we set during our time working together.

Special thanks to former clients Jim McMahon, Deion Sanders, Michael Westbrook, and Richmond Webb for allowing me to be your agent, your years of friendship, and for helping make this book possible through sharing stories and memories.

Thanks to everyone who worked on publishing this book. I am grateful to all of you. Thank you Ira Berkow, content editor; Howard Schlossberg and Suzanne T. Isaacs, line editors; Dorey Kronick, cover designer; and David Robson, page designer.

I also owe a tremendous amount of gratitude to my lovely wife, Shelly, whose loving support has allowed all of this to be possible.

Steve Zucker
Winnetka, Illinois